Rose Smith

Four Stages
of Life

*A Comparative Study
of Women and Men
Facing Transitions*

Marjorie Fiske Lowenthal
Majda Thurnher
David Chiriboga
and Associates

FOUR STAGES OF LIFE

Jossey-Bass Publishers

San Francisco · Washington · London · 1975

FOUR STAGES OF LIFE
A Comparative Study of Women and Men Facing Transitions
Marjorie Fiske Lowenthal, Majda Thurnher,
David Chiriboga, and Associates

Library of Congress Catalogue Card Number LC 74-27911

International Standard Book Number ISBN 0-87589-248-5

Manufactured in the United States of America

JACKET DESIGN BY WILLI BAUM

FIRST EDITION

Code 7503

The Jossey-Bass
Behavioral Science Series

Special Advisor in Adult Development
MARJORIE FISKE LOWENTHAL
University of California, San Francisco

*This book is gratefully dedicated
to the memory of Katherine Wolf*

Preface

This is a study of adults as they experience a particular pretransitional period in their lives and anticipate and prepare for their expectable future.[1] Our subjects are women and men at four life stages: high school seniors, young newlyweds, middle-aged parents, and an older group about to retire. While not usually in the same family, they share a long residence in a particular subcommunity within an urban setting, and we have found many similarities among them that seem to reflect a uniform context to their lives. At the same time, we have located distinctive styles of coping, dramatically different for men and women within each stage. We cannot predict from this study that the younger group will subsequently become like the older cohorts we studied at the same time, since obviously the data are cross-sectional and the particular period in history the young cohorts will live through will differ from that of the old. On the other hand, we have been able to identify certain sociopsychological characteristics conducive to successful coping at some life stages but not at others.

A major objective of this work is to delineate the parameters and identify concepts useful for the study of adaptation to the

[1] This research was made possible by grants from the National Institute of Child Health and Human Development (HD03051 and HD05941).

ix

inevitable changes that occur across the adult life course. As the first phase of a longitudinal study, it also constitutes the baseline from which we shall eventually test out certain hypotheses about the developmental nature of such changes (or lack of them) as do take place. Some of these hypotheses will be our own; others will be derived from certain conceptual stances which now pervade the professional literature, the field of mental health practice, and the literary and mass media scenes as well.

The prevailing frameworks within which the adaptive processes of adulthood have been examined range from the classically psychoanalytic (for example, Fromm's [1966] concept of the ever recurring life plot, firmly entrenched in the Freudian concept of repetition); the equally static views of some traditional fields of sociology, where social structure is viewed as the major source of differences between life-stage or age cohorts; to humanistic concepts of self-realization, as in the works of Allport ([1937] 1961), Gold-stein (1963), Erikson (1968), Bühler (1968), and Maslow ([1962] 1968). These appealing self-actualization theories were in large part drawn from studies of Harvard students, upper-middle-class patients, and other talented and privileged individuals—including, perhaps, a measure of introspection about the talented and privileged selves of the authors themselves. This is a major reason for our having chosen to study cohorts in the middle and especially the lower-middle class.

The life changes anticipated by high school seniors (first job, college, marriage) and by newlyweds (parenthood) are often viewed as "voluntary" and tend to be socially valued. Those expectable in later life, the postparental (or "empty-nest") and retirement stages, are more often than not perceived as involuntary and negative. The prevailing view, with which we agree in principle, is that all such changes, whether incremental (involving role gain) or decremental (involving role loss), are potentially stressful. The anticipation of an impending transition often serves as a stimulus to examine, and possibly to reorient, goals and aspirations, and to reassess personal resources and impediments in the light of the probability of their attainment. In searching out commonalities and differences in such coping processes among persons about to undergo four very different types of transition, we hope also to contribute to the understanding of the more gradual adaptive processes evoked by less dramatic changes that most people sense in themselves, their immediate milieu, and the broader society as they grow up, mature or do not mature, and grow old.

Insights derived from our previous intensive studies of mentally well and ill older subjects were important guides in the formulation of the research design. A primary task was to translate these insights into methods designed to introduce analytic rigor to propositions useful in studying the adult life course. While this report is restricted to data gathered at one point in time, another of our major intents was to provide methodological building blocks useful for the longitudinal phase of this study, and hopefully for other investigators who may conduct studies of change across the life course. The original framework for the research (including the longitudinal phase) has been reported elsewhere (Lowenthal, 1971). Like most conceptual schema developed for the study of relatively unexplored processes, the original parameters and foci of emphasis have subsequently been somewhat altered as the incoming data led us to modify our preliminary constructs.

The fieldwork consisted of a series of intensive interviews, lasting an average of eight hours, which included the administration of several structured research instruments (described in Appendix A). The open-ended material, subjected to rigorous quantitative analysis, has enabled us to identify certain rather complex characteristics associated with the adaptive process which would have otherwise escaped us, such as degree of preoccupation with stress, the nature of what people at various life stages perceive as stressful, and retrospective and prospective views of the life course (these derived measures are described in Appendix B). Through the operationalization of such comparative abstractions as life-style configurations, complexity of self-image, a dual model of adaptation, and value-goal continuity and discontinuity, we hope that the work makes a useful methodological (as well as conceptual) contribution to the as yet little explored questions centering on growth, stabilization, and regression in adult life. In the longitudinal phase of the research, just underway at this writing, we use several of these newly structured measures to assess their relative importance for adaptive level after the individuals making up the sample have undergone the expected incremental or decremental transitions.

Our approach differs from survey models at the one extreme and experimental models at the other. The survey model attempts to establish population values, and the experimental approach attempts to confirm or disconfirm a theoretical position. The goal of our research is to generate hypotheses and constructs from empirical data, models later to be tested by one of the other two methods. Levels of statistical significance are therefore not systematically reported in the text, but the reader should bear in mind that no findings are interpreted unless they reach significance at the .05 level. Significances between .05 and .10, when logically supportive of related findings, may be reported as trends. Some findings are reported that do not appear in the tabular material provided in the text. Tables relating to them are available from the respective authors.

There are two major subdivisions in the book. Part One, essentially an in-depth description of people at four pretransitional periods, develops the two-step proposition that (1) characteristics in the behavioral, perceptual, and intrapersonal spheres often reveal underlying commonalities such as degree of simplicity or complexity, or degree of futurity; and that (2) the significance of these deep-seated characteristics for the individual's adaptive level varies both across successive life stages and even more so between the sexes.

The sample is described in Chapter One. Although this chapter extends beyond conventional demographic characteristics to include involvement in the broader sociopolitical milieu, the prevailing theme is that of actual or anticipated family-centeredness at all four life stages. In conclusion, a tentative typology of life styles is offered, one which is provocative in part because of the marked convergence of the sexes at some life stages and dramatic divergence in others. Chapter Two describes the family context of this highly family-centered sample, in terms of marital and intergenerational conflict and confluence. It concludes with an analysis of themes relating to heterosexual intimacy, where we again find a reflection of the divergent needs of men and women at some life stages.

Chapter Three analyzes patterns of friendship, not only in

the usual terms of the structure of friendship networks and frequency of interaction, but on some rather more innovative dimensions, such as simplicity and complexity. To our surprise, variations in the concept and functions of friendship across the life course proved to be minimal, and, in any case, of far less significance than the considerable differences between men and women. An exception to this recurrent finding that differences between the sexes are far greater than those between life stages within each sex group is reported in Chapter Four, devoted to self-concept. In these self-assessments, variations according to stage of life are nearly as impressive as sex differences. Chapter Five focuses on self-reports of general happiness and recent emotional experiences; some evidence is found for a decline in emotional complexity, but none for a decline in happiness across the adult life course, at least to the preretirement stage. Chapter Six proposes a dual model of adaptation, a model that includes psychological resources as well as deficits. We have found such a model to be far more enlightening than the customary degree-of-impairment model. It is especially useful for studying variations across the life course, since particular resources and deficits have different implications for the subjective sense of well-being depending on what stage of life the individual is in.

The underlying theme of Part Two is the sense of time as continuity, discontinuity, or intrusion. Several of the new measures described in this section of the book were also developed from quantified analysis of detailed protocol material. They in turn enabled us to explore how intrusions from the past and expectations of the future influence adaptive level in the present. Perhaps not surprisingly, lack of futurity in time perspective is associated with blockages in the adaptive process, especially during periods where developmental changes may be occurring, and time perspective is strongly associated with preoccupation with stress. The individual's perception and anticipation of past and future continuities and discontinuities in goals and values also is associated with his adaptive level. Finally, the extent to which a person is preoccupied with past stress, apart from whether he or she was exposed to little or much, has as much bearing on adaptive level as does whether much or little of it was actually experienced.

In Chapter Seven, devoted to life-course perspectives, we explore stage and sex differences in preoccupation with the past and orientation to the future, as well as in attitudes toward death and in intrusive thoughts about it. There prove to be some interesting correlations between death attitudes and time perspectives, and they are by no means as stage-linked as might be anticipated from a commonsense view. Chapter Eight describes the personal characteristics of four stress types derived in part from a structured instrument measuring presumed stress. The Chapter concludes with an analysis of the relationship between stress type and physical and mental health, suggesting one type that may be at risk in later life. In Chapter Nine we turn to the respondents' own ideas about the kinds of events and circumstances that are stressful, and trace variations across the four pretransitional stages. Here again, differences between the sexes are far more pronounced than those across the four stages; in this context, as in many others, men and women in a given life stage resemble each other far less than the youngest men or women resemble the oldest people of their sex—an age range of nearly fifty years. Of special interest is the extent to which stresses undergone by others are a source of stress for women, especially middle-aged women.

Chapter Ten analyzes the complex issue of values, ranging from philosophy of life to value hierarchies. Interestingly, many individuals perceive their value systems as quite flexible, and there are few indications that the old are any more rigid in this respect than the young. The people who report that their values have changed greatly, in comparing the present with the past, are not usually those who anticipate the most value change in the future. In fact, there are two clearly delineated groups which prove to be quite different in their psychological resources and exposure to stress. Moreover, the sense of consistency or of change in values is associated with good adaptation at some life stages and poor adaptation at others, and once again men and women differ considerably.

Chapter Eleven reports on our subjects' orientation toward the next major transition they envisage. The principal dimensions of their anticipation were planning, problems, positive or negative attitude, and the sense of control, the latter being far and away the most salient. Whether the pending transition was incremental or decremental, some anticipated it as an opportunity for growth or expansion, others as surrender to the socially required or the personally inevitable. Once more, stage differences were minimal and sex differences paramount, and the nature of the pretransitional stance proved to be correlated with a number of other personal characteristics.

Certain themes tend to recur throughout the volume, and these are summarized in the final chapter. Most notable, perhaps, are criss-crossing trajectories of men and women at successive stages, which may eventually (in the future longitudinal phase of the research) prove to reflect differing types of developmental change, as well as different scheduling. For example, while the girls and young women in this middle- and lower-middle-class sample bear some distressing resemblance to the prototypes illustrating Freud's theory of an early and abrupt halt in the development of young women, there is some evidence that women confronting the postparental stage of life may be undergoing a change which perhaps eluded classical psychoanalytic theorists. In part, this oversight may have resulted from the fact that in the nineteenth and early twentieth centuries the postparental stage of life was often a brief one.

Another consistent set of findings, also reflecting marked sex differences, is the possibility, notable among middle-aged men, that a particular type of male is prone to physical illness at this life stage. Whether this type is the one primarily accounting for the morbidity and mortality differential between men and women at later life stages will be further explored in the longitudinal phase of the research. Two additional and rather intriguing differences between the sexes are (1) that parental deprivation in childhood has an effect on the adaptive level of women but not of men at midlife and beyond and (2) that there is either a selective survival factor operating, or a developmental change, in men between middle age and the period in which they confront imminent retirement. Whatever the explanation, men close to retirement were considerably more relaxed and philosophical than middle-aged men. The chapter concludes with a summary of the implications of our findings for research and for public policy.

So far as we are aware, the study reported here represents the first systematic attempt to assess the extent to which resources and impediments fostering or hindering the adaptive processes of the individual differ or resemble each other at successive stages of the adult life course. As we report in the succeeding chapters, while there are great differences between men and women, within each sex group there are some characteristics which appear to foster or hamper adaptive processes among both young and old, others which are a help at one stage and a hindrance at another. In examining the sociostructural and situational characteristics of these individuals and their own *perceptions* of and affective involvement in their immediate and more remote social milieu, we are in effect beginning to assess the little-explored interstices between the individual and his society and culture. Our findings, we believe, reflect processes of individuation and of socialization at successive stages of the adult life course.

We therefore believe that people in a variety of disciplines may find material in the book which will be of both practical and theoretical use. Anthropologists may discover life-course similarities between mainstream Americans and a variety of cultural groups here and abroad. Sociologists may be surprised to read about the enormous variations, within a very homogeneous population, in how individuals perceive and respond to their immediate and remote social networks and institutions. Psychologists, we trust, will at least not be offended at our assessments of cognitive and affective processes that clearly mediate between stimulus and response. We hope, too, that mental health practitioners and indeed professionals in all health fields will be as impressed as we are with the extent to which one psychological (or physical) resource may offset impairment and serve to motivate the individual to greater growth and health. We think, too, that we have located a few groups across the adult life course which are at a potential health risk (physically, mentally, or both), and that policy makers and clinicians alike may find in these pages suggestions helpful for the development of preventive health and educational programs.

Other professionals—lawyers, architects, the clergy, and criminologists—may find these perspectives across the adult life course professionally rewarding. Most especially, we hope that students in all the fields we have mentioned will become as challenged by the complexities and rewards of such a perspective as we are. By no means least, we would like to think that this report is not too technical to be of interest to lay readers, young and old alike, who may find in the retrospections and anticipations reported by these men and women in four life stages a means of enriching their own lives.

The quality of an in-depth sociopsychological field study such as this is as fully dependent on the sophistication, skills, and sensitivity of the interviewers as it is on the qualifications and talents of persons who analyze and report on the data. Indeed, to some extent these roles were performed by the same individuals. Three of the chapter authors—Majda Thurnher (who was responsible for the training of interviewers), David Chiriboga, and Elinore Lurie— also did considerable interviewing. Other interviewers were primarily graduate students in the social and behavioral sciences: Lotte Dolby, Peter Lewis, Thomas Lonner, James Stoll, and Eileen Schreffler (the coordinator of fieldwork). Phyllis Ogino coordinated the transcription of protocols; she was assisted by Vira Hileman, Alice Klink, and Starr Naines. Marjorie Fiske Lowenthal, who directed the study, and most senior staff members read all 216 protocols and held continuing discussions about their conceptual and theoretical implications. For a period of months, protocols from each of the eight transitional groups were also discussed at a life-history seminar led by Leonard Micon (psychoanalyst and lecturer, Langley Porter Neuropsychiatric Institute, University of California, San Francisco) and Marjorie Lowenthal. All interviewers and other project staff members attended these seminars, with interviewers presenting individual life histories. Additional cases were reviewed with psychoanalyst Robert Butler (Washington School of Psychiatry). Out of these two analytic procedures, criteria and methods for assessing psychological resources and deficits were developed.

While senior professional staff developed and tested codes for the analysis of the qualitative dimensions within their own specific research areas, the bulk of the arduous coding tasks was undertaken by research assistants Eileen Schreffler, Thomas Lonner, Lotte Dolby, Susan Kamins, Peter Drachsler, Rosiland Solomon, and Ray Launier. During the first half of the data-analysis period David Chiriboga served as consultant and coordinator of quantitative data processing. Robert Pierce subsequently assumed this task. Lynn Gigy and Judith Stein conducted many of the statistical analyses and played a vital role in the coordination and maintenance of a burgeoning data base.

Phyllis Olsen's task as supervisor of manuscript production was a prodigious one. Her patience and competence, and that of Linda Shearin, Susan Marks, John S. Foster, and Candiss Ivanova, contributed considerably to the equanimity of an occasionally temperamental and generally overstressed professional staff.

The authors wish to express their appreciation for the helpful consultations of many colleagues and associates: Herta Herzog, who influenced our decision regarding the nature of the sample and how it was to be drawn; Laurel Glass, who gave invaluable assistance in gaining the indispensable cooperation of the school board; Wayne Holtzman, Bernice Neugarten, and John Clausen, who provided valuable advice during the planning phase of the study; David Gomberg, who served as computer program consultant; and Warner Schaie, who made several helpful suggestions on longitudinal research design. Our heartfelt appreciation goes to Irving Rosow, who played an indispensable role in the development of the research design and throughout the course of the study continued to be a vigorous and insightful critic. Finally, and perhaps most important, our thanks go to the 216 people who shared important experiences with us in a truly generous and collaborative fashion. We believe they have made a major contribution to our understanding of how people cope with the often drastic changes of adult life.

San Francisco   MARJORIE FISKE LOWENTHAL
January 1975   MAJDA THURNHER
                                   DAVID CHIRIBOGA

Contents

    David Chiriboga   84

6. Complexities of Adaptation
    David Chiriboga, Marjorie Fiske Lowenthal   99

    TWO: TIME AS CONTINUITY AND INTRUSION

7. Perspectives on Life Course
    David Chiriboga, Lynn Gigy   122

8. Responses to Stress
    Marjorie Fiske Lowenthal, David Chiriboga   146

9. Perceived Stress Across Life Course
    Diane Beeson, Marjorie Fiske Lowenthal   163

10. Continuities and Discontinuities
    in Value Orientations
    Majda Thurnher   176

11. The Pretransitional Stance
    Marjorie Fiske Lowenthal, Robert Pierce   201

12. Summary and Implications
    Marjorie Fiske Lowenthal   223

A. Interview Schedule and Description
    of Structured Instruments   247

B. Scales, Typologies, Ratings,
    Derived Variables   250

C. Variables Examined in Relation
    to Stance Toward Transitions   261

    Bibliography   263

    Indexes   283

Authors
and Associates

DIANE BEESON, *graduate student, Human Development Program, University of California, San Francisco*

DAVID CHIRIBOGA, *assistant professor of psychology in residence, Human Development Program, University of California, San Francisco*

LYNN GIGY, *staff research associate, University of California, San Francisco*

MARJORIE FISKE LOWENTHAL, *professor of social psychology and director, Human Development Program, University of California, San Francisco*

ELINORE LURIE, *lecturer in medical sociology, University of California, San Francisco*

xxi

ROBERT PIERCE, *assistant research psychologist and lecturer, University of California, San Francisco*

DONALD SPENCE, *coordinator of gerontological programs, University of Rhode Island*

MAJDA THURNHER, *assistant adjunct professor of anthropology, Human Development Program, University of California, San Francisco*

LAWRENCE WEISS, *doctoral candidate, Human Development Program, University of California, San Francisco*

Figures and Tables

Four Stages
of Life

A Comparative Study
of Women and Men
Facing Transitions

Style of Life

The 216 men and women who took part in our study live in the central city of a large metropolitan area, are largely Caucasian, and were selected to be as homogeneous and representative of the middle and lower-middle class as possible. They include that segment of American society whose origins may have been that of a traditional blue-collar working class, and who indeed may themselves occupy such positions, but whose life styles increasingly resemble those of the middle class (Berger and Berger, 1971). Their position in society may be less the result of self-motivated advance over that of their parents than of the more general mobility, both geographic and social, of a developing society (Lipset and Bendix, 1959).

For the most part, these blue-collar, white-collar, and middle-range professional or managerial workers have succeeded economically. They own their homes in an area where not only the population but the architecture is strikingly of a kind; with few exceptions the manner in which they decorate and care for their

This chapter was coordinated and rewritten by Majorie Fiske Lowenthal after chapter authors left the program for other positions, in 1973 and and 1972, respectively.

1

property reflects the standards established by the women's home-making magazines. They are, for the most part, not leaders of the community, but in a very important way they represent its center. Policemen, firemen, nurses, schoolteachers, small businessmen and minor executives, housewives, civil servants, craftsmen, and sales personnel—it is their votes that determine how the city will be governed.

A senior high school was our central source for locating people in four pretransitional stages. The geographic boundaries of this school defined the district from which all four groups were drawn. The senior class of the school constituted the universe for the youngest group. From school records, we determined which of these students were the youngest members of their families and thereby identified a second group, parents who were facing the "postparental" or "empty-nest" stage of family life. The group representing a stage intermediate between these two consisted of newlyweds who had been married less than twelve months and who had not yet started a family. The fourth stage was made up of older persons who were planning to retire within the next two to three years. These latter two groups were composed of friends or relatives of the subjects in the student and the postparental groups, as well as persons whom we found by consulting marriage license records and local organizations which maintained records of the probable retirement status of their employees. All persons so selected resided or had resided within the boundaries of the sample district.

The high school seniors (twenty-five boys and twenty-seven girls) were sixteen to eighteen years old and were the only cohort to include nonwhites (seven in all, including one black, two Filipino Americans, two Chinese Americans, one Japanese American, and one Mexican American). The newlyweds (twenty-five men and twenty-five women) ranged from twenty to thirty-eight years of age, with an average age of twenty-four (these were all first marriages). The mean ages of the two older groups were fifty for the middle-aged parents (twenty-seven men and twenty-seven women) and sixty for the preretirees (thirty men and thirty women, slightly oversampled to allow for morbidity or mortality in the longitudinal phase of the study). The sample thus encompasses two groups facing what might be called "incremental" transitions, characterized predominantly by role gains, and two facing "decremental" transitions, where losses or changes in familial or work roles were imminent. A five-year follow-up of these four groups will eventually provide the data for a longitudinal sequential design (Baltes, 1968: Schaie, 1965).

As Table 1 shows, most of our subjects had some education beyond high school, either technical or general, but not usually to the completion of a bachelor's degree. They viewed education primarily as a necessary means of entering the work world. Unlike the upper-middle class, where it is assumed that one will attain a degree independent of career considerations (Seeley, Sim, and Loosley, 1956; Keniston, 1965, 1968; Westley and Epstein, 1969), the older subjects usually entered college only when they considered it necessary for some previously planned occupational objectives (Komarovsky, 1962). Some take jobs and return to school later if continued advancement demands it. Only a few of our subjects said that, in their opinion, general, nonvocational education should continue beyond high school; and even these subjects usually meant by "continuing education" work at a two-year college rather than a four-year university or college. In keeping with general social trends (Riley and Foner, 1968), the newlyweds were better educated than the middle-aged, and the middle-aged more so than the oldest group. Similarly, all of the people in our study generally had had more education than their parents of the same sex.

Most of our subjects (89 percent) were born in the United States and were raised and went to school in the neighborhood of their birth. Some geographic mobility was associated with the period following high school, but after that they tended to move very little. Almost all of those with children had lived in the Bay Area for more than ten years. If there is a second life period within which geographic relocation occurs with any major frequency, it will probably prove to be at the time of retirement. Almost a third of those confronting this life stage had already taken some action toward this end.

Our subjects tended to come from small stable families. About two thirds had one or two siblings, one fifth were from larger families, and 12 percent were only children. The older the subject, the more likely was he or she to come from a large family. The

Table 1.

Selected Characteristics of Sample

	High School		Newlywed		Middle-Aged		Preretirement	
	Boys (25)	Girls (27)	Men (25)	Women (25)	Men (27)	Women (27)	Men (30)	Women (30)[a]
Mean Age	17	17	25	23	52	48	61	58
Percent Some College	NA	NA	92	92	48	41	36	37
Percent Married	NA	NA	100	100	96	89	83	73
Religion (%):								
Protestant	36	26	28	24	41	44	60	40
Catholic	20	44	36	52	18	30	23	30
Jewish	12	4	4	12	18	22	7	10
Fundamentalist	12	4	8	12	11	4	3	17
Other/none	20	22	24	0	11	0	7	3
Percent Working Part Time	56	18	0	12	0	4	0	10
Percent Working Full Time	0	0	92	72	100	48	97	53
Socioeconomic Status[b] (percent high)	52	30	24	28	44	37	67	50
Activity Scope[c] (percent high)	64	78	64	64	22	37	33	37
Social-Horizons Complexity[c] (percent high)	44	30	48	20	63	74	33	37
Social-Role Involvement	124.8	123.2	140.9	135.9	124.4	115.9	126.1	119.3

[a] Henceforth, subsample sizes will be omitted unless the missing data exceed 10 percent, in which case the sizes of all the relevant groups will be presented.

[b] Based on trichotomized scores.

[c] Based on dichotomized scores.

families of procreation were much like those within which these respondents were raised. Again, the average family size was two or three children (86 percent having three or less), with only two families having more than four children.

A religious identification was mentioned by nearly all, and they come from church-related families, reminding one of Herberg's (1955) religious America of the 1950s. Whether or not the parents belonged to a church or synagogue, the young were sent to Sunday School. Among men, religious involvement was considerably less among the newlyweds. Among women, there was a more consistent religious participation across the four stages. Church membership for men was 76 percent, 24 percent, 59 percent, and 50 percent as we move through the four stages, while for women it was over half in all groupings except preretirement, where it increased to 60 percent. These trends hold whether we use church membership or participation as the main indicator. With the exception of the oldest men, more people participated in religious activities than held church or synagogue memberships, 70 percent indicating attendance of some sort.

Nearly three fourths of the respondents were employed in either part-time or full-time positions at the time of the fieldwork. The high school senior girls had the lowest rate (18 percent) while the middle-aged men were all employed. The women in the preretirement stage who were working at the time of the fieldwork included four widows and four divorcees. Aside from them, the proportion of employed women was half, the same as the rate for the spouses of the men in this stage, and quite consistent with that of the middle-aged women.

Whereas one might expect that the women, particularly in the two older samples, would be working part time, perhaps returning to work after their children left home or to supplement their family income prior to retirement, this was not the case; the majority of women who were employed worked full time (80 percent). Among those working women, 86 percent of the newlyweds, 93 percent of the middle-aged, and 84 percent of the oldest women were employed full time. As one would expect, in the sample as a whole more men than women were employed, and men tended to have longer and more stable employment histories than women; but among the older working women, half had work histories fully as stable as the men's, the majority having been on the same job for over ten years.

A measure of the socioeconomic status of the family of each respondent was derived from a combination of three factors: the occupation and education of the principal breadwinner, and the family income. The occupational scores were based on our own adaptation of Bogue's (1963) socioeconomic indexes of occupations. By design, socioeconomic status had a limited range, and the variations which occurred largely reflected career development. The newlyweds had the lowest status, the preretirees the highest. The only subgroup that showed some slight inconsistency between the sexes was within the student category, where there were a few more girls than boys on the lower level. We believe that this difference resulted from a higher refusal rate among lower-class boys.

A marked characteristic of the people attracted to this residential area was that, like the working class, they had a very family-centered leisure pattern. Relatively few of these men and women have adopted the patterns of organizational membership, cultural, and civic activities which tend to characterize people whose ancestral roots are more firmly middle class (Seeley, Sim, and Loosley, 1956). In many ways, they more closely resemble the working-class East Londoners moved to the suburban "estates," whose emerging patterns of family-centered leisure were reported by Young and Willmott (1957), or the Levittowners studied by Gans (1967). Except for the high school seniors, this family-centeredness is strongly reflected in their daily and weekly activity pattern, as assessed by thirty-three activities (Checklist of Activities) to which the subjects responded in terms of frequency of participation. Somewhat to our surprise, the hierarchy of activities was very similar across all stage and sex groups. Activities reported by the great majority included radio listening, reading, household chores, shopping, visiting, being visited, and helping others. Those seldom reported included playing a musical instrument, dancing, solitary games, picnics, and physical exercise.

High school seniors and newlyweds undertook the greatest

variety of activities and were involved in them more frequently than persons in the older life stages. On a scale that combines number of activities with frequency of participation, 64 to 78 percent of the high school seniors and newlyweds were rated high in activity scope (see Appendix B), as compared to 22 to 37 percent of the middle-aged and those facing retirement (Table 1). High school students seemed to be trying out all the various leisure pursuits generally within reach of young people of their social class. To the extent that resources (both time and money) permitted, newlyweds were "on the go." Because many were working and going to school, and because most had not yet begun to accumulate any financial resources, their activities were simple and inexpensive. Some of them, mainly the men, complained a bit, jokingly or otherwise, about feeling restricted.

By midlife, both time and energy seemed to require a more selective use of leisure. The middle-aged men, who had assumed the greatest number of roles, had the least variety in their regular activities. As we shall document in later chapters, these middle-aged men, who were already anticipating retirement with some apprehension, were preoccupied with their jobs and financial security. Some were making a last-ditch stand, an almost desperate effort to attain a promotion, in hope of ensuring an adequate postretirement income. This preoccupation, combined perhaps with some loss of energy, resulted in a sloughing off of accustomed leisure activities, such as participation in clubs and church affairs. They may have retained their affiliations as Elk, Mason, or church member, but at this life stage these roles were often more symbolic than real. The behavioral pattern of middle-aged women also was more restricted than that of younger groups, but for different reasons. Although about half of these women had jobs, they were working primarily to supplement the family income, and revealed none of the job preoccupation or sense of financial press characterizing the middle-aged men. Since they were almost exclusively family-centered, these women may in part have been merely accommodating to the more restricted styles of their husbands. This family- and job-centeredness of most of our sample will be further elaborated in the ensuing sections on roles and familial involvement of our subjects. But first we shall sum-

marize its consequences for their perspectives on the broader social
world in which they live.

Social Horizons

To obtain a picture of social perceptions and involvement,
subjects were asked to discuss what they considered to be the major
social issues and problems on local, national, and international levels.
The nature of the individual's political ideology, his sophistication
or naiveté, was of lesser concern than his general views on how the
wider social system affected his life, and his sense of control of and
responsibility for inducing desired social change. The interviews
took place during a period of heightened sociopolitical unrest: the
escalation of antiwar protest and civil rights movements, the intensification of racial conflict, and the peaking of youth's counterculture. Voiced often was a sense of unprecedented sociohistorical
change and the belief that an era had ended.

Social problems mentioned bore a direct relationship to the
individual's life style and his or her personal commitments and
aspirations. The Vietnam war was viewed as critical across all
groups but was given primary emphasis by high school boys, the
group most immediately affected. Concern over race relationships
was highest among high school girls and lowest among subjects
facing retirement. The high school girls were most apprehensive
about the increasingly frequent racial confrontations occurring at
school; the oldest subjects were least exposed to interaction with
minority groups and believed that they would be less so when they
actually retired. Parents facing the empty nest were most likely to
express distress over the changing values and behavior of the younger
generation. The two older groups shared concern for increasing
violence in the streets; the middle-aged were primarily anxious about
the security of their children, and those facing retirement worried
about possible injury to themselves and the constraints on their
activities that avoidance of streets would impose on them.

Similarly, certain differences among stage and sex were noted
regarding methods of solving social problems (Lurie, 1972). High
school girls and middle-aged women tended to point to the need for
personal change: people should change their attitudes and values,

become kinder, better, and more responsible. They were also most likely to suggest informal community action. The middle-aged were most likely to state that solution of social problems requires action on the federal level. Lastly, men in this group deviated from others in their higher endorsement of law and order and their belief that the underprivileged should help themselves.

In general, subjects had greater ease in depicting problems than in offering solutions, and those who perceived severe and numerous problems were not necessarily the ones who had given the most thought to their solutions. The measure used to investigate group differences in sociopolitical concerns, a social-horizons-complexity score, was based on the number of ways the individual felt his life was affected by social conditions, the number of possible solutions he envisioned, and the active steps he had taken or had planned to take. As Table 1 shows, complexity scores were highest among the middle-aged (more so among women than men), the stage most directly involved in meeting familial or occupational responsibilities. High school boys, newlywed men, and the oldest women occupied an intermediate position. High school girls and newlywed women paid least heed to the wider world around them, this in part because of their greater preoccupation with the emotional dimensions of interpersonal relationships.

Factors associated with the scope of an individual's social horizons and his involvement with social problems are complex and varied. Involvement in social problems may reflect exposure to and familiarity with the wide range of social institutions. Involvement may be affected by the degree to which social conditions impede an individual's aspirations or impinge on the welfare of close others. To explore the determinants of sociopolitical involvement within different stage and sex groups, we examined the social-horizons-complexity scores in relationship to familial and extrafamilial roles.

Among high school seniors, awareness of social problems and concern for remedial measures was related to activities extending beyond family and school. Among boys, complexity scores were correlated with active participation in organizational activities; among girls, they were correlated with the number of extrafamilial roles; that is, with church and organization memberships and with employment. No correlates were noted for newlywed men and women. Among middle-aged men, high involvement in social problems showed an inverse relationship to number of familial roles; that is, with absence of living parents and lesser contact with siblings and children. A tendency was further noted for those who participated in organizational activities to show greater involvement—in this instance resembling high school seniors. Among the middle-aged men, paucity of family ties and commitments seems to permit the direction of attention to the wider segments of society; men with heavy family responsibilities, immersed in work and the pursuit of security, are less likely to express such concerns.

Middle-aged women were most concerned about social problems. While this heightened involvement was in part engendered by solicitude for family members, it was also shown to be correlated with a wide range of social activities (both familial and extrafamilial) and particularly with high interaction with friends. Although men facing retirement were considerably less involved, correlations indicated a pattern similar to that found among women facing the empty nest. High involvement was correlated with high number of familial roles, high number of social activities, and numerous joint activities with their wives. No notable correlations were apparent for women in this stage.

Role Scope and Involvement

Many authors have suggested that wide range of roles is positively related to the individual's development and adaptation. Simmel (1955), for example, noted that membership in dyads or groups which make conflicting demands provides an increased opportunity for the development of a complex, individualized personality. A number of recent studies have suggested that breadth of role scope in middle age is associated with greater flexibility in adapting to the demands of old age and, when necessary, to institutional living (Birren and others, 1963; Granick and Nahemow, 1961; King and Howell, 1965; Lowenthal, 1964; Tec and Granick, 1959–1960). Older people who have occupied many roles in earlier life apparently experience more conflict over age-linked social losses, but eventually come to enjoy family roles in old age more than do those whose role scope has been more limited (Lurie, 1970).

Other studies have been devoted to the relationship between socioeconomic status and social roles. Babchuk (1965) found that middle-class men had a wider range of friendships than women. Booth (1972), in comparing the breadth and depth of involvement with kin, friends, and voluntary associations, reported both sex and age differences. Women had broader ties with kin when younger; as the women grew older, however, these ties grew narrower, eventually resembling those of men. He also found that women had more restricted friendship roles and, further, that their organizational participation was more limited. However, women revealed greater affect and spontaneity in their relationships with friends; and when they were involved in organizational activities, the depth of their commitment resembled that of men.

Cumming and Henry (1961) found that people tended to reduce the amount and intensity of social interaction as they aged. They propose that a process of "disengagement" takes place, the relinquishment of given roles (such as brought about by retirement) leading to withdrawal from other roles and activities. Similarly, Zborowski and Eyde (1962) suggest that, with increasing age and diminution of energy, social participation may be narrowed to those role relationships and activities which are most necessary or rewarding. Accordingly, we might expect role scope and involvement to be lower among those about to retire. But high school seniors, who are unmarried, childless, and not yet in the job market, would also be expected to have lower scores. In short, if these assumptions are correct, the scope of one's roles and role involvement in terms of time devoted to them should have an inverted U-shape in relation to the life course.

To develop a measure of social-role involvement for this study, we assessed participation in the roles of spouse, child, parent, grandparent, sibling, friend, and organization member. The "spouse" score consisted of the number of activities carried out jointly with husband or wife; scores for the other roles consisted of the number of relationships one had with other people in each role category, weighted by frequency of interaction. The number of organizational memberships was weighted by frequency of attendance at meetings. These weighted scores were converted to be comparable and summed to produce the social-role-involvement score for each person.

As Table 1 shows, the expectation that social participation would present an inverted U-shaped curve, with high school seniors and preretired people being low and newlyweds and empty-nest people high, was not realized. Although there was some difference in mean role-involvement scores and range for each sex and stage group, the difference was not statistically significant. The mean scores of men, however, were consistently higher than those of women, and these differences between the sexes were more pronounced in the two older than in the two younger groups. Since, in terms of roles occupied, these women had as much potential for high involvement as the other groups, one wonders whether this is a temporary state or a long-term trend. Except for newlywed men, who ranked highest, all men scored about the same.

As in previously reported studies, among all stage and sex groups there was a slight tendency for greater role involvement to be associated with some education past high school (Gans, 1962; Nie, Powell, and Prewitt, 1969a, 1969b; Seeley, Sim, and Loosley, 1956). For newlyweds and middle-aged people, higher participation was also associated with higher income; but among high school seniors and people about to retire, this was not the case. Thus, the expected rise and decline of role involvement appears to be modified by income. Although most of the roles measured were interpersonal ones, men averaged higher scores than did women who were mothers (about 90 percent of women in the older stages), regardless of whether the latter were still active in the maternal role. This result is consistent with other studies, especially those of Babchuk (1965) and Booth (1972).

The components of the role-involvement scores differed for the sexes and between sexes within each stage. Older people were more likely than younger to belong to organizations. At the same time, in these later stages of life sex differences became more pronounced, with men engaging in more organizational activities than women. Unlike the findings in the midwestern samples of Babchuk (1965) and Booth (1972), the sexes resembled each other in their contacts with friends. Newlyweds, as might be expected, scored highest for spouse-related activities. The low scores of the middle-aged men in this respect are quite remarkable and suggest, as we shall discuss in detail later in this volume, that their attention was directed elsewhere at this time of life. Contact with parents diminished over the life course; and contact with children, as one might expect, diminished in the postparental stage. In accord with previous studies (Adams, 1968; Booth, 1972), women in this sample did not appear to have an edge over men in maintaining contact with children (or grandchildren) in the later stages. Lastly, men and women differed in their interaction with siblings. Among men, interaction dropped markedly upon marriage and was followed by a further decline at the preretirement stage. Women had more stable relationships with siblings, with contact remaining similar across all stages except for middle-aged women, who were most engrossed in meeting the responsibilities of raising a family.

Toward a Typology

By combining the activity-pattern measure derived from the Checklist of Activities with a dichotomized role measure based on number of roles (see Appendix B, Role Scope), we developed a fourfold table which, in a simplified way, reflects the structural dimensions of four kinds of life styles. The first type, which we call the "complex," includes those subjects who have many roles and a varied pattern of activities. The opposite of this, few roles and a limited range of activities, we have called the "simplistic." Those who combine few roles with a varied activity pattern are called "diffuse," while those with a wide role scope and a narrow range of activities have been labeled the "focused."

For the sample as a whole, we found no relationship between the number of roles occupied and the breadth of the activity pattern: about half of the subjects with low and high role scope, respectively, ranked high on breadth of activities. The four types, however, were distributed quite differently at the successive life stages (Figure 1). For men, there were marked differences: high school senior boys and newlywed men tended to be complex, having many roles and varied activities. The middle-aged men, on the other hand, were least likely of all men to maintain a complex life style, and even among men in the preretirement stage there were less than half as many complex as among the younger men. The modality for middle-aged men was the focused style, reflecting no doubt their

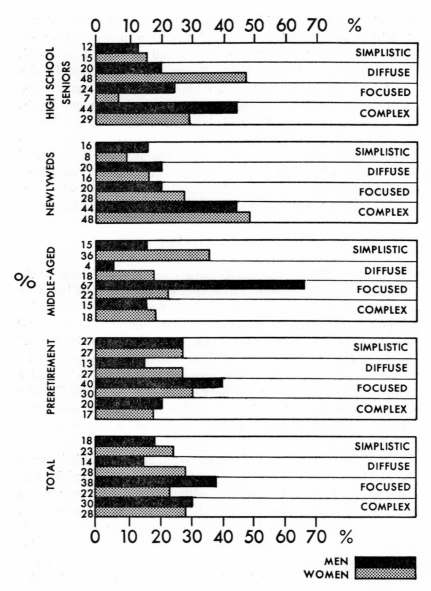

FIGURE 1. Roles and activities combine to produce life career styles.

preoccupation with establishing maximum financial security (and, for some, occupational status) before retirement. Among men in the preretirement stage, there was a decrease in the focused life style, with concomitant increases in the simplistic and, to a lesser extent, the complex.

Among women, the life-style patterns were quite different. High school girls were much less likely than high school boys to have a complex style; nearly half of these girls were in the diffuse category, with few roles and varied activities. Newlywed women, on the other hand, were at least as likely to have a complex style as newlywed men. By midlife, the modality for women, though not a marked one, was the simplistic. Perhaps these women had withdrawn, to retool for the next, postparental, life stage. In any event, we found that women in the preretirement stage had patterns more similar to those of men, with the diffuse and the complex predominating, the simplistic and focused styles close behind.

Finally, looking at the differences between the sexes across the stages, we see that about twice as many men as women tended to follow a focused life style and that, conversely, twice as many women followed a diffuse pattern. The simplistic and complex life styles were not clearly sex-linked. The major sex differences occurred at midlife and during adolescence. At marriage in particular, but also at preretirement, men and women tended to converge in life styles.

This typology is indeed one of style and not content. To elaborate on its substantive components, we turn to an assessment of the "careers" which contribute to these changing configurations. To do so, we shall present analyses of qualitative data, since sample size did not permit operationalizing substantive dimensions within the life-style typology.

The concept of career has been useful for examining certain dynamic aspects of adulthood (Becker and Strauss, 1968). Its developmental potential is particularly evident when it is defined as "a progression of statuses and functions which unfold in a more or less orderly though not predetermined sequence in the pursuit of values which themselves emerge in the course of experience" (Foote, 1956, p. 31). And, although the term has been traditionally applied to occupation, it is applicable as well to family concerns and leisure pursuits. Collectively, these three domains and their subdivisions provide a means of tracing variations in the "life career" across the four stages. (In order to determine whether, and to what extent, the "developmental" potential is indeed realized, we must await the longitudinal phase of our study.)

To begin with, the emergent class structure from which we drew the samples, although relatively homogeneous, nevertheless contained varying patterns of occupational, family, and leisure activities and concerns—some linked to working-class norms, others to middle-class norms, and still others to the rural heritage of the western migrants. As a result, many of our subjects pursue career configurations representing multiple strata of society. One individual may be pursuing the family course of one stratum and the occupational course of another. Further, some individuals may move from the pattern of one stratum to that of another in the course of his or her life span, in one or more of the family, occupational, or leisure spheres. Finally, the relationship between generations tends to be complicated by the possibility that the pace of their respective movement from one stratum to another may differ (Thurnher, Spence, and Lowenthal, 1974).

Family career. Among high school seniors, the boys are primarily of two types: those who barely mention family roles and activities, because they are primarily involved in the task of finding their life's work, and those for whom a future family already appears as central. All of the girls see marriage and family as primary in their lives, but they differ in terms of when they see these roles and behavioral patterns emerging. The differences among boys reflect their level of maturity. The first group have no specific content to their educational objectives at this time. Most of the second group have already decided on specific careers; they want to settle down quickly in a job such as fireman or restaurateur (like their fathers before them). Then they can continue with the facets of life they consider most important; namely, starting a family, traveling, and enjoying their leisure time. The differences among girls relate to their educational objectives. Those who feel that graduation from high school will complete their education are ready to marry as soon as they find the "right" man. For those who are going to college, the choice of a mate does not loom large.

Family involvement peaks for both men and women among newlyweds, despite the fact that they are not yet parents. For some young men, marriage seems to be the stabilizing influence in an otherwise chaotic existence. Such men seem to be moving in every direction at once. They marry thinking that marriage will simplify their social world, without realizing that marriage will also influence other spheres of their lives. They find themselves with responsibilities which affect their day-to-day and long-term decisions. The pressure of these responsibilities may eventually produce the focused life style characterizing the middle-aged.

Most of the young women entered into marriage with the expectation of becoming mothers. However, they are part of a segment of society that attaches considerable importance to the notion that an infant must be cared for by its own mother (Veroff and Feld, 1970). Therefore, these women realize, even before they become pregnant for the first time, that motherhood will demand the redirection of their attention from their husbands and the marriage relationship, from a job, and from leisure pursuits. Most of these newlywed women are fully prepared to redirect their attention in this way, but at the same time they are acutely conscious of the changes such a shift will bring about. It is as though the rather remarkable shift from a diffuse life style (noted among high school girls) to a complex style resembling that of their husbands represents a conscious effort on their part to make the most of their opportunity for expansion in the period between marriage and motherhood.

Men, on the other hand, tend to anticipate parenthood in terms of their role as provider (Veroff and Feld, 1970). Although many of our newlywed women also mention financial readiness for parenthood, they see it as involving the costs of having a baby rather than a continuing increase in the expenses of family life. Men's concern involves the reciprocal commitment between having a family and an occupation. They may remain in a prolonged state of unreadiness for parenthood if they do not feel that their present job is something they want to spend their lives pursuing. Considerable marital strain can be created by the differential readiness for parenthood between spouses (Taylor, 1972).

In retrospect it is the early years of child rearing which the middle-aged women see as most rewarding. As children grow and begin to reach a point of independence, women feel frustrated by the fact that their success as a mother is dependent upon the decisions of their children—when, at the same time, their influence on these decisions is declining or has disappeared altogether (Spence and Lonner, 1971). Since young people remain relatively unsettled until they have established a home and family of their own, the middle-aged women's anxieties and frustrations may be prolonged, and the relief which they associate with the departure of children from home (Lowenthal and Chiriboga, 1972a) delayed.

Men, on the other hand, look back on their early years of child rearing with some regret for not having spent more time with their children. Retrospectively, many wish that their career configurations had been different. They generally give their wives credit for the personal development of successful children. However, if these men are disappointed in their children, they generally do not blame their wives but, instead, justify any inadequacies they might feel as fathers by the fact that they met the financial needs of the family.

By retirement age, unless the independence of children has been delayed, concerns with family are centered in the pleasures that grandchildren can bring. If there are still problems with dependent children, women's concerns are with the future of the children while men face the complications of arranging for educational and wedding expenses in the face of their loss of income at retirement. Those parents who confront retirement and whose children still are not settled are often acutely aware of being "off schedule" (Neugarten, Moore, and Lowe, 1965). The fact that some persons at preretirement still have children at home obviously contributes to the heterogeneity of life styles characterizing this group. Between the middle-aged and the preretirement stages, there is a significant increase in the proportion of women working (from about two fifths to nearly two thirds). This heightened participation in the occupational career helps bring about a convergence of the life styles of men and women.

Occupational career. High school seniors have little awareness of the course their occupational career is likely to follow. Many, if not most, in speaking of their future careers, convey the impression of a "fantasy trip." They talk about "making it big" and of an early retirement (when they will really begin to live). Although they recognize the inevitability of work in their future, it is not something they look forward to with any great anticipation. There are exceptions among the boys, a minority who seem to know where they are going and how to get there. For most girls, work is only a period of marking time between school and marriage. Generally, however, both the boys and girls seem unaware that getting an occupational start may involve something of an effort.

By the time of marriage a degree of realism has set in. Many men are still in school, but now there is purpose to their education. For most, it is related specifically to a job they have or one they hope to obtain as a result of this education. They are acutely aware, unlike the high school seniors, of the time that it takes to attain a position with rewards commensurate with their ambitions. They have also learned that another dimension in the world of work is the non-material components of the job. Basically they are asking, "Is this something I am willing to spend a lifetime doing?"

Newlywed women who work generally do so primarily to enable their husbands to go to school or at least to shop around for work they can accept. In addition, two incomes make possible a more affluent standard of living. Most newlywed women (84 percent) do work. From among this group will emerge a smaller one who will become working wives and mothers (see Fogarty, Rapoport, and Rapoport, 1971).

Among the older married women who work, half returned to the work force after their children were grown. The other half, as we have noted, have work histories that are as stable as those of the men in the study. This latter type of woman may have taken a few years out from her occupational career to have her children, but this time out does not appear that much different from the time out for education, career searching, or military service taken by men.

Men, particularly in the middle-aged group, differ from women in their career stance. Men seem to believe that their work should be more important to them than it is. Like Chinoy's (1955) automobile workers, they entered the work world with the assumption that their efforts and diligence would somehow bring them "success." Most of the middle-aged men of our study clearly had reached a plateau in their occupational career, a situation which

provoked some of them to question the extent to which they are
responsible for their own success or lack of it.

The working women of our sample, on the other hand, are
for the most part not committed to their work. They entered the
work world secondarily to their role of wife, mother, homemaker.
They were satisfied with the financial rewards, the increased affluence
that their contribution made to their families' style of life. They
would pass up chances for advancement if advancement meant increased obligations and a possible drain on the energy they could
direct to their family responsibilities. Since they never really strived
for success in their work role, there is no lowering of sights as there
was for men. Women's liberation may be changing the stance of
some women toward their careers, but we doubt if it will have any
immediate effect on the segment of the population being studied
here.

Differences in the way that men and women relate to their
work careers continue to manifest themselves in their handling of
retirement. For men, the organization of the pending retirement can
be a means for feelings of continued achievement; knowing that
they have adequately prepared for the financial, housing, and other
demands of retirement provides a sense of control over their own
fate. For most married women, work has been and continues to be
a means of contributing to the financial objectives of the family.
Since it has never been a principal source of self-satisfaction, retirement does not have the significance it has for men.

Leisure career. The developmental course of a leisure career
is somewhat different from the course of family or occupational
careers. There is neither the normative scheduling imposed by age
nor the imperative imposed by necessity. Leisure careers begin and
end throughout the life course. Some are short-lived; others extend
beyond the period of family development or work demands.

Leisure is by definition that aspect of one's time which is
left over after the fulfillment of primary roles (Kaplan, 1961).
Therefore, one would expect the course of leisure development to
be accentuated during the periods prior to and after primary adult
responsibility. This proved to be only partially true among our subjects. The stance toward leisure varies more between the sexes than
it does across the life course. While the men generally emphasize

"play," women generally emphasize sociability. The stage differences which do exist are among the men. The younger are regretful that the demands of adulthood will limit their play time, and the older men are anticipating pleasurably the increased play time of retirement. Men's play over the years may decline in amount of active participation, but it continues to exhibit the same outdoor, athletic orientation.

Career configurations. The interplay of career trajectories at a given time might be called a career configuration, consisting of the roles one occupies, the activities in which one engages, and the stance one takes with respect to his various careers. In addition, and perhaps fully as important, the career configurations of career partners must be taken into account. In discussing the family careers of newlyweds, we alluded to the possible differences between men and women in expectations regarding the appropriate conditions for parenthood. If either partner dominates the decision making, it can be at the expense of the other. A woman, for example, insisting on starting a family, may lock a man into a work career that is not only inconsistent with his basic aims or ambitions but may jeopardize his own standards of meeting family responsibilities. In this final section we will present the general characteristics of the different career configurations common to each of the subgroups.

High school seniors are unique in that their present family and work roles have only a limited relation to their future family and work careers. School is the work component of the career configuration at this stage, but the expectations concerning school are as much those of the parents as of the students. Most students, good and poor, question the relevance of school as they experience it; yet they seem to accept their parents' judgment that it is necessary for a successful future. They seem to be existing in a kind of suspended state, not at all certain in which direction to move.

Jobs are available, primarily for boys, but not the kinds of jobs at which one makes a living or out of which careers develop. Girls are more restricted than boys in the number of roles they occupy. Most girls seem to be limited to home, school, and a weekend social life. Either jobs are not available for girls or parental restrictions concerning the type of work, hours, and the like, severely limit the work possibilities. Fewer girls than boys are involved in nonschool club activities, such as the Y or Scouting, and the school structures many activities (such as athletics) for boys but not for girls. It is in large part the difference in opportunities which makes for the complex life style of boys and the diffuse style of girls.

Athletics provides one of the few systematic links to a future work career. Every football, baseball, and basketball player is well aware that the lines of development which begin in high school may eventually end with an opportunity to play professional ball. Since college scholarships are a part of this course of events, there are generally favorable parental sanctions. Even if their son does not make the ranks of the professional, he has still met the requirements for significant opportunity through the associated education. If he does make it, what was leisure at one time in the life career becomes work at another time.

At marriage, as we have seen, the structural dimensions of the life styles of men and women converge. As many women as men are working, and the activities engaged in outside of work, including family activities, are generally undertaken with spouse. The critical characteristics of this period are its temporary nature and its continuities and discontinuities with the future. The problem is one of working out the desired balance between work, family, and leisure activities at a time when some roles are reversed and others are being sought after—as, for instance, when a wife is the principal provider while she would prefer to be a mother.

A few of our newlyweds seem to be aware of the critical nature of this period for the development of their family careers. They are using the period prior to their having children for personal development and the development of a relationship with their spouses. Others seem to focus mainly on the prospect that children make a family career, unaware of the difficulties this may produce later in life, when children are grown and on their own. But most, if not all, newlyweds are well aware that having children will produce significant changes in their lives.

By the time one's children have reached maturity, the consequences of the interplay or lack of interplay in the configuration of family, work, and leisure careers are very evident. Men at this period have more roles than at any other stage. They are fully engaged in society, and yet they rank low in the variety or scope of the specific activities in which they engage. We believe that this is the consequence of the attitudes men of this stage have toward their primary roles. For example, when asked to describe a typical day, most men responded in terms of going to work and returning from work, without any mention of what took place in the interim. In addition, although a few men approach their family roles in terms of the interpersonal responsibilities and relationships involved, most men, as we have noted, respond to their family roles in terms of the general economic function they perform.

Most middle-aged women have few extrafamilial roles or activities because their energies are consumed in their interdependency—primarily with their children but also, to some extent, with their husbands. The interpersonal demands of the motherhood role limit the energy that women have to invest in roles and activities, accounting in part for the shift to the simplistic career style. We have already suggested that work commitment is limited by the motherhood responsibilities of women in this sample. It might also be argued from these same data that the psychic demands of motherhood will limit the women's personal development and acquisition of roles even when time is available (Spence and Lonner, 1971). It is at this stage that the greatest difference occurs between the life styles of men and women.

A major concern for people confronting retirement is to find common concerns and interests with the marriage partner. It is not as if these older subjects were striving for the personal closeness of newlyweds, since both men and women usually have interests of their own which they hope to pursue into retirement. It is an underlying worry that the years of work and family, with the relatively independent roles for men and women, have left them without a common basis for their life together after retirement. Women have been absorbed in the problems of others, men in those of work; and life becomes empty for them both unless they have inner resources as well as constructive outlets in a broader community.

While the substantive dimensions of life style remain to be fully operationalized in a larger study, some of the consequences of these career configurations and their changing juxtaposition within the marital dyad will become apparent in the ensuing chapters.

Family Confluence,
Conflict, and Affect

CRID CRID CRID CRID CRID CRID CRID CRID

In this chapter we are concerned primarily with emotional aspects of family relationships: how members appraise one another and get along with one another. For this study of family relationships, we developed a series of measures. Developed first were measures of affect toward individual family members (spouse, mother, father, son, daughter, brother, and sister), affect toward family of origin (parents and siblings), affect toward family of procreation (spouse and children), and overall familial involvement (based on all family members). Subjects were asked to describe each family member and to tell how they got along with him or her. The answers to these two questions were rated separately on a three-point scale of positive-negative affect, and the average of these two ratings was used as the affect score for the given family member. These affect scores for individual family members were used to derive measures of affect toward broader categories of kin. Thus, for example, measures of affect toward parents were obtained by adding the affect scores for mother and father and dividing by two. Scores for affect toward family of origin were derived by summing the affect scores for each member of the subject's family of origin and dividing by number of members. The same procedure was followed in obtaining affect scores for family of procreation and for overall familial involvement.

Marriage Relationships

In their descriptions of spouses, the subjects differed not only in their positive or negative evaluations but also in the dimensions emphasized—the respective importance given to the role and interpersonal components of the marital relationship (Kerckhoff and Bean, 1970). Newlyweds, both men and women, gave almost exclusive attention to personality characteristics and emotional responsivity and made minimal references to roles and statuses, norms which they were still in the process of clarifying. They were eager to convey the unique features of the partners they had just chosen, and dwelt on themes of mutual understanding, caring, shared interests, and enjoyment of each other's company. While the two older groups also touched upon personality attributes (such a wife's gregariousness, compassion, or attractive appearance), their descriptions were set within the framework of normative role expectations. More so than those of others, the middle-aged men's descriptions of spouses were centered on their performance as wives and mothers, with equal emphasis given to the tasks and duties and the feeling aspects of these roles (for example, good housekeeper, effective manager of the family budget, or "devoted" wife and mother). Their female age peers invariably touched upon the husband's role as family provider but also tended to include his behavioral idiosyncrasies (such as moodiness or wasteful hobbies), which demanded understanding and indulgence. In comparison, men and women in the preretirement stage expressed what appears to be a renewed interest in the personalities of their spouses, and their descriptions were more expressive. Though these oldest men also paid tribute to the roles of housewife and mother, they were more likely to mention companionship and the wife's personal talents and qualities (both nurturance and independence of mind were admired). Similarly, the women, while not omitting the husband's role of worker and provider, gave greater consideration to emotional ties and to the individuality of the spouse.

Kerckhoff and Bean (1970) suggest a functional link between role structure and the interpersonal components of a dyadic relationship. In their view, the interpersonal qualities of the partners become salient when role definitions are lacking; obversely, when role expectations and obligations are clearly defined, the partners need not become "personally involved." The newlywed and middle-aged groups would represent the two extremes of this continuum, with the groups facing retirement occupying an intermediate position. The renewed attention given to personality attributes and affective bonds by these men and women would, in some measure, reflect the decreasing clarity of the role structure following the diminution of responsibilities and tasks related to family and work. The responses of men and women at this stage would also accord with Fengler's (1973) conclusion that values of expressivity and companionship invariably rise to the fore once the fulfillment of basic economic and family requisites is assured.

Table 2 lists the various descriptions of spouses on a three-point scale (predominantly positive, neutral or ambivalent, and predominantly negative). As the table shows, respondents of all groups except middle-aged women gave very similar evaluations: roughly four fifths described their spouses primarily in positive terms. The middle-aged women were conspicuously more critical: only two fifths gave predominantly positive portrayals, two fifths were neutral or matter of fact, and about one fifth stressed only negative attributes. Neither men nor women among the preretirees gave negative portrayals, and they were also exceedingly rare among newlyweds. Evaluations of spouse were, not surprisingly, significantly correlated with descriptions of the marriage as satisfying or unsatisfying. Thus, consistent with their critical portrayals of their husbands, the middle-aged women mentioned the most difficulties in getting along with their husbands.

When asked "How do you think your spouse would describe you?" the newlyweds, actively concerned with their feelings for one another, were quick to reply. In contrast, one third of the pre-

Table 2.

Perceptions of Spouses (percentages)

	Newlywed		Middle-Aged		Preretirement	
	Men	Women	Men	Women	Men	Women
Description of Spouse						
Positive	72	76	85	42	82	82
Neutral/ambivalent	24	16	15	42	18	18
Negative	4	8	0	16	0	0
	(N = 25)	(N = 25)	(N = 26)	(N = 24)	(N = 27)	(N = 22)
Spouse's Description of Subject						
Positive	75	61	33	54	57	55
Neutral/ambivalent	8	30	43	31	31	27
Negative	17	8	24	14	11	19
	(N = 24)	(N = 23)	(N = 21)	(N = 24)	(N = 19)	(N = 11)
Family Authority						
Male dominant	64	75	54	44	41	50
Egalitarian	36	17	31	26	44	10
Female dominant	0	8	15	30	15	40
	(N = 25)	(N = 24)	(N = 26)	(N = 23)	(N = 27)	(N = 20)

retired men and over half of the preretired women found it impossible to answer, partly from genuine lack of awareness and partly from greater reticence (and possibly modesty). Newlywed men and preretired men seemed considerably more confident of their spouses' positive evaluations than women in these groups (the optimism of the men in this sample will be a recurrent theme). Among middle-aged men, however, only one third would expect predominantly positive descriptions, as compared to more than half of the women. In other words, while the middle-aged men stressed their wives' virtues, they were ready to admit that they did not meet their wives' expectations. The women shared this view: they were not only more critical of their husbands but more confident of their own role performance (a trend noted also by Gurin, Veroff, and Feld, 1960). In terms of fulfilling emotional needs, these sex differences appear to mirror actuality. Middle-aged men, by and large, did not question their adequacy as family providers but seemed aware—though not necessarily contrite about it or moved to change—that they were often inconsiderate and unheeding of the wife's desires for attention, companionship, or diversion. Moreover, in describing daily activities, these men made fewer references to spouses than did women, tending to disregard the many commonplace interactions and discussions, integral to the domestic scene, which were stressed by women.

Men in every stage tended to describe themselves as "boss" in the family or to describe their marriages as egalitarian, and were considerably more reluctant than women to ascribe dominance to the wife (Table 2). Among men, the idea of male dominance declines across the three life stages, accompanied by a marked increase in female dominance in the reports of older women. Given the recent search for new patterns of conjugal relations (see, for example, Skolnick and Skolnick, 1971), the marked adherence to traditional norms of male authority among the newlyweds (reported by two thirds of the men and three fourths of the women) was unanticipated. Though ideological supports for traditional sex-role differentiation may be waning, emotional allegiance to traditional patterns remains strong (Komarovsky, 1973). For people facing a critical role transition and the integration of multiple new experiences and tasks, perhaps traditional rules of decision making prove reassuring and expedient. Then, too, male dominance is implicit in the romanticism characteristic of this life stage—viewed by some as part of the normal maturational process (Kephart, 1970), by others as a necessary condition for the formation of enduring unions (Spanier, 1972). The newlyweds' endorsement of male dominance may also allay anxieties about their masculine and feminine identities. Their views on marital authority may best be regarded as a passing phase, and longitudinal data may allow us to examine the specific events which bring about a reorientation. Marital authority has been shown to be influenced by socioeconomic factors (Goode, [1963] 1970), though the effects of women's rise in the occupational hierarchy remain to be determined. Nevertheless, one would venture that women are granted, or assume, increasing authority when they become responsible for the welfare and socialization of children and again when the husband relinquishes the role of family provider.

Married subjects were asked about marital changes since the prior stage and those anticipated for the next (see Table 3). Thus, newlyweds reported on changes during the first year of marriage and on the changes that they expected in their marriage when their children were grown; middle-aged respondents were asked to review changes since marriage and to anticipate changes after the children had left home; people in the preretirement stage were asked to describe changes since their children had left home and changes anticipated following retirement. Men and women at all stages tended to perceive their marriages as changing and growing rather than static, although there was a progressive decline in this attitude by life stage.

Across all groups most people felt that their marriages had improved, with newlyweds and preretired men giving somewhat more positive evaluations than others. Predictions for the future varied considerably more across the life course. Newlyweds were strikingly more optimistic than all other groups, offering positive to neutral descriptions in ratios of 2:1; the older groups, except middle-aged women, tended to give neutral responses as often as positive ones. Again, middle-aged women were most pessimistic, with neutral or ambivalent expectations vastly outnumbering positive ones.

The ideals of emotional intimacy and of loving, enduring

Table 3.
CHANGES IN MARITAL AND SEXUAL RELATIONS (percentages)

	Newlywed		Middle-Aged		Preretirement	
	Men	Women	Men	Women	Men	Women
Marital Relations						
Retrospective change						
Positive	54	62	46	48	59	46
Neutral/ambivalent	12	14	25	14	4	4
Negative	12	14	12	24	7	14
No change	21	10	17	14	30	36
	(N = 24)	(N = 21)	(N = 24)	(N = 21)	(N = 27)	(N = 22)
Anticipated change						
Positive	64	61	36	17	23	27
Neutral/ambivalent	27	26	28	44	23	27
Negative	0	9	8	9	12	5
No change	9	4	28	30	42	41
	(N = 22)	(N = 23)	(N = 25)	(N = 23)	(N = 26)	(N = 22)
Sexual Relations						
Retrospective change						
Better	96	61	33	44	29	32
Mixed/ambivalent	4	13	0	16	4	14
Worse	0	13	21	24	50	32
No change	0	13	46	16	18	21
	(N = 20)	(N = 18)	(N = 21)	(N = 15)	(N = 19)	(N = 22)
Anticipated change						
Better	55	50	5	0	0	6
Mixed/ambivalent	5	6	14	20	10	6
Worse	30	6	57	33	63	33
None expected	10	39	24	47	26	56
	(N = 20)	(N = 18)	(N = 21)	(N = 15)	(N = 19)	(N = 18)

solidarity, often described as the distinctive features of the American family (Goode, [1963] 1970; Schneider, 1968), emerged clearly. In depicting past change, newlyweds stressed heightened sensitivity to the partner's emotional needs and a rising sense of commitment which permitted increasing openness. Both sexes expressed relief at their ability to express negative feelings, and admitted to greater frequencies of spats and quarrels, which they tended to regard as promoting growth; they seemed predisposed to evaluate all changes as maturation. The few who said that their marriages were less satisfying than formerly attributed such decline to external rather than personal factors. Newlywed men and women pointed to the disruptive effect of job requirements on their relationship (voiced by about one fifth), commenting that long or irregular work schedules kept them apart and hindered joint activities. The newlyweds' expectations for the future were contiguous with the past: the relationship would become closer, warmer, and happier. While most felt that children would enhance the sense of closeness, some believed it important to work out the best possible relationship before the arrival of children, who might deflect attention from the marital bond and impede the achievement of genuine understanding. Some observed that "most couples either stay the same or lose their closeness"—and hoped that their marriage would prove an exception.

Middle-aged respondents shared the newlyweds' concern for closeness but gave a sense of gradual settling down with time, of coming to terms with the exigencies of marriage and family and making allowances for temperamental or value differences. Women were somewhat more negative about the course of their marriage, alluding to conflict over children and at times to general disillusionment. Both men and women at this life stage tended to look forward to the departure of children (Lowenthal and Chiriboga, 1972a) as an event which would improve marital relations. The emphasis was not on better understanding but on companionship and mutual dependency. Though, as will be discussed later (see Chapter Ten), values relating to marriage and family ranked highest in the value hierarchy of middle-aged men and women, and though they were appreciative and generally supportive of their offspring, the disruptive influence of teenage children on marital relations was a recurrent theme. Bohannan (1971, p. 58) states that, unlike people in other societies, "middle-class Americans establish a sort of antithesis between parenting and spousing," where parenting is perceived to "interfere with the capacities of a spouse either to give or receive attention and love from the other spouse." This attitude was often implicit in statements from older subjects, who appeared anxious for an end to parenting and a return to spousing.

Marital relationships seem indeed to improve in the period between the departure of children and retirement, though more from the perspective of men than women. The oldest men resembled the newlyweds in their positive evaluations of past change within marriage. The greater companionship and closeness were attributed to increased opportunities to spend time together and the renewal of the wife's undivided attention. Women also noted improvement since the departure of children, though they did not voice as high a degree of satisfaction. These older subjects were less likely than the middle-aged to anticipate further change in their relationship, conveying the impression that major adjustments had already been made. Men tended to look forward to increased sharing of activities, though aware that increased exposure following retirement might bring new problems if they were to become inactive and not develop interests of their own. Both men and women often commented on the increased potential for friction and irritability. Men seemed conscious that they would be intruding into the wife's domain; women were concerned that the husband's presence and demands might disrupt their own preferred routines and activities.

The results of our cross-sectional analysis accord with those of other researchers (Blood and Wolfe, 1960; Burr, 1970; Rollins and Feldman, 1970): marital dissatisfactions tend to peak during the period preceding the empty-nest stage and are followed by increased satisfaction in the postparental and early retirement stages. Troll (1971), in reviewing the literature, concludes that while the data presented show a trend toward a "passive-congenial" type of marriage in later life, writers differ in their valuations of this trend. The changes reported and anticipated by our older groups might appropriately be described as converging toward a "passive-congenial" orientation; and while the newlyweds would undoubtedly regard this as disenchanting, the older subjects themselves viewed it with favor.

The changing dependency needs of the two spouses across the life span, and the modes in which these needs are fulfilled, would appear to be a critical issue requiring further study. Older women in our sample at times felt that their spouses were overdependent, whereas among the newlyweds men were more likely to express such feelings. The transition to the "empty nest" has been described as an unhappy time for women (Spence and Lonner, 1971), and the heightened marital dissatisfaction expressed by these women may constitute but one of many interrelated factors—both intrapersonal and interpersonal. However welcome, the cessation of parenting functions seems to leave a vacuum and demands major reorientation of purposes and goals. This situation could enhance the wife's need for emotional support—a need which husbands are not ready to fulfill because the demands of the work world still engage their energy and attention. (In a certain sense, the preretirement stage brings a reversal of this situation.) Also relevant is Bohannan's (1973) proposition that the adolescent child may have a critical impact on marital relations, evoking in the parents memories of their own adolescent turmoil and bringing their unresolved oedipal problems to the fore. As shown in Chapter Seven, women had a considerably more negative recollection of adolescence than did men.

In the study of marriage we were also concerned with changes in the quality of sexual experiences. Whether reporting changes during the short period of marriage or contrasting marital and premarital sex, newlywed men invariably reported high, newly discovered satisfaction (Table 3). For them sex had become more all-encompassing; they contrasted "mature" and "mutual" love with earlier views of sex as a matter of athletics or entertainment, and often mentioned a decline in "hang-ups" and anxieties and an increasing sense of "competence." Newlywed women responded similarly: sex had become more "emotionally satisfying," a "more complete giving." They differed from men in not alluding to earlier anxieties. Also, considerably more women (about one fourth) than men (only 4 percent) reported ambivalence or a decline in satisfaction. Thus, one woman missed the excitement of illicit sex, one felt that her husband's interest had waned, and yet another commented, "I don't like it very much. . . . I can think of better things to do."

For the older groups, questions of sexual intimacy and optimal sexual adjustment had been supplanted by other existential concerns, and changes were no longer as consistently positive. In general, middle-aged men tended to be more positive, the older men less positive, than women in these groups, who were roughly similar to each other. Middle-aged men were most likely to state that no change had occurred (almost one half), while the men facing retirement tended to report a decline in satisfaction (one half).

Older people who did report increasing sexual satisfaction (about one third) pointed to changes similar to those of newlyweds. Men spoke of heightened "enjoyment" and "appreciation" deriving from growing emotional involvement and compatibility. Women spoke of "better understanding of one another," of becoming more "honest and comfortable," and made explicit references to early inhibitions, a problem not voiced by newlywed women. Accounts of negative change were considerably more varied. Here women tended to comment on change in attitudes and feelings, while men focused on decline in interest in and frequency of intercourse. Women blamed their husbands, explicitly or implicitly, for shortcomings in satisfaction: husbands were "not considerate," or their "critical behavior during the day made it difficult to feel affectionate at night." While some women regretted the absence of earlier passion and "excitement," others occasionally welcomed the decline in wifely duties: "I'm happy about it. I'm not a sexy person and never have been."

Middle-aged men, the group most likely to perceive no change (or to deny change), tended to stress waning interest rather than declining potency when reporting negatively: "The thrill is gone. I just don't look at girls the way I used to. You look at a woman just like a person." The men facing retirement were explicit about declining potency, which they viewed as an unavoidable concomitant of aging. They admitted to not having the "same urge" and not being as "ambitious" as when younger. Some commented that gains in other areas compensated for this loss, or that the decline in potency was fortunately accompanied by a commensurate wane in interest. As one man put it, "Nature has a way of not letting things you can't do affect you too much."

Themes of declining interest in and frequency of sexual intercourse predominated in the men's discussion of anticipated changes. Only about one fourth of the middle-aged and older men expected no change, over half mentioned a decline, and almost none foresaw heightened satisfaction. Though the majority of newlywed men were confident of growing satisfaction, about one third anticipated changes similar to those reported by older men. They thought that sex might become less absorbing and anticipated possible "stretches of boredom." Compared to men, women more often anticipated no change; this was the predominant view of the older women (about one half) and one also frequently expressed by the younger.

Our findings support those of Pfeiffer and his associates (1972), who noted an overall decline in sexual interest and activity with advancing age, along with a tendency for men to assume direct responsibility for the change and for women to attribute it to their husbands. Our data are also congruent with the traditional view that sexual relations are more important to men than women—a view which, whether valid or not, has the real consequence that for men self-worth is more critically linked to this area. This could account for the tendency among men to veer toward extremes in their evaluations of change, while the greater tendency among women to report no change suggests lesser concern and differentiation and may be a consequence of their more passive stance. Whatever importance they attached to sexual relations, the older groups of women conveyed the impression that husbands were responsible for whatever satisfactions they experienced. Older men seemed to agree, since they never alluded to their wives' attitudes or behavior. Though newlyweds appeared consciously striving toward sexual equality and mutuality, the relative differences in evaluations given by men and women tended to conform to the pattern observed among the older groups.

Many subjects believed that changes in sexual relations would not affect the meaningfulness of marriage, and this view was not invalidated by the data. No significant association was found between reports of past change in sexual relations and past change in the marital relationship, nor was there an association between ratings of anticipated changes in these two areas.

Nuances of Projection

The direct approach to perceptions of heterosexual relationships was supplemented by free associations evoked by a pertinent card (10) from the Murray (1943) Thematic Apperception Test

(TAT). The latent stimuli of the card, which shows a woman's head against a man's shoulder, consist of themes of physical closeness and love objects, as well as views of spouse and parental marriages (Henry, [1956] 1967). In assessing the dimensions of the stories told by subjects, we sought to keep inferences at a minimum and focused on their manifest content. Categories developing from the analysis included the age and role relationships of the characters, the attitudes and affect of the man and woman vis-à-vis one another, sexual behavior, and plots and their outcomes. Despite extensive and varied use of TAT material, the relationship between the imagery contained in the stories and actual behavior remains subject to considerable debate. We concur with Neugarten and Gutmann (1968), who conclude that TAT imagery, although not informative about daily role behavior, does evoke central issues and affective components of roles. On the whole, the projective material corroborated findings derived from direct questioning, but it also revealed subtle differences in attitudes and concerns.

Subjects almost uniformly identified the figures as representing love or marital relationships, and very seldom other dyads—a sharp difference from the low frequencies noted by Henry ([1956] 1967), possibly because of the higher family orientation of our sample. The themes centered on affiliation, consolation, reunion, separation, and courtship. Affiliation stresses ongoing, mutually satisfying relationships as ends in themselves; consolation carries the connotation that the primary value of the relationship rests on having someone to turn to when in need or distressed. High school and newlywed women and middle-aged men and women gave greater emphasis to affiliation than to consolation; newlywed men and preretired men mentioned both in roughly equal proportions. Women in the preretirement stage conveyed a more negative outlook than did the remaining groups: they were more likely to portray themes of consolation than affiliation and were most likely to allude to permanent disruptions of unions. Lastly, themes of courtship occurred frequently in the stories of high school boys and preretired men (one fourth) and rarely among other groups.

The stories of newlywed men encompassed a wider range of themes and plots than did those of the remaining groups, and were more individualistic and attuned to their personal marital experiences. The stories took the form of expressive and hopeful accounts of love and caring, most often limited to moments of intimacy, or of reaffirming the relationship after discord. Consistent with the description of their marriages, newlywed men and women were more likely to describe the woman as dependent than were other groups. Newlywed women stood out from the rest of the sample in referring to parental nurturance—with themes of a child's happy return home or of mothers giving love and assurance to the child. Some were clearly anticipating their future roles as parent; however, the prominence given to the mother-son relationship suggests they may have been, less consciously, commenting on their relationship to their husbands. Thus, while the husbands were portrayed as protectors, they were also seen as persons dependent on their wives for emotional support and understanding.

Middle-aged men tended to tell stories of married couples of indeterminate age, with the focus on the conjugal relationship and with conspicuously few references to parental roles. For the most part, relationships were described as tender and comfortable. Feelings of affiliation and reciprocal nurturance seemed important to these men. In contrast, in their description of their own marriage they emphasized the wife's instrumental role performance and admitted their shortcomings as husbands. The concern to maintain a strong masculine image may have made them reluctant to expose their need for nurturance and also deflected overt displays of affection. Possibly such feelings could more readily be expressed in fantasy, where they could picture themselves as loving and caring and could feel at ease in describing tender emotions. Their stories also suggest that closeness with children was of less importance to them than love and support from the wife.

Whereas middle-aged men left the age of the characters indeterminate, their female peers tended to specify middle-aged and elderly couples, suggesting that unlike men they were keenly aware of the permutations of the family cycle and the particular stage which they themselves presently occupied. Themes of happy marriages occurred about as frequently as among men but were more likely to be attributed to the very elderly. These women's stories more often touched upon familial roles; in consolation themes the losses experienced were more severe and more deeply felt, and the consolation offered was less warm and less effective. In general, the women were more inhibited and sparing in telling of emotional bonds between men and women, placing emphasis on a relationship that provides support and mitigates against loneliness. The word *tender,* often used by men, was infrequent among women, who more often used the term *clinging.* The women's stories suggested that men fell short of meeting their wives' emotional needs; the stories also indicated anticipation of increasing dependency and greater closeness in the future. In general, the feelings that these women portrayed in the projective material were very consistent with those shown in their answers to direct questions.

Men at the preretirement stage, in sharp contrast to middle-aged men, more frequently described nonmarital relationships, and their stories had greater sexual content. Their stories most often portrayed love relationships, either courtship or monents of emotional or physical intimacy. In contrast, when they identified characters as husband and wife, the stories tended to contain themes of grief and consolation; comfort was proffered, but nurturance and warmth were lacking, and their narrative style suggested some rejection of the theme the picture had evoked. The satisfying companionable bonds contained in their description of their actual marital relationships were missing; and some nostalgia about youthful romantic and passionate encounters was apparent. Although their discussion of sexual relations yielded few depressive comments, their stories suggested some distress and apprehension about declining virility.

Women in the preretirement cohort were less likely than other groups to portray simple themes of affiliation. Their stories of consolation were accompanied by notions of "leaning on one another" and the idea that "life must go on." While among other groups losses generally affected both partners equally, these women tended to single out the woman as the person experiencing the misfortune. Their stories, too, occasionally strayed outside the framework of marriage; and there were indications, as among older men, of reaction to the sexual stimulus of the card. However, while men were explicit about physical intimacy, women tended to deny it ("I would say they don't look sexy") and to focus on romantic sentiment instead. At times there were shades of cynicism; and, on the whole, the older women tended to comment more coldly on male-female relationships than did middle-aged women.

Finally, we developed a measure of overall emotional content, which we felt would usefully summarize the key feature of the narrative and also serve as an indicator of the individual's openness in the handling of feelings and emotional intimacy. As will be discussed later, this measure further provided a means of exploring the association of projective material to other parameters of the study. TAT responses were evaluated for the intensity of feelings (both positive and negative) contained in the story, such evaluations based primarily on the use of affect-laden terms in the depiction of heterosexual relationships or in the descriptions of emotional reactions of characters to a given event. The resultant four-point scale included, at one end of the scale, instrumental responses totally devoid of affect and, at the other end, portrayals of deep emotions (for example, "very tender moment," "deep sorrow"). Average emotional-content scores showed no significant group differences except that high school boys had lower scores than any of the other groups. Newlywed women gave the highest number of glowing, loving relationships (over one half), considerably more than newlywed men. A reversal, however, was noted among middle-aged subjects, where men (over one third, and the second highest in the sample) more often gave sensitive portrayals of relationships than women. Men in the preretirement stage generally told stories with moderate or minimal expression of affect, in contrast to women, who tended toward extremes: while their stories often contained high emotional content (about one third), these women were also the group most likely to avoid any display of feeling (over one fourth).

Intergenerational Relationships

The literature on parent-child relationships is voluminous; the concepts and theoretical issues vary not only by discipline but also by the phase of the family cycle under scrutiny. In studies of early phases, most extensively conducted by psychologists and psychoanalysts, the problem is phrased in terms of the parents' influence on the psychological development or psychopathology of the child; in later phases, the domain of social gerontologists, the focus shifts to the effect of the child on the morale and well-being of the elderly parent. Some studies of the middle phase of the family cycle—that is, of the relationship of the adolescent or the college student to the middle-aged parent—are clinically oriented (Westley and Epstein, 1969; Douvan and Adelson, 1966); others have investigated the universality and dynamics of intergenerational conflict (Erikson, 1970; Bengtson and Kuypers, 1971). Specific studies have examined similarities and differences in values and ideologies, and the associations of these domains to socialization practices and the affective aspects of parent-child interaction (Block, Haan, and Smith, 1969; Bengtson, 1971; Keniston, 1968; Thurnher, Spence, and Lowenthal, 1974). Works that focus directly on the permutations of parent-child relationship across the life cycle (for example, Pressey and Kuhlen, 1957) remain rare; our own study has such a focus. We tried to discover how parents' perceptions of their children vary over the years and how, in turn, the individual's perception of his parents changes as he rears a family and grows older.

Middle-aged subjects and those approaching retirement looked back to the time when their children were infants as the period of greatest parental happiness. In so doing, they may in part be indulging in pleasant recollections of their more youthful selves, or reflecting more contemporary experiences of carefree interaction with grandchildren. For the most part, they were nostalgic for a period free of parent-child conflict, a period when, whatever the stresses, the child's dependence on the parents is unquestioned and his expressions of love most frequent and direct ("Little children are such a delight and everything is so new to them; they are capable of such happiness and such sorrow, and their troubles are so easy to fix"). Middle-aged men also recalled with fondness the years when their children were five to twelve years old, whereas for older men the next most satisfying relationships occurred after the children had fully matured. More attuned to the complexities of child development, women were more likely to comment that each period of growth had its own gratifications and frustrations.

Both the middle-aged, who were still contending with a high school senior (and at the height of the so-called "generation gap"), and those in the preretirement stage considered teenage children especially trying for parents (see also Clausen, 1972). Most groups experienced somewhat less difficulty in relating to daughters (a daughter was most often mentioned as the child they got along with best); the oldest group of men formed an interesting exception in often according preferred status to the oldest son, suggesting an emergent concern for succession (Bengtson and Kuypers, 1971), which contributes to increased closeness and respect between father and "heir."

About three fourths of the middle-aged parents and those facing retirement reported some conflict with children. For the most part, these conflicts could best be termed "mild" or "moderate" and only rarely amounted to resentment or rejection of the child. The reasons for conflict included problems of tidiness, lackadaisical attitudes toward studies, difficulties in communication, and troublesome personality traits. Differences in goals and values played a lesser role than anticipated, being mentioned no more often than any of the other problem areas. The presence of conflict did not detract from the positive descriptions and appraisals of children (Thurnher, Spence, and Lowenthal, 1974).

Parental descriptions of children, including teenage youngsters, were predominantly benign. About half of the parents had only positive things to say about their children, and only about one tenth of the middle-aged and almost none of the older men and women made strong negative comments. The remaining descriptions can most accurately be described as "mixed indulgent," recognizing frailties or irritating idiosyncracies—often viewed as temporary—but stressing the overall likeableness of the child. (For example, one woman described her daughter as a "petite," "selfish," and "very loving person," and mentioned "lying" as her weak point.)

Given differences in family size, and the fact that not all children are equally loved or equally trying, a series of summary affect scores were developed: affect toward sons, affect toward daughters, and affect toward children. Except for men in the preretirement stage, all groups tended to have more satisfying relationships with daughters. It is not that these men valued daughters less than did other groups, but that, perhaps because of concerns for successors, they were more appreciative of their sons. Affect-toward-children scores, which capture overall attitudes and feelings, showed that middle-aged parents had less positive feelings than those in the preretirement stage.

In general, portrayals of mothers were more positive than those of fathers—partly, perhaps, because the concept of a "good mother" is more clearly and narrowly defined than is that of a "good father." Thus, respondents tended to evaluate mothers in terms of nurturance, caring, and understanding, and generally to see them as meeting these expectations. Fathers, on the other hand, were appraised in terms of their occupational competence and performance as family providers, as well as their mood and personality and their capacity to relate to others. Similarly, mother-child relationships were seen as smoother than father-child relations. When asked which member of their family of origin they felt closest to, men and women in every life stage mentioned mother almost twice as often as they did father, the sense of closeness often transcending negative appraisals or reports of friction in the relationship.

Summary scores (affect toward mother, affect toward father) proved the mother to be the favored parent across all groups, except for high school boys and middle-aged women. Reflecting perhaps the urgency of establishing a male identity, which at this stage may require conscious rejection of feminine traits, the high school boys tended to elevate the father and to devaluate the mother. This suggested need to identify with the father figure is further reflected in the answers to the question "Do you think you are more like your mother or your father?" High school boys reported that they were like their father more often than did other groups.

Newlyweds displayed a certain rejection of parent figures; both men and women were particularly critical of fathers and reported greatest difficulties in relating to them. The dynamics underlying this seeming severance of ties appear to be different for the two sexes. The young men seem pressed to denigrate their fathers as one means of asserting their comparatively new adult male status. Among women, the devaluation of fathers may reflect a need to resolve (possibly unconscious) conflicting loyalties, with guilt being fanned by the father's negative reaction to the loss of his daughter to another.

Compared to the newlyweds, the older groups (except for

middle-aged women) had predominantly positive perceptions of parents. In retrospect, they recalled relating equally well to both parents, though descriptions of the mother tended to be somewhat more favorable than those of the father. Middle-aged women, in contrast, had very negative perceptions of their mothers (the second lowest in the sample) and positive perceptions of the father (highest in the sample). If the pattern shown by middle-aged men and the older groups represents normative and stereotypical perceptions, which emerge with increasing physical distance and psychological independence, then the deviation of the middle-aged women would reflect continued, or resurgent, emotional involvement. One can but suggest interpretations: perhaps the heightened marital dissatisfaction which characterized this group leads to a compensatory glorification of their fathers. Drawing upon Jungian theory and assuming that parental figures reflect masculine and feminine components of one's psyche, we might conclude that the middle-aged women are expressing a need for reorientation—namely, to be more like their fathers and less like their mothers, the unconscious awareness that wholeness would demand greater acknowledgment of their instrumental and active functions and a veering away from nurturant passive functions. As will be shown in Chapter Four, a reorientation in this direction does in fact appear to take place in later life.

To complete the study of dyads within the nuclear family, we traced perceptions of same- and cross-sex siblings across the life course. In this area—reflecting, perhaps, the relatively low salience of the sibling bond in the American kinship system (Rosenberg and Anspach, 1973)—our respondents showed fewer and less pronounced stage and sex differences than in their perceptions of parents or children. Nevertheless, a consistent trend toward more positive evaluations of cross-sex siblings was shown across all groups. This trend suggests the continuation of rivalry with siblings of the same sex into later years of life—a field of inquiry which has been neglected. Our findings deviate from previous research, which has shown that the closest relationships prevail between same-sex siblings, particularly between sisters (Adams, 1968; Irish, 1964). These differing results are not irreconcilable if one assumes that rivalry and ambivalence do not necessarily rule out emotional closeness.

In our attempt to assess the feelings invested in family membership and, more important, to provide a method for examining the implications of the family sphere for other areas of adult life, we devised a summary measure of familial affect. Stage and sex differences in familial-affect scores were not significant. This finding suggests that, although the composition of family networks and perceptions of individual family members fluctuate in the course of the life span, the overall emotional involvement potentially remains relatively constant, at least for this family-oriented, middle- and lower-middle-class sample.

Intrafamilial Perceptions

Observations of family interaction readily suggest the proposition that the way an individual perceives one family member may influence his perceptions of other family members. Having noted variations in perceptions of family dyads, we proceeded to explore systematic associations between these perceptions. As a further step, we also assessed the relationship of these perceptions to the feelings conveyed in the projective material. (An intercorrelational analysis of all measures of familial affect and emotional-content scores of TAT stories was undertaken for this purpose.)

Perceptions of mother showed a significant association with perceptions of father among all men except the newlywed men; among women this association was noted only for the middle-aged group. These findings suggest that men are more prone to view parents as a unit, appreciating or rejecting both equally, whereas women tend to be more discriminating and are more likely to respond to and evaluate each parent independently. Noted among high school girls was what might be construed as a tendency to equate same-sex parents and siblings; affect toward their mother, whether positive or negative, tended to be reflected in attitudes toward sisters, and attitudes toward their fathers paralleled those toward brothers. A similar linkage between perceptions of parents and perceptions of siblings was found among newlywed men, though in their case it was limited to a strong association between affect toward father and brother.

Except for the close relationship between perceptions of father and mother, significant associations among the older groups were not linked to interaction within the family of origin but were derived from the family of procreation. (Measures of overall affect toward family of origin showed no relationship with overall affect toward family of procreation.) Among the older subjects, except middle-aged women, perceptions of spouses paralleled perceptions of children. Love or approval of one's child would tend to promote love and approval of the child's other parent, while frustration over a child's behavior could well evoke some sense of dissatisfaction with one's spouse. On the other hand, one must also consider the reverse causal relationship—namely, that feelings about one's spouse affect feelings toward children. It is possible that a sex difference prevails in this regard and that, among men more than among women, the rejection of a spouse is likely to lead to rejection of children. This sex difference appears to decline after the children have left home and may account for the fact that among middle-aged women, in contrast to other groups, feelings toward their husbands showed no relationship with feelings toward children. Though these women were often dissatisfied with the conjugal relationship, this dissatisfaction seemed not to contaminate appraisal of their children.

The ratings of emotional content in TAT stories provided a simple method of tapping the individual's overall expressivity and his capacity, or need, for emotional intimacy. In order to further our understanding of family dynamics, we explored the relationship between feelings conveyed in fantasy and those expressed in the portrayals of family relationships. The analysis yielded significant associations between emotional content and affect toward family members among all groups except high school boys and women in the preretirement phase. Most interesting was the finding—one which points to the cardinal role of women in the shaping of an individual's emotional responsivity—that, with only one exception (newlywed men), all associations involved female family members— mother, sister, or wife. However, while high emotional content was consistently related with positive affect among women, it was linked with negative affect among men.

High school girls and newlywed women who told stories with high emotional content expressed warm feelings toward their sisters; newlywed women, as well as middle-aged women, also expressed warm feelings toward their mothers. The associations found among married women suggest that the feeling dimensions of the early home environment, particularly the emotional ties with the mother, influence a woman's attitude toward intimacy and closeness. Satisfying relationships with the mother, possibly also a sense of identification, seem to foster expressivity and openness to feelings; negative experiences with the mother, on the other hand, may contribute toward the inhibition of feelings and unease or fear regarding close interpersonal relationships.

The psychodynamic processes suggested above were not applicable to men, among whom associations were more disparate and attempts at explication more difficult and speculative. Newlywed men diverged strikingly from the other groups, for in their stories the father emerged as the critical figure. Those who tended to be critical or rejecting of their fathers revealed deep emotions in the fantasy material; those who valued fathers highly told stories devoid of feelings. This constellation suggests problems relating to masculine self-identity, the acceptance or rejection of traditional male roles as represented by the father. Again, perhaps fathers are more appreciative of and relate better to sons whose orientation is instrumental and pragmatic, and are less responsive to sons who show emotional sensitivity and high affiliative and nurturant needs. Among middle-aged men, high emotional content was associated with negative evaluations of wives. Earlier, when contrasting the very warm relationships depicted in fantasy with the relatively low display of feelings in the description of marital relationships, we commented that this difference may stem from the need to project a strong masculine image. The present analysis suggests further that their fantasies may have been compensatory in nature, reflecting unconscious (or conscious) wishes arising from emotional nurturant needs that their wives failed to meet. The men in the preretirement stage presented yet another configuration, an association of high emotional content with negative affect toward the mother. This configuration may reflect a repression of threatening intimacy and sexuality, which sometimes accompanies strong attachment to the mother (the TAT picture was more likely to evoke sexual imagery among the older men than among other groups). It also suggests that men who have experienced some maternal deprivation may be particularly prone to feel strong emotional needs in late life. A general trend for older men to become more tolerant of their own nurturant impulses is reported in Neugarten and Gutmann's (1968) study of TAT material and is also noted in our analysis of self-concept data in Chapter Four.

Life-Course Perspectives on Friendship

At least four types of dyadic relationships may be envisioned: (1) acquaintanceship, (2) friendly interaction, (3) friendship, and (4) intimacy. In the foregoing sequence, each type is distinguished by an increment of knowledge about the unique individuality of the other, as contrasted with a role-reliant or stereotyped conception. Thus, friendship is more personal and less role reliant than either the friendly interaction or acquaintanceship. The intimate relationship is even more personal and, ideally, totally free of the formal, involving a higher degree of closeness, spontaneous interaction, emotional commitment, responsibility, and mutuality.

Friendship, in this discussion, is defined as a voluntary, unique, dyadic relationship. Implicit in this dyad are the assumptions (1) of continued interaction by the two persons involved and (2) that they view themselves as the sole members of a collectivity (Weber, 1947; McCall and others, 1970). This collectivity may be formal, whereby norms and roles define and constrict the pattern of the interaction; or it may be highly idiosyncratic and flexible, whereby mutual recognition and knowledge dictate the style of interaction. Although these two extremes are theoretically pure forms, everyday associations may swing back and forth between them. For instance, one's physical attributes may contaminate the 'pure' formal relation; one's stereotypical role concepts may hamper the development of spontaneity and uniqueness. The importance of role and other more formal behaviors obviously will lessen as spontaneity increases (McCall and Simmons, 1966). This chapter is devoted to an exploration of those qualities that people in this middle- and lower-middle-class sample attributed to their friends. Both the structural components and the qualitative substance of friendship are considered.

A first step in searching out the quality or substance of the relationship between friends is to describe the friendship structure. In the present study, the respondents described their friendship networks (see Table 4) with respect to number of friends, their age and sex, relation to subject's spouse, and length and frequency of contact. Each subject listed his friends, and the range was from none to 24; the mean was 5.7, considerably higher than the 3.7 figure obtained by Booth (1972). This difference is no doubt in part accounted for by Booth's greater proportion of blue-collar subjects, who generally report fewer friends than do white-collar respondents. In addition, Booth's subjects were all over the age of forty-five, which probably tends to lower the mean number of friends a bit more. In the sample reported on here, the newlyweds had the most friends (a mean of 7.6), the preretirement group ranked second highest (6.0), and the middle-aged and high school groups had the fewest friends (4.7 and 4.8). On the average, however, the two older groups had about one less friend than the two younger. One possible explanation for the newlyweds' having the highest number of friends is that they usually counted a couple as two friends, whereas the other groups tended to consider only the same-sex member a friend.

Table 4.
Friendship Networks by Life Stage and Sex

	High School	Newlywed	Middle-Aged	Preretirement	Men	Women	Total
Mean Number of Friends	4.8	7.6	4.7	6.0	5.2	6.3	5.7
Percent Reporting Contact:							
Daily	75	24	33	26	38	37	33
Weekly	19	52	44	41	36	34	38
Monthly/less	6	24	23	33	26	29	29
Percent Reporting Duration of Friendship:							
At least 5 yrs.	73	53	12	7	30	39	35
More than 6 yrs.	27	47	88	93	70	61	65
Friend Considered Important to Spouse (%)	NA	61	81	82	79	70	75
Percent of Respondents Who Have An Opposite-Sex Friend:							
Among 3 friends listed	62	66	30	18	39	46	43
For closest friend only	9	12	0	5	8	4	5
Age of Closest Friend (%):							
Younger	3	3	2	12	6	2	5
Same	94	90	93	85	90	94	90
Older	3	7	5	3	4	4	5
High Friendship Complexity (%)	38	56	37	70	46	56	46

In all the stages, women consistently reported a greater number of friends than did men (a mean of 6.3, compared to 5.2). In contrast, Booth (1972) found that white-collar men have more friends than white-collar women and that there are no significant sex differences in the blue-collar group.

Not surprisingly, three quarters of the high school seniors reported daily interaction with friends. People in other stages tended to see their friends on a weekly or monthly basis, with about one third of the preretirement group having contact once a month or less. This interactional decline becomes even sharper when the frequency of contact is weighted by mean number of friends to produce a friendship-participation score (Lurie, 1972). Blau (1961, 1973), who studied interaction with friends among elderly widows, also found that it declined with age. Her criteria for friendship were rather modest: to have a high score in friendship participation, one needed to confide in, see more than once a month, or possess a group of common friends. Despite the different operational criteria, however, our work corroborates Blau's finding. The friendship-participation score decreased with stage, with the high school seniors having the highest scores and the middle-aged the lowest scores. The group facing retirement—perhaps because they were largely relieved of parental obligations, or because they were strengthening friendship networks in anticipation of retirement—reported slightly more involvement with friends than did the middle-aged.

A clear, and perhaps obvious, relationship prevailed between age and the duration of friendship: the older the respondent, the longer the friendship. About three quarters of the friends reported by the high school group had been important for five years or less; among the two older groups, nine out of ten reported friends of six or more years' standing. This trend held for both men and women.

Another component of friendship networks, explored with the married couples, was the extent to which they believed that their friends were important to their spouses. This importance increased from the newlywed group to the two older groups, with men consistently placing slightly more value on their friends' relationship to their spouses than did women. The relative lack of importance of one's friends to one's spouse among the newlyweds may relate to the continuing importance of premarital friendships, even though they are not necessarily perpetuated by the newly married couple. For example, several newlyweds reported an old boy or girl friend, whom they had previously dated, as a close friend. The older couples, having had more time together, have established and developed more friends in common.

Four fifths or more of the men and women in each stage reported their closest friend to be close to their age, a finding supported by Faunce and Beegle (1948) and Koch (1957). Further, the majority of these closest friends were of the same sex. Opposite-sex friends were more frequently cited by the young, almost two thirds of the two younger groups having at least one opposite-sex friend, compared with only one fourth of the two older groups. This trend, of course, reflects traditional norms for the life stages with which we are concerned; the high school seniors (especially the girls) are intermingling courting behavior and friendships, and the newly married are in transition between former heterosexual relationships and the establishment of new joint friendships. We may also be seeing some historical change in normative friendship behavior, reflecting greater tolerance for opposite-sex friends among the younger groups, but this conjecture can be supported or rejected only when we enter the longitudinal phase of the study.

The overall categories or domains and the specific dimensions into which the descriptions of friends fit are listed in Table 5. These varieties of friendship were obtained from the subjects' own subjective descriptions of their real friends, as well as responses from a more abstract question dealing with the "makeup" of an ideal close friend. The respondents' specific and detailed descriptions were content-analyzed and classified into nineteen dimensions, which in turn were grouped into six logical domains or broad categories. The interrater reliability for these nineteen dimensions was .79. The most important broad rubric is *similarity,* encompassing two fifths of all the discrete characteristics mentioned by the respondents (left side of Table 5). This category includes five dimensions, or specific attributes, and is limited to commonalities in behavior and interests, of which *shared experiences* was the most important. Such experiences were often vividly described: "We went through a lot of things together in high school; you know, parties, drinking, all that. You have all these experiences and it just sort of binds you" or

"We've gone through thick and thin together." Sometimes, more recent or current activities were emphasized: "We go to dinners and to cultural events with them." "We take acid trips together and we play music together." "We do a lot of stuff together. . . . I work with him. . . . We fool around at lunch time, too."

The sense of similarity was also often reflected in terms of ease of communication: "He seems to be a person I can talk to pretty well, I guess. We're pretty much the same and communicate well as far as our ideas are concerned" or "She's just the type of person you commune with." Having similar characteristics ("We're the same type of personalities, so we get along pretty well," "He's basically the same type I am," or "He's got a streak of devilment just like I do—that's why we get along so good together") was not cited quite as often as shared experiences and ready communication. Nor, interestingly enough, was the sense of shared interests, ideas, values, or attitudes of great relevance. When mentioned at all, this dimension was described in rather general terms: "We have the same interests . . . in religion and the way we look at things" or "He believes a lot about the same things I believe in."

These findings for our middle- and lower-middle-class sample are not very supportive of Lazarsfeld and Merton's ([1954] 1964) concept of "value homophily" as an important component of friendship, except insofar as shared experiences and activities may reflect shared values. According to Homans (1961), similarity in sentiments does develop through increased interaction, such as reflected in past shared experiences reported here; but similarities are obviously also predisposing factors involved in the beginnings of friendship as well. That perceived similarity among friends is the most emphasized quality generally supports the empirical findings reported in the literature (see, for example, Lott and Lott, 1965; Byrne, 1971).

Reciprocity is the second major area, accounting for about one fifth of all the specific descriptions applied to particular friends. Here, the emphasis was on helping and support. A supportive type of relationship was the one most frequently singled out, accounting for over half of the dimensions falling within this domain and ranking second among all dimensions cited. Our respondents described this characteristic in simple, concrete terms, with the concept of reciprocity often more implicit than explicit: "I can depend on

Table 5.

REAL AND IDEAL QUALITIES OF FRIENDSHIP (percentages)

Domains and Dimensions	Real		Ideal	
	Percent Within Domain	Percent of All Dimensions	Percent Within Domain	Percent of All Dimensions
Similarity				
Shared experiences	34	12	6	1
Sharing activities	24	8	17	5
Verbal communication	19	7	28	8
Similar general behaviors	12	4	21	6
Similar interests	11	5	28	8
Total	100	36	100	28
	(616)[a]		(141)	
Reciprocity				
Supportive/dependable	52	11	34	15
Understanding/accepting	26	6	35	16
Confidant	16	3	19	9
Trustworthy	6	1	12	5
Total	100	21	100	45
	(362)		(230)	
Compatibility				
Likeability	69	11	82	14
Enjoyment	31	5	18	3
Total	100	16	100	17
	(268)		(87)	
Structural Dimensions				
Duration	78	8	90	2
Proximity	22	2	10	0
Total	100	10	100	2
	(174)		(10)	
Role Model				
Respecting	45	2	67	2
Learning/advice	41	2	27	1
Instrumental/useful	14	1	6	0
Total	100	5	100	3
	(93)		(15)	
Other				
Personality	23	3	63	4
"Just good friends"	32	4	0	0
Other	45	5	37	2
Total	100	12	100	6
	(204)		(30)	

[a] Parenthesized numbers refer to the number of descriptions.

her. . . . I know that if I ever needed help with anything, I could always go to her." "Someone I could go to if I were in trouble." A second attribute, understanding or accepting, accounts for about one quarter of the responses in the reciprocity category. Here the reciprocity is made more explicit: "We have a mutual understanding . . . total acceptance." "We have an understanding and we're somewhat closer in that way." Being a confidant reflects a similar reciprocity. "She is someone to confide in. Maybe she cannot do anything for you, but you can cry on her shoulder, get it out of your system. It does not seem so big a mountain if you can talk it over. I talk over everyday problems." "She is one person I can tell anything and everything, no holds barred, and she can tell everything and anything to me. And that's it." In our earlier work (Lowenthal and Haven, 1968) we relied entirely on the respondents' own definitions of confidant and found that these "confidants" ranged from a room clerk to a spouse with whom mutual trust was at least implicit. In the study reported here, we included only the relatively few responses where trust was made quite explicit: "We are close and trusting in thought . . . based on mutual trust." "She listens and you know that it is not going any further."

Altogether, this domain of reciprocity is probably the most complex, involving a higher degree of involvement, commitment, and understanding than the others. Giving and receiving is the central theme. One offers trust, receptiveness, and openness in order to have another share his private self. Differentiations among the four dimensions are not easily discernible. It may well be that all four reflect the level of mutual trust that we are trying to tap, and that happenstance or semantic style rather than degree of intimacy accounts for the emergence of the four dimensions within the reciprocity domain.

The third broad category, *compatibility,* accounted for 16 percent of all responses. Here, the emphasis was on the comfort and ease of the relationship and the likability of the friend. The descriptions tended to be laconic: "He's important as a friend because I like to be with him." "He is a good companion." "He's a likable guy." Also expressed here is the enjoyment, fun, or active entertainment with the other: "She is my fun friend" or "He can take a joke. . . . I enjoy seeing him. I enjoy going to his place." The underlying feeling tone is one of simple pleasure in being with the friend.

The fourth domain is that covering *structural dimensions,* emphasizing nonsubstantive aspects of the relationship, such as duration, geographic closeness, or convenience: "He is important to me because I have known him a long time" or "because we're neighbors" or "because we spend a lot of time together." The simplest of all friendship descriptions, this domain accounted for one tenth of all types of attributes ascribed to friends. If there was substance or feeling tone in the relationship, the subject was unwilling or unable to describe it. Duration of the relationship contributes most to this domain, accounting for over three fourths of the responses within it and ranking fifth among the total nineteen attributes. Proximity or geographic convenience was not perceived by the respondents as a very important quality among friends. In other studies, proximity has been found to be an important quality of friendship, particularly for the working class and the aged (Rosow, 1967; Rosenberg, 1970). Our findings are not contradictory, however, since our sample was neither as old nor as poor as those in the major works cited.

In the *role-model* type of relationship, the emphasis is on attributes to which the respondent himself aspires or which he "looks up to" or respects in his friends: "I respect and value his intelligence." This domain also includes learning experiences where one member of the dyad benefited from the interaction: "He taught me everything I know, from how to handle women to the making of drinks." Conceptually, the domain supports Shapiro's (1953) notion that individuals tend to choose "ideal-self" friends, but for this middle- and lower-middle-class group the role-modeling type of relationship accounts for a mere 5 percent of all descriptions of friends.

The sixth rubric does not constitute a conceptual area but is a catch-all which includes miscellaneous attributes such as specific personality characteristics and a motley range of identifications, such as "He's one of the few friends I have" or "She's a friend of a friend" or "a friend of my wife." These identifications often include references to a familial role: "She's like a sister to me." "He's like a father." This role has a symbolic quality of closeness attached to it but still remains somewhat detached and comfortable. These miscellaneous attributes, accounting for little more than one tenth of all descriptive items, include the ultimate in tautological response: "just good friends."

The first and most important difference between the qualities attributed to real friends and those of an ideal friend appears in the reversal of emphasis on the first two domains (right side of Table 5). Reciprocity is regarded as by far the most important quality in an ideal friend, while similarities predominate in perceptions of real friends. In other words, while a reciprocal relationship is the most desirable (accounting for about half of all characteristics of ideal friends), it is not often realized (accounting for only a fifth of the descriptions of actual friends). Conversely, friendships based on similarities are more important in descriptions of real friends than of ideal. A glance at the shifts in the specific attributes falling within these domains provides further insight into the felt needs accounting for this difference. All dimensions of reciprocity increase in importance as one moves to the descriptions of ideal friends. The greatest increase in emphasis bears on understanding or acceptance. In fact, this is the most important ideal attribute of all nineteen, with its companion, supportive-dependable, a close second. In the similarities category, shared experiences and activities are clearly not as valued as good communication and similar interests. Perhaps when a person talks about his actual friends, he finds it easier to focus on the past and to extract experiences which are dominant in his memory, readily accessible to his consciousness, and easily communicated. On the other hand, when he is encouraged to talk in more abstract terms, about friendship in general, there is no time span or recollection of events or circumstances to draw upon, and there is more freedom of expression. The alternative explanation, of course, is that our subjects are simply making the best of the realities of opportunities for friendship open to them.

The remaining qualities desired in hypothetical friends follow a pattern similar to that evolved from descriptions of real friends, except for the structural dimension, which is of almost no importance. Apparently, at least some of our respondents have settled for what they perceive as "realities" of life, though they attach little value to them.

Perceptions of the qualities of friends and of friendship are surprisingly similar across the four life stages. There are virtually no stage differences in the perception of real friends, one significant distinction in an ideal friend, and one further distinction when real and ideal friends are compared. (Tables showing variations by stage and sex are available on request.) The first finding, that qualities associated with real friends are constant across the four life stages, suggests that the functions of real friendships may be established at an early age and maintained throughout life. The second finding bears on conceptualizations of ideal friends: similarity, a very important attribute of an ideal friend for high school seniors, decreases in importance at successive life stages. These late adolescents are in the process of attempting to establish a separate, unique identity, but they also still have dependent family relationships; their self-concept may well be strengthened by a recognition of similarities with their peers. In the newlywed stage, a clearer self-concept is apparent (Chapter Four), so that the importance of similarity with one's friends is reduced. Other than this difference in the importance attached to similarity, all other ideal concepts of friendship were quite similar across life stages, as were descriptions of real friends.

There was, however, a stage difference in the degree of discrepancy between qualities associated with real friends and those conceived in an ideal friend. A gradual decrease in such discrepancy can be traced across the first three stages: about half of the high school seniors had high discrepancy, compared to about two fifths of the newlywed group and one third of the middle-aged group. A reversal occurred in the group about to retire, however, where the highest discrepancy scores of all (two thirds) prevailed. The decrease in discrepancy noted across the first three stages may reflect an *increase* in selectivity with maturity. That respondents in the oldest group reveal the greatest discrepancy may be explained in part by the idealization of real friends lost along the way through deaths or geographic moves. An alternate explanation for this phenomenon, and one for which we shall shortly provide preliminary evidence, is that the group about to retire, perhaps because of fewer familial and occupational pressures, become more concerned with interpersonal relationships and more interested in the complexities of human nature. Such an increase in perceptual and conceptual sensitivity would, of course, allow for a greater discrepancy between the real and the ideal.

When comparing the various qualities associated with friends, we found sex differences more pronounced than life-course differences. Generally, women responded in more detail than men with respect to their real and their ideal conceptions. This finding may reflect the higher verbal level of the women in this sample, as reflected in the WAIS verbal scores, as well as their deeper involvement in interpersonal relations, which we have seen reflected in their familial relations (Chapter Two). Again, the main differences lie between the first two domains. Men emphasized similarity more frequently than women, across all four stages. Women, again across the four stages, singled out reciprocity. To take the most marked sex difference as an example: only two fifths of the high school boys considered reciprocity important, compared with three fourths of the oldest women. This finding supports Booth's (1972) observation that friendships among women are affectively richer. The men's emphasis on similarity with their real friends centered on common activities, which may reflect a preponderance of on-the-job friendships. In describing their ideal friends, on the other hand, men focused on similar interests and beliefs. Women emphasized good communication with both real and ideal friends, especially with an ideal friend.

Our empirically derived dimensions also enabled us to develop two separate measures of the complexity of friendship patterns: (1) degree of homogeneity or heterogeneity among the three closest friends of the same respondent; (2) complexity of friendship descriptions, regardless of to whom they are attributed. The first issue, then, is whether different friends serve similar or dissimilar roles for the same individual. A heterogeneous friendship pattern might include one person who, out of the three friends selected, is mainly described in the similarity domain, one who is reciprocal, and one who is compatible. For example, a middle-aged woman perceived her first friend as "[like me] in some ways because we have both chosen to retreat from life"; her second friend as "a good person . . . not wise but . . . good"; and her third friend as "my fun friend . . . we go to horse races." Each of these friends clearly assumes different functions for this woman, reflecting a heterogeneous pattern. A homogeneous pattern of friendships was reported, for example, by a high school boy who characterized all three of the friends he selected to describe as "just a good friend." Similarly, a man about to retire depicted his three closest friends as "very compatible; we like to do the same things."

Three quarters of all descriptive categories mentioned were attributed to only one of the three friends described. One fifth were attributed to two friends; and only one twentieth of the descriptive items characterized all three friends. Clearly, the three closest friends described met different needs in the lives of the individual. This heterogeneous pattern held for all subgroups, except for a slight trend toward homogeneity in the preretirement group (two thirds, compared to three quarters for the other three stages). If degree of homogeneity alone is taken into consideration, there is a gradual lowering in the proportion of people who score high across the first three stages: from half of the high school seniors to two fifths of the newlyweds to one quarter of those in the empty-nest stage. The preretirement group, however, significantly reversed this pattern, with three quarters of them ranking high in the homogeneity of their friendships. This pattern is parallel to that found in comparing real and ideal stage differences; that is, the preretirees reversed what appeared to be a stage trend.

While at first glance this shift toward homogeneous friendships might be taken to indicate a need for simplicity, or reduction of diverse elements in one's life, such an assumption would be premature if we do not take into account the *variety* of attributes assigned to friends. The second issue, then, bears on the range of characteristics attributed to friends, regardless of the degree of similarity among the descriptions of three friends. In a sense, this measure reflects the complexity of interpersonal perceptions. This measure was developed by totaling the number of different perceived attributes or dimensions, regardless of to whom they were attributed, for each subject. For example, one older woman about to retire used twelve out of the nineteen dimensions to describe her friends, and they fell in all six of the broad domains. A middle-aged woman, on the other hand, mentioned only one (similar interests) as important in her friends. Marked differences in complexity were manifest across the four stages and were, in fact, highly significant.

In general, friendship complexity was higher in the preretirement group than in the high school seniors. The middle-aged men and women, however, were quite simplistic in their perception of the important qualities in friendship, deviating from the gradual increase in complexity by stage. This lowering in friendship complexity among the middle-aged may in part be explained by the strong familial focus of the women (Chapter Two) and the almost obsessive concern of the men with building up security for the retirement phase (Chapter One). In other words, the parents' time and emotional energy were diverted elsewhere, and they perceived their extrafamilial relationships with less cognitive and affective richness. (As Table 4 shows, people in this stage also have fewer friends than those in the stages before and after them.) This lack of individuation virtually disappears among those in the preretirement phase. In fact, the overwhelming majority of people in this later stage of life have highly complex or multidimensional friendships. In sum, there is an increase in perceptual complexity in relation to actual friends across the four life stages, except for the critical midlife period. Perhaps Jung's ([1916] 1953) concept of individuation is applicable here. He contends that, with advancing age and an increased awareness of approaching death, one grows to know and accept the various qualities that make up the self. This increase in perception of the complexity of the self may well in turn enhance awareness of the subtleties in the makeup of others. If so, such a process of increasing awareness of individuation could also account for the finding reported earlier, namely, that the preretirement group revealed a wider discrepancy between an ideal friend and their actual friends because they were concerned with more dimensions in which differences could occur. Women, it should be noted, tended to perceive more complexity in their friendships than did the men. These sex differences, interestingly enough, were notable not only in the oldest (preretirement) group but in the youngest group as well. This finding lends yet further support to the frequent observation that women are more involved with interpersonal relationships than men are. It also hints at the possibility of greater affective and perhaps cognitive complexity, about which we shall have more to say in subsequent chapters.

IV

Concept of Self

The youth orientation of American society creates potential conflicts for those in the later stages of the adult life cycle, conflicts additional to the general losses attendant on aging. An apparent corollary of the youth culture, for example, is the negative image of aging and the aged reportedly held by those still in the productive years (Rosenfelt, 1965; Bunzel, 1972). If the self-concept is not "fixed" once and for all in childhood, but rather continues to evolve (as one might infer from Mead, 1934; Sherif and Cantril, 1947; Sarbin, 1954; or Morse and Gergen, 1970, for example), it seems reasonable to assume that with age the self-concept will become increasingly negative, and self-esteem will consequently decline.

Evidence for an age-related shift to self-depreciation, however, is equivocal. While Giedt and Lehner (1951), Wallach and Kogan (1961), Ziller (1967), and Rose (1965) found an increasing negativism associated with the aging self-image, Mason (1954), Thomae (1970), and others found that the aged may actually view themselves more positively than do those who are younger. Moreover, to complicate matters further, there is a suggestion that sex differences may affect results. For example, men may be more likely than women to deny negative attributes, or what they consider to be undue emotionality (Grant, 1969).

This chapter explores differences in the self-concept among men and women in successive stages of adult life. The primary source of data is a seventy-item Adjective Rating List. The adjectives, the same as those in the Block Modified Q Sort for Nonprofessional Sorters (Block, 1961), were rated according to whether they were perceived as like or unlike the self, or in between.

We first looked at the social desirability of adjectives espoused by men and women at different stages of adult life. Desirable and undesirable traits were distinguished from each other by means of factor analysis. We found ($p < .05$) that eighteen attributes declined systematically by stage. Sixteen of them were undesirable: absentminded, dependent, disorderly, dissatisfied, easily embarrassed, guileful, helpless, lazy, restless, sarcastic, self-pitying, stubborn, suspicious, timid, undecided, unhappy; only two were not: dramatic and shrewd. Three attributes, all of them desirable, increased by stage: frank, reserved, self-controlled. Both positive and negative attributes, however, fell within a narrow spectrum of the self-concept, that dealing with what Neugarten (1968a) calls the "executive" functions of the ego. Thus, in the area of instrumental behavior, one notes improved efficiency (decline in absentmindedness, disorderliness, laziness, and restlessness); in the area of interpersonal relations, there is a decline in vulnerability (suspicion and embarrassment); there is a decline in the need for misrepresentation and manipulation (less guile, shrewdness, and drama, coupled with an increase in frankness), and in conflict-evoking behavior (sarcasm, stubbornness); lastly, there is an increase in overall self-reliance (less timidity, helplessness, indecisiveness, and dependency) and in self-control.

While the general direction in self-description is toward the positive and socially desirable as we move through the stages of the adult life course, the substance of the differences also includes an increase in what might be called rational self-limitation. For example, the older respondents considered themselves less disorderly, restless, sarcastic, and stubborn than did the younger respondents. A decline or restriction of the free flow and expression of psychological and physical energy is indicated, along with the rejection of the more vulnerable, volatile, or emotional components of personal existence. In other words, the data suggest a deenergizing of the perceived self with age, a process which may be associated with psychological disengagement (see Havighurst, Neugarten, and Tobin, 1968). Differences shown in the self-concepts of men and women support earlier findings (Grant, 1969; Rosenkrantz and others, 1968), where women have been more likely than men to ascribe expressive attributes (both negative and positive) to themselves. At all stages, the men provide classical examples of the instrumental role player. They described themselves ($p < .05$) as ambitious, assertive, calm, competitive, confident, guileful, hostile, reasonable, self-controlled, shrewd, sophisticated, unconventional, and versatile. Women rated themselves comparatively high (higher than the men rated themselves) on the following characteristics: charming, cooperative, easily embarrassed, easily hurt, friendly, helpless, sincere, sympathetic, timid, touchy (younger women only; older are equal to men), undecided.

We began to explore the meaning of sex differences in more detail by constructing two indexes, one of masculine and one of feminine traits, on the basis of those attributes which significantly differentiated men from women.[1] As would be expected, men scored higher on the Masculinity Index, and women scored higher on the Femininity Index (Table 6). In addition to the sex differences, however, a stage difference was found for the Femininity Index, with women in the later stages appearing less feminine in their self-conceptions than the younger.[2] The self-conceptions of preretired women more closely approximated those of their male stage peers than those of the other women in the study. While women ranked consistently higher than men on the Femininity Index in the high school, newlywed, and midlife stages, the preretirement men and women were not significantly different. The reason seems to be that,

---

[1] The prototypes of these indexes were developed with the help of Stephanie Dillon. Ranking high on either the Masculinity Index or the Femininity Index is associated with ranking low on the other; the correlation is low ($r = -.26$) but significant for the overall sample.

[2] Three homogeneous subsets of women (high school seniors and newlyweds; newlyweds and the middle-aged; the middle-aged and the preretired) with progressively lower rankings were found when Duncan's New Multiple Range Test (Dixon, 1970) was computed.

Table 6.

MEASURES OF SELF-CONCEPT (means)

	High School		Newlywed		Middle-Aged		Preretirement	
	Men	Women	Men	Women	Men	Women	Men	Women
Masculinity Index	29.1	25.7	28.9	24.7	28.0	24.7	27.8	25.2
Femininity Index	21.9	25.9	22.0	25.1	21.9	24.1	21.6	22.9
Self-Criticism	4.1	7.1	4.8	6.9	5.0	7.6	5.4	6.3
Ego Diffusion	21.8	18.7	17.8	16.4	13.0	17.6	10.2	14.0
Respondent-Interviewer Agreement	.45	.48	.53	.49	.55	.53	.58	.53

	Younger[a]		Older[b]		Total	
	Men	Women	Men	Women	Men	Women
Masculinity Index[c]	29.0	25.2	27.9	24.9	28.4	25.1
Femininity Index[c,d]	22.0	25.5	21.8	23.4	21.8	24.4
Self-Criticism[c]	6.0	7.0	5.2	6.9	5.6	6.9
Ego Diffusion[d]	19.7	17.6	11.6	15.6	15.2	16.6
Respondent-Interviewer Agreement	.49	.49	.56	.53	.53	.51

[a] High school and newlyweds.
[b] Middle-aged and preretirement.
[c] Differences between men and women are significant with $p < .05$.
[d] Differences between stages are significant with $p < .05$.

as mentioned above, stage differences among men were not marked, while there was a definite drop by stage among women.

The preretired women also differed from other people in the kinds of things associated with a traditionally feminine self-concept. For example, among the middle-aged men and women, the higher the score on femininity, the greater the scope of activities (see Chapter One). For the preretired women, however, the relationship was in the opposite direction: the higher the score on femininity, the more restricted the scope of activities. These results underscore the highly distinct self-concept of these women, a self-concept in which the traditionally valued attributes may be in the process of being redefined. Indeed, the qualities which preretired women were more apt to attribute to themselves, and which approximate those of the men, tend to be those that *both* men and women perceived as socially desirable.

The sex differences reported above would be of little consequence if they arose simply because of sex differences in the definition of adjectives. If, for example, women viewed qualities such as being easily hurt or indecisive more positively than men, then the apparently greater willingness of women to discuss these "problem" areas would be suspect. In order to assess the amount of overlap in definition, we computed principal components analyses (Dixon, 1970) separately for men and for women. Similarity for the first three factors was high: on social desirability (Factor I), assertion-competitiveness (Factor II), and sensitivity to interpersonal relations (Factor III). This close approximation supports the conclusion that the sex differences in adjective ascription were not contaminated by differential evaluation. Perhaps most significantly, men and women shared remarkably similar perspectives on the social desirability of adjectives, supporting the conclusion that the negative traits more often espoused by women were actually perceived by them to be less desirable. More concretely, ten of the thirteen adjectives on which men scored higher than women were perceived to be socially desirable by both men and women; only five of the eleven adjectives on which women scored higher were similarly desirable.

Further support for a consensus was provided by "ideal-self" ratings on the Adjective Rating List, where subjects indicated the kind of person they would wish to be (these ratings were available only for the high school and middle-aged stages). A remarkably high agreement was noted: of the twenty-four adjectives comprising the Masculinity and Femininity Indexes, differences were found on only two. Almost all men and women were shown to place extremely high value on ambition, calm, and confidence; on self-control, reasonableness, and versatility; and on cooperativeness, friendliness, sincerity, and sympathy. Almost all rejected timidity, helplessness, indecisiveness, hostility, and also touchiness and the propensity to be easily hurt or embarrassed. Equal proportions of men and women saw value in sophistication and shrewdness (about half).

Assertiveness and competitiveness, the two ideal traits with different evaluations, seem to pinpoint conflict-laden issues in the female self-concept. Women valued these traits less than men did. From the women's perspective, the possession of desirable attributes in which men traditionally surpass women (a pattern replicated in the self-ratings) may enhance the worth of women, but only if these attributes supplement rather than replace traditional roles and relationships. While the recognition of equal capacities is approved of, the challenge of assuming male prerogatives or dominance evokes considerable ambivalence among our female subjects. Similarly, Neugarten and Gutmann (1964, p. 85) suggest that aggression and self-assertion are viewed as "inimical to the central function of motherhood"; and Miller (1973) and Moulton (1973) found that self-assertion and achievement invoke self-doubt in women.

We next isolated those traits which significantly distinguished each stage from all others within each sex (Table 7). The results suggest that the developmental pattern of self-concept formation differs for men and women. Men, consistent with the more pronounced shifts in male social-role norms (Hauser and Shapiro, 1973), showed sharper differentiations and fluctuations through successive life stages than did women.

The themes which emerge in the analysis of the men are fairly clearcut, with the stage differences in basic accord with such developmental theoretical statements as those of Erikson (1963), Cumming and Henry (1961), Neugarten (1968b), and Gutmann (1964, 1966). In essence, there is reflected through the successive stages a change from an insecure and discontented self-image through a buoyant and sometimes uncontrolled phase, to the stage

Table 7.

ADJECTIVES DIFFERENTIATING EACH STAGE FROM OTHERS
OF SAME SEX[a] ($p < .05$)

High School Men	Newlywed Men	Middle-Aged Men	Preretirement Men
Dissatisfied +	Cautious —	Cautious +	Ambitious —
Frank —	Cruel —	Disorderly —	Dissatisfied —
Friendly —	Dramatic +	Frank +	Hostile —
Persevering —	Hostile +	Lazy —	Reasonable +
Timid +	Impulsive +	Masculine +	Restless —
Unhappy +	Poised —	Sarcastic —	Unhappy —
	Reserved —	Self-pitying —	Uninterested —
	Restless +		
	Sarcastic +		
	Self-controlled —		
	Unconventional +		
	Versatile +		

High School Women	Newlywed Women	Women Middle-Aged	Women Preretirement
Dependent +	Energetic —	Absentminded +	Absentminded —
Guileful +	Jealous +	Unhappy +	Assertive +
Helpless +	Warm +		Dependent —
Idealistic —			Disorderly —
Intelligent —			Dramatic —
Lazy +			Easily embarrassed —
Restless +			Guileful —
Sentimental +			Helpless —
Suspicious +			Intelligent +
Undecided +			Lazy —
			Self-indulgent —
			Stubborn —
			Suspicious —
			Undecided —

[a] A plus sign after an adjective indicates that this adjective is more
characteristic of this stage than of others; a minus sign indicates
that the adjective is less characteristic of this stage than of others.

of control and industry, to a later point of decreased demands on
the self and greater acceptance of others and one's environment.

The most characteristic self-appraisals of high school boys
could be construed as shortcomings. Industry and intimacy, two of

Erikson's (1963) epigenetic stages, are apparent areas of conflict for these students. They rated themselves comparatively low (lower than the other men rated themselves) in perseverance. A reading of their protocols brings forth numerous examples of this felt deficiency. Here is one senior discussing his goals: "I don't feel that I'm far enough along in life to have goals and to follow them. . . . I used to want to be a veterinarian, but then I found out that math and science were involved and I decided that I wouldn't be a good one."

In interpersonal relations the high school seniors rated themselves as less friendly, less frank, and more timid than the other men rated themselves. As the following comment indicates, the high school boys were painfully aware of their social inadequacies: "Socially I have lots of room for progress. I'm the kind of person that most people don't think one way or the other about. I'm not hated. I don't know what you'd call it. I'm not really popular, I'm right in the middle." Relations with the opposite sex, of course, provide their share of anguish: "It just happens that when I go to lunch I don't see any girls that I have in any of my classes. So I have a hard time meeting them. It just hasn't worked out. . . . I'm just not in the right places. Sometimes I feel like walking down the halls, run into a girl, actually run into her and knock the books out of her arms, and then while I'm picking them up, get to know her. Man, I would try anything in order to get started." Perhaps because of their perception of shortcomings in intimacy and interpersonal relations, the boys also manifested greater discontent than the other males, scoring higher on dissatisfaction and unhappiness.

The self-concepts of newlywed men suggest qualities of diffuse dynamism, of free—at times uncontrolled—energy to be expended in diversified or unconventional pursuits. While more hostile and sarcastic than other men, they also rated themselves as less cruel—as if hostility and sarcasm arose from a lack of inhibition or reserve, reflecting a certain impatience in their social interactions rather than real animosity toward others. Having resolved the early crises of what Erikson (1963) calls the stage of intimacy versus isolation, they are riding on a wave of confidence. One gets the sense of an almost explosive burst of energy, as if their newly won independence from parental authority, as symbolized and formalized by their marriage, has prompted a burgeoning outward in many directions.

For example, in discussing his daily activities, one man remarked: "I like to move constantly, I love to keep going. Sitting still, staying in one place, that's the worst thing. Working, that's really bad, too; I just hate anything that holds me down, that keeps me from moving. That's why I don't like my job; it's so routine."

For many there is a growing awareness of new worlds to conquer, and the energy and enthusiasm with which to try it. At some point they will face the task of learning how to regulate their energy; but for now, as the following quote illustrates, many are more than happy to take on the world: "There's never enough time. I could easily put two weeks into one week. I could use about twice as many hours. . . . I'd take a double load at college. I'd double the time I'm taking right now. I'd keep the same work schedule, but I'd spend more time at home. I'd take more time in the morning. I'd also try to get a program going like I did at college before I went into the service. You know, working with kids."

The aggressive and acutely conscious sense of mastery manifested by these newlywed men recalls the ego-mastery styles formulated by Gutmann (1964). Focusing on later life, Gutmann has shown that middle-aged men exhibit a more active sense of mastery in Thematic Apperception Test productions than do older men. Our own TAT data provide some complementary evidence, validating the existence of the energy that newlywed men perceived in themselves. In her analysis of directional activity in stories told in response to one of the same cards (17BM) employed by Gutmann, Hodges (1972) found very striking differences between the younger and the older men. The stories told by the younger men displayed an active manipulation of the environment; for the two older stages, activity was somewhat removed from the environment, and the energy displayed had a static quality.

The self-image of the middle-aged men presents an antithesis to that of the newlyweds. Among them, expansiveness and diffusion is replaced by orderliness and caution. Their feelings of masculinity, frankness, and industry perhaps reflect the attainment of power and authority which the middle years often bring (Neugarten, 1968a). Although they certainly exhibit a self-concept congruent with Gutmann's active-mastery type, in the sense of feeling in control of their milieu, the control is also extended to the self. Thus, in addition to feeling more masculine and frank, middle-aged men, compared to all others, rated themselves as less lazy, less self-pitying, less disorderly, more cautious, and less sarcastic. In some sense, then, their control over the environment is gained by the exercise of a considerable degree of self-restraint.

An examination of those adjectives which border on significance helps to clarify how these middle-aged men perceive themselves. For example, they rated themselves as dull, reserved, and uninterested and as lacking in sense of humor—suggesting that to some extent they find their position in life tedious. Persevering and not rebellious, they are also suspicious, often touchy, and sometimes cruel. In short, many are busy about the common, unexciting, but critical task of keeping their own small worlds going, their bosses and their families satisfied: they are plodding along and perhaps feel that there is something missing from their lives. The attitude expressed below seems typical of these men: "I'm forty-five years old and I've reached the situation where I don't have to kill myself to make money. And I'm happy compared to other people. I just don't want to be in the rat race. But I'm not a happy person. The money doesn't mean a goddamned thing. If I could find something else, I'd love to get out of it. Let's say I'm a successful failure. I'm bored with the routine of it all. Basically, it's the same routine; you know, buy it [property], fix it up, sell it, and start all over again."

The preretired men are mellow—and significantly less dissatisfied and unhappy—compared to men at earlier stages. While their self-image reflects less drive, there are compensatory factors and fewer rough edges: they see themselves as less hostile and more reasonable. They feel less ambitious but also less restless than any of the younger men. Unlike the middle-aged, they do not seem to feel the need to control others or to drive themselves. Rather, they manifest a concern for warm interpersonal relations. For one man, the chief satisfaction with work is "watching people under my supervision develop and grow—to become eligible for higher jobs." Another had this to say in evaluating the interview: "It's entirely fair to say that I enjoyed meeting you [interviewer], and if nothing else has occurred, I still cherish personal relationships above everything. There's no mystery about it. So, when I suggest that you come

over to the club or come over here to the house, I will be glad to see
you." Perhaps most important, these men reject the image of being
uninterested, which suggests that whatever solution to the problems
of life they have found, it is not one of withdrawal. In sum, the preretired men seem the group most comfortable, not only with others
but with themselves as well.

The themes of high school girls are very similar to those of
boys in their negative content. The girls are even more likely to
question their ability to lead an independent life; they see themselves as helpless and dependent. Closely connected with dependence
is their perception of being less intelligent and lazier (compared to
the self-assessment of women in the other groups). In short, more
than any other women, they see themselves as the "helpless" female:
"I don't know what I'm going to do. . . . My biggest fear is going
out in the world 'cause I'm not ready for it, you know. . . . I want
to be financially secure for the rest of my life. Wow! Yeah, that's
what I'd like. . . . But I couldn't do it, how am I going to do it?
I'd like to marry a rich guy, yeah and have money, just live off
him." This negative and dependent self-image carries over into the
interpersonal domain, where the girls rated themselves as more guileful and suspicious than the other women rated themselves. Linked to
their feelings of powerlessness is the apparent belief that direct action
and independent achievement are not within reach and that the
only way to obtain gratification is through trickery and guile. Finally,
this sense of frustrated achievement is accompanied by a lack of
idealism.

Few traits distinguish newlywed women from other women.
The two that do, greater jealousy and greater warmth, may be
linked to the insecurities and expectations of their newly acquired
marital status. Interestingly, about two fifths of these women considered themselves both warm and jealous. For many, the jealousy
was directed not so much toward other women (although there was
some of that as well) as toward anything that separated the couple.
As the following comment illustrates, the separation was often the
result of action by the husband: "Usually on Thursday nights I'm
left to myself. My husband goes out. He has these friends who insti-
gated this ridiculous idea of playing basketball or cards every
Thursday night. It's sort of a young marrieds' escape league." The

newlywed women spoke often of being with their husband as their most important activity and seemed very dependent on this relationship. One woman with an M.A. in physiotherapy confessed that she had lost interest in keeping up with her profession: "I'd rather be with George than go to a weekend seminar." Such dependency may cause conflicts: "We mostly disagree on our concept of marriage . . . because I am more dependent on him than he is on me. I want to spend a lot of time with him while he would rather talk with friends or do things by himself."

Since, in a general sense, jealousy and warmth can be placed in the realm of impulse life, newlywed women, in an attentuated way, parallel some of the self-conceptions of newlywed men. They do not, however, show the high energy level typical of the newlywed men, and in fact consider themselves significantly less energetic than do other women.

Greater absentmindedness and unhappiness, the two traits distinguishing the middle-aged women from others, hint at greater situational distress. Within most of the psychological and sociological domains examined, this group tended to emerge more negatively than the others. They were not, as one might conjecture, distressed by the pending departure of their last child (Lowenthal and Chiriboga, 1972a), and few seemed disturbed about the menopause. The reasons for their diminished sense of well-being are complex but often center on relations with their spouse: "I thought I was happy. Then, all of sudden, I realized my husband was unhappy, so I became unhappy too." The self-concept of middle-aged women stands in sharp contrast to the generally positive attributes espoused by middle-aged men. Moreover, these women apparently feel deficient in the very areas where men regard themselves as strong (or in which they are compelled to deny deficits). For see p. 83 example, the heightened sense of orderliness among men contrasts with the heightened sense of absentmindedness among women; the rejection of self-pity among men contrasts with the open admission of unhappiness among women.

A similar polarization appears to exist among newlyweds, where the men's self-image is distinguished by high energy and the women's by its very lack. At the preretirement stage, moreover, the women's assertiveness contrasts sharply with the more expressive orientation of the men. Considering how heavily an individual's self-image is influenced by the evaluations of and interactions with significant others (Brim, 1966; Mead, 1934; Sherif and Cantril, 1947), some influence by the spouse is to be expected, and our data suggest the development of a certain complementarity in self-images. Responses made by both the newlyweds and the middle-aged parents further suggest the proposition that when one partner appropriates for himself a strong configuration of desirable traits (whether for personal reasons or because of conformity to social expectations), the other is likely to experience a sense of inferiority in comparison.

It is in the preretirement stage that women seem finally to hit their stride. The problems with competence, independence, and interpersonal relations (evident in the earlier stages, particularly among high school seniors) appear resolved. The preretired women see themselves as less dependent and helpless and as more assertive: "I don't have the fears and tragedies that I had when I was younger. I can say what I feel, I am not embarrassed by many things any more, and my personality is better." This heightened feeling of effectiveness may occur at some psychic cost, for these women also indicate more than other women a sense of constraint or self-control: they feel less disorderly, less dramatic, and less self-indulgent. In this area, as well as in the areas of competence, women in the preretirement stage resemble the middle-aged men more than they do those facing retirement. Changing patterns of dominance are found not merely in the Adjective Rating List data but in many other instruments and questions. As reported in Chapter Two, both men and women agree that in the later life stages fewer men are "boss" in the family and that more women are.

Neugarten and Gutmann (1964), using a TAT-like card depicting a family scene, report a similar shift between respondents who are forty to fifty-four years old and those who are fifty-five to seventy years old. In stories centered on the figure of an old man, older respondents depicted him as more passive, easygoing, and submissive than the younger. In marked contrast, stories told about the figure of an old woman showed a shift from a subordinate role to one of authority and dominance. While Neugarten and Gutmann (1964, p. 88) caution against attempting to apply their findings directly to actual behavior, they conclude: "For both men and women respondents, it is almost always the old woman, not the old man, to whom impulsivity, aggressivity, and hostile dominance are ascribed. This consistency cannot be explained by chance. The assumption seems warranted that there is something common to the actual role behaviors of older women that elicits this consistency in respondents' fantasies."

These themes, derived from such divergent sources as the Adjective Rating List of western urban residents collected in 1969 and projective responses from a midwestern sample collected in the 1950s, give empirical support to earlier formulations of developmental change found in Jungian theory. Jung (1933) proposes a psychological transformation in the second half of life, wherein women give increasing emphasis to masculine components, and men to feminine components, of their psyche; that is, men give greater recognition to the world of feelings, and women show a rise in instrumentality and incisiveness. Although Jung regards these changes as part of an intrinsic developmental process, he also alludes to concomitant changes in social tasks and settings. There remains the critical question of why these shifts occur.

One possible explanation is that these shifts reflect differences in social stage of life—that, for instance, many women confront the "empty nest" not with a sense of dismay but with a sense of relief (Lowenthal and Chiriboga, 1972a). Reasoning that the departure of children might be associated with positive change in their self-concepts, we compared those preretirement women who still had children in the home with those whose last child had left. When the effect of age was controlled, women whose children had not been launched reported more self-pity and stubbornness and being more easily hurt and less shrewd than did the women who had reached the postparental stage. They also tended to portray themselves as more affected, dissatisfied, guileful, selfish, and touchy, and as less sincere. In short, the self-concept of the oldest group of women who still remain in the "nest-emptying" stage is much less positive, particularly in respect to characteristics bearing on interpersonal relationships.

These results accord with those of Back (1971) and support our contention that social stage of life is more helpful than chronological age in explaining life-course differences. In an analysis of men and women aged forty-five to seventy, Back reports that controlling for the presence or absence of children virtually eliminated age differences in the self-concept of women. He concludes: "During the aging process, women tend to shift their self-image from their relationships to others, the social characteristics, to their own abilities and feelings; the separation from children can be viewed this way. Freed from daily obligations, they may feel that they can be much more easily accepted for what they are" (p. 303).

In contrast, children did not affect the self-image of men (Back, 1971)—probably because men have less immediate emotional and behavioral involvement in the family domain, or, more specifically, in parenthood. For men, analogous conditions and influences must be sought in the permutations of their occupational careers. It has been shown, for example, that critical life reviews, which often set in at the completion of the family cycle for women, occur at the termination of the male work cycle (Thurnher, 1974). A relevant question for men is the extent to which changes in personality configurations and self-perceptions are directly traceable to retirement. Our interviews do not permit a controlled examination of this question. However, the characteristics observed in the self-image of the preretirement men would theoretically foster favorable adjustment to retirement and may reflect anticipation and preparation for this new status. Possibly, as Back (1971) has argued for women, the relief from responsibilities and pressures of work allows men greater freedom to be themselves. In contrast to early childhood and very old age, where chronological age is a key determinant of identity and self-concept, during most of adulthood social life stage may become more important than age.

The impact of life stage was also manifest in the area of self-criticism. The systematic decline in the self-ascription of socially undesirable traits across the life course, noted earlier, raised the question of the extent to which it reflected increasing self-acceptance. In our examination of self-acceptance, we focused on its opposite—namely, self-criticism, for which measurable self-report data were available.

In the administration of the Adjective Rating List, subjects were asked to circle attributes they disliked about themselves. Surprisingly, no significant stage differences were found in average number of traits circled, suggesting relative constancy in self-criticism over the life span. On the other hand, consistent with their generally more negative self-assessment, women tended to be more critical of themselves than men. Again there was evidence of increased convergence between the self-concepts of men and women in late life, for while sex differences in self-criticism were significant among high school seniors, they were almost nonexistent in the preretirement stage.

While the level of self-criticism remained constant, we noted, as Kaplan (1971) has, that its content varied by both stage and sex. Some traits seemed to present potential problem areas for all members of a given sex; others reflected stage-specific preoccupations.

Desired changes common to all women centered on questions of social vulnerability and of mastery. They wished that they were less easily hurt and touchy, as well as more confident and shrewd. Further attributes troublesome to women (the preretirement stage notably excluded) were easy embarrassment, stubbornness, absentmindedness, worry, laziness, and indecision; put together, these attributes convey a lack of what is commonly referred to as ego strength.

Certain stage-specific concerns and values were also voiced by women. High school girls wished that they were less dissatisfied; in keeping with a stage wherein issues remain diffuse and ambiguous (Erikson, 1963), and autonomous strivings are unchanneled (Angyal, 1965), these girls focused on a generalized emotional state rather than on traits more directly linked to role performance. Newlywed women wished that they were less selfish (thereby placing further emphasis on the ideal of subordinating personal inclinations), but also that they were more energetic and ambitious and less dull, a configuration that suggests role conflict. That is, while anxious to fulfill the nurturant functions entailed in the traditional female role, they are also opting for personal competence in areas reaching beyond the family confines. The ideal of these newlywed women matches what Epstein (1973) describes as the image of the "new" woman, the "perfectly balanced person who does a little of everything" (p. 27). Our middle-aged women felt that they should be more introspective and persevering, and also more reserved and poised. Striking was their expressed need to be more imaginative (voiced by about one third). Most of these traits can logically be linked to the anticipation of future change and the call for new modes of adjustment. About to enter the postparental phase, these women appear to be shifting their attention away from family members onto themselves and the wider social milieu. The preretired women resemble the middle-aged women in their concern for a social persona, but seem closer to their goal. Rather than desiring a social barricade of poise and reserve, they wished for greater charm and sophistication; and they were unique in their focus on assertiveness and competitiveness.

On the whole, men admitted to fewer shortcomings and appeared more accepting of and comfortable with themselves. Their concerns with self-image change were more stage-specific, and no traits presented a problem for men in all stages. Those most commonly acknowledged as leaving room for improvement were laziness and disorderliness (mentioned by all except the middle-aged); American work ethics and the stress on "doing" (Kluckhohn and Strodtbeck, 1961) all too frequently leave men with a sense of not being sufficiently active or productive. High school boys were most troubled by their absentmindedness and dependency. In contrast, newlywed men wished that they were less easily hurt and also less stubborn, defensive, sarcastic, and impulsive. This attitude reflects an increasing awareness that impulsivity may hinder them from meeting familial and career responsibilities, and presages the rigorous control of energy that characterizes middle-aged men. Like the newlyweds, middle-aged men admitted to being too easily hurt, stubborn, and defensive. In addition, they wished that they were more assertive and had greater emotional control (for example, they wished to be more calm and poised and less worried), qualities which would further enhance their effectiveness. Finally, the preretirement men wished that they were less touchy and more shrewd (changes desired by women in all stages) and resembled the middle-aged women in desiring to be more imaginative. Since both the middle-aged women and the preretirement men were confronted with problems of rechanneling their energies into new goals and activities, the heightened value attached to imagination—or heightened awareness of its lack—is understandable.

A further approach to the study of self-criticism was to examine its relationship to the Masculinity and Femininity Indexes. Among men, no consistent relationship existed between self-criticism and femininity; there was, however, a tendency for men who ranked themselves high on masculine traits to score lower in self-criticism. Among women the associations were stronger and more consistent. Women high on femininity were generally more self-critical, with the correlations rising from nonsignificant among high school seniors to highly significant among preretirement women. Moreover, among women facing retirement those who ranked higher on masculinity ranked lower on self-criticism. These findings suggest that, along with the progressive decline of feminine self-perceptions across the life course, endorsement of the feminine role or rejection of the masculine role among women becomes increasingly associated with feelings of unacceptability about one's self.

Previous research has shown that men are more likely to deny problems (Lowenthal and Chiriboga, 1972a; Grant, 1969; Shanas and others, 1968); this tendency toward denial may account for the consistently lower rate of self-criticism among men. While a certain degree of self-criticism may be viewed as normative among women, the same degree would represent deviancy in men, and hence self-criticism among women may be less reflective of mal-adaptation than among men. Some supporting evidence for sex differences in the implications of self-criticism is presented in Chapter Five. Here we would simply mention that while self-criticism bore no relationship to friendship patterns among women, it did for men. Men high on self-criticism reported fewer long-term friendships (particularly high school seniors and the preretirement men) and showed a propensity to seek gifted and successful persons as friends they could admire and learn from.

In the preceding analyses we have focused on the substantive content of the self-concept and addressed ourselves to the problems of self-criticism. We now examine two different dimensions. The first deals with problems of diffusion and individuation, the integration of the individual's self-concept and the clarity with which he perceives his identity. The second dimension deals with the relationship between the individual's private image and the image he projects onto the outside world.

Self-awareness and integration are important dimensions of the self-concept. For most people the accumulation of experiences and crises may be expected to bring about better self-understanding. Neugarten (1964), for example, proposes that self-awareness and self-differentiation increase throughout adulthood. An increasing integration of the self-concept through advancing life stages is also implicit in the theories of Erikson (1959), Werner ([1940] 1948), and Lecky (1969). The goals of organization and synthesis, toward which people consciously or unconsciously strive in many aspects of intrapsychic functioning (Werner, [1940] 1948; Lecky, 1969), encompass the self as well.

We measured integration of the self-concept by the number of times a respondent was able to report whether traits on the Adjective Rating List did or did not apply. That is, we assumed that a respondent's inability to do so reflected ambiguity and, as an extension thereof, diffusion. We found that, among the men, each succeeding stage exhibited a lower diffusion score, whereas women maintained a moderately high average (relative to men) at all stages (Table 6). Thus, men were slightly more diffuse than women in the high school and newlywed stages but significantly *less* diffuse in the two older stages.

These results suggest that self-image of men becomes increasingly crystallized as they move through life, whereas among women uncertainties continue. Our findings accord with Constantinople's (1969) longitudinal study of college students, which showed that men mature in the area of identity versus diffusion and women do not. That standards of performance are less distinct in the sphere of family than they are in the sphere of work (Schneider, 1968) may in part contribute to this sex difference. Or perhaps women's greater awareness of the complexities and ambiguities in interpersonal relationships (noted in earlier chapters) may foster ambiguities in their own self-image.

Regarding private versus public images, several of our older subjects commented on the paradox that they themselves felt little had changed, whereas others seemed to view them as older. High school seniors, in turn, seemed preoccupied with questions of peer appraisals; they spoke frequently of being "watched and talked about," a symptom common and normal in their age group but one which in any older group might be judged to border on psycho-pathology. Notwithstanding these problems of misperception, pecu-liar to both the young and the old, there is evidence that with age individuals become more aware of themselves and more able to regulate the outcome of their self-presentations (Neugarten, 1964; 1968b). We hypothesized that the degree of discrepancy between the private and public images would decline by stage but that the implications of such discrepancy would become increasingly negative.

Although it would be preferable to use so-called "significant others" to acquire data on the public image of our respondents, this possibility was lacking and we chose the interviewer as a substitute. Interviewers were asked to rate subjects on the Adjective Rating List. Since each spent from seven to nine hours listening to, observ-ing, and interacting with the respondent, a considerable degree of familiarity was established. A measure of fit between private and public images (the agreement score) was based on correlations be-tween self-ratings and interviewer ratings.[3]

Among men, respondent-interviewer-agreement increased systematically by stage (Table 6), their self-concept becoming in-creasingly consistent with the self presented to others. The relative absence of difference in agreement scores among women may relate to the fact that, unlike men, their self-concept shows no decrease in diffusion with age, the diffusion continuing to impede clear projec-tion of the self.

One possible explanation for the increase in agreement among the men is that the greater social control that accrues to individuals in middle age may permit them greater freedom of self-expression. There is considerable evidence that the more an individ-

---

[3] A methodological issue in the use of respondent-interviewer agree-ment scores involves the possibility of systematic bias between interviewers in the general scoring of the Adjective Rating List and also bias in their evaluation of specific stage and sex groups. Analysis of variance of agreement scores indicated that while interviewers differed from one another, these biases were not related to specific stage and sex groups. We next tested the effect of interviewer differences in agreement scores on the relationship of agreement scores to other variables. An intercorrelational analysis of select variables (life satisfaction, affect balance, and adaptive ratings) with indi-vidual interviewer agreement scores showed that systematic interviewer dif-ferences did not affect the intercorrelations to any significant degree.

ual lacks control over the social situation, the less likely is his behavior
to reveal his actual intentions (Rosow, 1965; Kelly, 1967; Thomas,
Franks, and Calonico, 1972; Organ, 1973). Social control tends to
fall to those in the middle period of life: "Middle-agers recognize
that they constitute the powerful age group vis-à-vis other age
groups; that they are the norm bearers and the decision makers;
and that they live in a society which, while it may be oriented
toward youth, is controlled by the middle-aged" (Neugarten, 1968a,
p. 83). We can see, particularly among the men in midlife but also
among the preretired men, a willingness to speak their minds and a
sense of control. The older groups of men may feel less pressure to
conceal their feelings and desires; this easing of pressure could lead
to a greater matching of their private and public images.

　　Interested in the implications of fit between private and
public images of the self, we next examined agreement scores in
relation to self-criticism and to social interaction. Those with less
agreement were generally more self-critical, the association increasing
by stage with the exception of the middle-aged women. For example,
while self-criticism was moderately related to agreement scores
among teenagers, a marked association (explaining 42 percent of the
variance) was found among men and women in the oldest stage.

　　As suggested earlier, discrepancies between one's personal
and public selves may have increasingly negative implications with
age; insofar as they lead to misunderstandings, discrepancies may increasingly give rise to problems in the sphere of interpersonal relations, and may rob the older person of the social supports that act
as a critical buffer against life's stresses (Lowenthal and Haven,
1968; Rosow, 1968). To investigate the effect of such discrepancies
on interpersonal relationships, we noted the number of times that
subjects reported feeling lonely during the past week. High discrepancy was associated with feelings of loneliness only among men
in the two later stages. The association was stronger among preretirement men than those in midlife, suggesting that discrepancies
lead to increasing vulnerability to loneliness with age. Discrepancies
also had negative implications for relationships within the individual's
most immediate social milieu, his family. For three of the four older
groups—middle-aged men were the exception—high discrepancy
was significantly associated with negative feelings directed toward

members of the family of procreation. In the younger groups, by way of contrast, significant associations were obtained only for newlywed women, those high on discrepancy again directing more negative sentiments toward their family. Thus, while discrepancy between the perceived and the presented self seems to decrease with age, the proposition that its presence in later life is likely to be associated with social maladjustment received partial confirmation.

In this chapter we have shown that men and women differ markedly not only in the substantive content of their self-image but also in the trajectories of self-image change through the adult life course. Sex and stage differences in self-image configurations could readily be traced to social-role norms, at times also to proximity to normative transitions of adult life. Role expectations appear to influence the content of self-criticality and may also account for its greater intensity among women. Adequate role performance among women, indeed, seems to be more closely linked to a wider range of personality characteristics than among men, whose evaluations are generally restricted to instrumental performance. Women's self-acceptance may also be viewed as more reactive to and dependent on the assessment of significant others (Mendelsohn and Gall, 1970; Garai, 1970). There is also the suggestion that women are more willing to recognize their shortcomings and men are more compelled to deny them.

Since it is well-nigh impossible to control for it in any research design, the question of intrinsic sex differences and age-linked change will long remain a matter of conjecture. Since intrinsic factors elude direct study, their clarification may rest on intensive studies of social and cultural influences. The effects of differences in the socialization of males and females is being given increasing attention—the scientists, not surprisingly, being predominantly women (Hochschild, 1973; Epstein, 1973; Hutt, 1972; Maccoby, 1963). Perhaps equally salutory would be a critical review of established psychological theories. Purporting to explain the psychodynamics of the human organism, they frequently appear to apply only to men (Carlson, 1972; Horney, 1967; Sarason and Smith, 1971).

V

Perceptions of
Well-Being

In several of the preceding chapters we have directly or indirectly referred to the "adaptive level" or "adjustment" of our respondents, and we will now examine this domain in more detail. Traditionally, adjustment has been evaluated in terms of the individual's subjective experience or on the level of overt behavior (Havighurst, 1963; Treanton, 1963; Rosow, 1963). In this chapter we shall focus on the former; that is, on self-evaluations of well-being; in Chapter Six the more objective indicators will be reported. In both we examine negative and positive indicators and the balance between them.

Happiness, life satisfaction, morale are but some of the categories used in assessing the sense of well-being, with happiness being perhaps the most common (Rosow, 1963). Large-scale surveys (which, incidentally, usually omit people who are over age sixty) reveal an impressive consistency in the proportion of adults who report themselves to be happy. As Bradburn (1969) notes after reviewing the literature, generally about one third of the respondents say that they are very happy, while from 5 to 15 percent report themselves as not too happy. The consistency is somewhat less impressive, however, when age differences are assessed from these same surveys. In an early study, Gurin, Veroff, and Feld (1960) looked at a cross section of Americans and found evidence that older people are less happy than younger people are. On the other hand, using a measure of life satisfaction purported to tap an inner feeling of happiness, investigators in the Kansas City study found essentially no evidence of an association between happiness and age (Havighurst, 1963). Cantril's (1965) survey, which included more than 23,000 people from fourteen nations, also found very little evidence of age differences. Bradburn (1969), however, in a pilot study which included people over age sixty, found a notable increase in unhappiness after age sixty.

Aside from inconsistencies in the self-reported happiness of people at different stages of life, another key issue is determining the sources of happiness and how these sources vary across the life course. There is very little in the way of causal inquiry in this field (Bradburn, 1969, and Wessman and Ricks, 1966, represent notable exceptions). Assessment of the correlates of happiness, however, does allow for some inferences. These correlates include higher socioeconomic status (Cantril, 1965; Bradburn, 1969; Edwards and Klemmack, 1973), better physical health (Bradburn, 1969; Edwards and Klemmack, 1973), greater self-esteem (Wilson, 1960; Laxer, 1964; Wessman and Ricks, 1966), and participation in a wider range of social activities (Bengtson, 1969; Edwards and Klemmack, 1973; Havighurst, Neugarten, and Tobin, 1968; Maddox, 1963). In addition, in this country, whites are generally happier than ethnic minorities (Bradburn, 1969).

Self-Appraisals of Experiences

We began our inquiry by asking our respondents the same question used by Gurin, Veroff, and Feld (1960) and by Bradburn (1969): "In general, how happy are you these days? Very happy? Pretty happy? Or not too happy?" The results, if we look at all life stages combined, are very similar to those of the earlier studies:

slightly more than one third saw themselves as very happy, 13 percent felt not too happy, and the rest were moderately happy. When we examined stage differences, however, we found little of the decline with age reported previously. As shown in Table 8, the high school seniors, who represent an age group not included in any of the earlier surveys, were the least happy, particularly the boys. In marked contrast were the newlyweds, among whom only two felt unhappy. People in the two later stages fell midway between, with those facing retirement being slightly happier than the middle-aged.

While generally consistent with previous research, from an analytic viewpoint the results from this general question on happiness were unsatisfactory due to the high proportion of people (over half) giving an in-between response. It has been suggested that such clustering stems from the respondents' perception of what constitutes a "desirable" response (Wessman and Ricks, 1966; Nowlis, 1965). In order to offset this tendency and to probe for greater subtlety, we developed a composite index which adds three indicators to the happiness measure. They consist of two affect items, dissatisfaction and unhappiness, from the Adjective Rating List (see Chapter Four), and satisfaction with the present year, as reported in a Life Evaluation Chart (see Figure 2) in which respondents rated their past, present, and projected lives. (The Life Evaluation Chart is discussed in greater detail in Chapter Seven.)

On this new measure, the Life Satisfaction Index (LSI), the high school seniors again turned out to be the least satisfied, followed by the middle-aged parents. In contrast to their in-between responses to the single question on general happiness, those in the preretirement stage were very satisfied—as much so, in fact, as the newlyweds. And men at the preretirement stage turned out to be the most satisfied of all. Far from displaying a systematic decline in satisfaction, then, our results suggest that there are peaks and valleys in satisfaction distributed throughout the course of adult life. Knowledge of the particular stage occupied by people may prove to be helpful in analysis of the circumstances surrounding these peaks and valleys.

Analysis of abstract subjective states such as satisfaction or happiness, however, is hindered by problems of validity. The pervasive influence of social desirability is a case in point. It has been

Table 8.

MEASURES OF PERCEIVED WELL-BEING
(means unless otherwise noted)

	High School		Newlywed		Middle-Aged		Preretirement	
	Men	Women	Men	Women	Men	Women	Men	Women
Percent Very Happy	25	26	48	52	37	33	52	37
Life Satisfaction[a]	26.2	28.6	30.9	30.2	29.6	28.1	30.6	29.9
Positive Affect[b,c]	8.6	9.2	9.5	10.6	7.6	8.2	7.7	8.4
Top of world[b,c]	1.8	2.1	2.3	2.8	1.7	1.9	1.9	2.0
Excited[b]	2.4	2.4	2.5	2.6	1.7	2.1	1.7	2.1
Pleased	2.4	2.4	2.5	2.8	2.3	2.2	2.2	2.5
Proud[b]	2.0	2.3	2.2	2.4	1.8	2.0	1.9	1.8
Negative Affect[a]	7.9	8.6	7.4	7.8	5.8	6.1	5.2	5.4
Lonely[b]	2.0	2.2	1.4	1.8	1.1	1.4	1.3	1.2
Depressed[b,c]	1.7	2.0	1.7	2.0	1.3	1.8	1.1	1.6
Bored[b]	2.1	2.4	2.1	2.4	1.6	1.2	1.4	1.3
Restless[b]	2.1	2.0	2.2	1.6	1.8	1.7	1.4	1.4
Affect Balance[b]	13.7	13.7	15.1	15.7	14.8	15.1	15.5	16.0

[a] Higher scores on the negative-affect items imply greater negative affect. For explanation of scoring system, see Appendix B (Affect-Balance Score).

[b] Differences between the stages are significant at $p < .05$.

[c] Differences between men and women are significant at $p < .05$.

[d] Life-satisfaction scores ranged from 10 to 36.

suggested that factual reporting of specific affective experiences may be a useful way of minimizing the tendency to offer socially desirable responses to queries about subjective states (Nowlis, 1965). Furthermore, it is important to tap both positive and negative experiences if one is adequately to assess affect (Bradburn, 1969; Wessman and Ricks, 1966; Nowlis, 1965). According to Bradburn (1969), an individual's reports on his general state of happiness are a consequence of the relative balance between positive and negative emotional experiences; therefore, Bradburn's original morale indicators (Bradburn and Caplovitz, 1965) include reports on four positive and four negative emotional experiences. Since the range of emotional experience which might be explored is, as James (1922) notes, limited only by the vocabulary of the investigator, for reasons of economy as well as comparability we elected to use the Bradburn measures.[1]

The measure of positive experience is a summation of four emotional states experienced during the past week: (1) feeling "on top of the world"; (2) "excited or interested in something"; (3) "pleased about having accomplished something"; and (4) "proud because someone complimented you on something you had done." In contrast to the Life Satisfaction Index, where no differences were found between the sexes, on this measure women reported more positive feelings than men. There were also differences across the four pretransitional stages, as shown in Table 8, with the high school seniors and newlyweds having more positive experiences than the two older groups. Intuitively, these differences by stage may seem contradictory to the results reported in the discussion of the LSI, on which the high school seniors ranked lowest and newlyweds

---

[1] In order to overcome some of the criticisms of the Bradburn battery, particularly its "either-or" nature (Mettee, 1971), we expanded the scoring response alternatives to include "never experienced, once, several times, and often" during the past week. When responses were subjected to a principal components analysis with orthogonal varimax rotation, the two factors contributing most to the total variance were positive and negative factors, indicating that the correlational matrix exhibited the same associations as Bradburn and Caplovitz (1965), using nonfactor-analytic procedures, found with the original version. The factors were not used in the subsequent analyses, however. Rather, the weighting system employed by Bradburn was incorporated, with modifications to take into account the extended range of possible response.

and preretirees highest. Before we examine some of the possible
reasons for this seeming contradiction, it will be helpful to report
variations in the individual items summarized by the positive-affect
score.

Newlyweds of both sexes and women were more likely to
feel on top of the world, while men, especially the middle-aged,
were least likely to feel this way (the youngest and oldest groups of
men closely resembled each other). The two younger stages were
more apt to report feeling excited during the past week; and there
was a trend for women, particularly older women, to have had more
such experiences than their male cohorts. The two younger groups,
newlyweds in particular, were most likely to report feeling proud
because someone complimented them, while the preretirees were
least likely to have had such an experience. There were no stage or
sex differences in regard to the feeling of accomplishment. Younger
respondents, in short, reported greater emotional intensity and sense
of personal recognition. The results parallel those of Chapter Four,
where people in the younger stages (especially newlyweds) projected
more energetic self-images, and those in the two later stages, particularly the men in the preretirement stage, had become mellow and
noncompetitive in their dealings with others. On the basis of this
kind of self-concept, it is not surprising that the preretirees may be
more concerned with giving compliments than with receiving.

Negative affect was assessed with the following items: (1)
feeling "very lonely or remote from other people"; (2) "depressed
or very unhappy"; (3) "bored"; and (4) "so restless you couldn't
sit long in a chair." There were no differences between men and
women in their total negative-affect scores, but there was a systematic
decline by stage: the high school seniors had the most, followed in
decreasing order by the newlyweds, the middle-aged, and, lowest
of all, the preretirees.

When each of the four items making up the total negative-
affect scores is examined separately, sex as well as stage differences
emerge. Women, particularly older women, were more likely to
report depression than men. More striking are the differences among
the four stages, which help to clarify the reasons for lower overall
negative-affect scores in the later stages. High school students were
more lonely than newlyweds. Newlyweds and high school students

were more lonely and bored than middle-aged parents; and the two younger groups were also more lonely, depressed, bored, and restless than were those facing retirement. The middle-aged and those facing retirement, on the other hand, were very similar—the only difference being that the middle-aged reported more restlessness.

Taking positive as well as negative experiences into account, it is apparent that the older groups reported fewer than the younger. This may be a reflection of the decreases in ego energy reported by Gutmann (1964) and by Havighurst, Neugarten, and Tobin (1968), which they construe as evidence for a process of inner "psychological disengagement." These investigators believe that such an inner withdrawal or shielding precedes behavioral changes in social relationships in later life; they are, in short, positing a developmental phenomenon. Their conclusions, however, are based on cross-sectional data, which limit the inferences that may be drawn about change over the life course. From our own cross-sectional study, similarly, we have no way of assessing whether the lower levels of emotional experience reported by our older respondents are due to indifference, to lack of opportunity, or to an intrinsic developmental process.

Whatever the underlying reasons are for the lower frequency of emotional experiences among older people, it has implications for their life satisfaction. According to Bradburn (1969), the proportion of positive to negative experiences, rather than the sheer frequency of such experiences, determines emotional well-being. To apply Bradburn's balance concept, we followed his procedures and computed the ratio of positive to negative emotions reported for the week preceding the interview. On the resulting measure, the affect-balance score, there were no differences between men and women, nor were there differences between any stages except when newly-weds, middle-aged parents, and those facing retirement were compared with the high school seniors. High school students, whom we have already reported as lowest in life-satisfaction scores, had higher proportions of negative relative to positive experiences than any other stage.

These results provide only partial support for Bradburn's hypothesized relationship between affect balance and life satisfaction. It is true that the low regard in which adolescence is held by many respondents (as reported in Chapter Seven), as well as the lower life satisfaction of high school seniors, may very well stem from their disproportionate share of negative experiences. On the other hand, the similarities between the remaining stages provide no clues to why, for example, middle-aged parents were less satisfied than either the newlyweds or those facing retirement. An obvious question is whether life satisfaction is related to affect balance in the same way across the stage and sex groupings. Our results in making this comparison do not help to explain the greater dissatisfaction of parents but do lend unequivocal support to Bradburn's thesis. Among men and women in each stage, the balance between positive and negative emotional experiences during the week prior to the interview was more closely associated with satisfaction than were high ranks on positive or low ranks on negative experiences considered separately.

Characteristics Associated with Affect

After an extensive review of the literature on happiness through 1966, Wilson (1967) reported a widespread relationship between higher socioeconomic status and happiness. Later studies report similar findings (cf. Bradburn, 1969; Edwards and Klemmack, 1973; Cutler, 1973). Our index of socioeconomic status is similar to that used by many earlier investigators, and includes education, occupation of the principal wage earner, and family income. At no life stage did we find a notable relationship with life satisfaction (or affect balance, for that matter). Only among younger women was there even a trend, in a direction which does support the general finding that those higher in socioeconomic status are more satisfied. This general absence of a relationship between socioeconomic status and satisfaction is probably due to the relatively restricted range represented by our sample. Those studies reporting a strong association included both the lowest and the highest socioeconomic levels, which were deliberately excluded from the present study. We did, however, cover blue- and white-collar workers in about equal proportions, and their similarity in life satisfaction lends further support to the thesis offered in Chapter One that the life styles and psychosocial characteristics of these two groups are becoming increasingly similar.

Ever since Cumming and Henry (1961) first posed their theory of disengagement in the late fifties, the relationship between satisfaction and activity has received considerable attention on the part of gerontologists. Contrary to what might be expected on the basis at least of the original statement of disengagement theory, higher satisfaction has been shown with great consistency to be associated with greater levels of activity (see Tobin and Neugarten, 1961; Maddox, 1963; Phillips, 1967; Havighurst, Neugarten, and Tobin, 1968; Bengtson, Chiriboga, and Keller, 1969; Bradburn, 1969).

Table 9 shows selected correlates of life satisfaction and affect balance for the respondents in our study. Among the younger, the most satisfied were those high in family role participation and those who had a broad scope of social activities. The more satisfied younger people, particularly among the newlywed women, were also involved in many more roles than their less satisfied peers. A seemingly discordant note was struck by the dissatisfaction of those more wrapped up in the occupational role. A closer inspection of the data revealed that this latter association was entirely caused by high school boys, among whom work apparently did not set too well: the happiest boys were those least involved in work-related activities. Dissatisfaction was also associated with greater participation in activities related to philosophical expression among the boys and to ease and contentment among newlywed women. These latter two activities, however, do not denote "activity" in the sense employed, for example, by Cumming and Henry (1961), and their association with dissatisfaction does not refute the conclusion that activity is related to satisfaction among our younger respondents.

Among the older people as a group, on the other hand, satisfaction was not associated with activity. There is generally no association between a relatively low level of activity and high satisfaction, as Cumming and Henry (1961) postulate (though mainly for older groups than ours), or between activity and high satisfaction, as others have reported. Our results, in fact, indicate that among the middle-aged and those facing retirement there may simply be a weakening of the tie between satisfaction and activity. If the relationship persists, it may be in altered form. As Chapters One and Seven suggest, middle-aged and older people may simply be more

Table 9.

SELECTED CORRELATES OF LIFE SATISFACTION AND AFFECT BALANCE[a,b]

	High School		Newlyweds		Middle-Aged		Preretirement		Younger	Older
	Men	Women	Men	Women	Men	Women	Men	Women		
LIFE SATISFACTION AND:										
Familial roles			(.37)	.54**					.42**	
Occupational roles									(—.17)	
Total role scope		(.33)		.51**					.22*	
Instrumental activities										
Expressive activities										
Philosophical activities	(—.37)	.39*								
Social-service activities				—.60**			—.57**			
Ease-contentment activities										
Hedonistic activities										
Growth activities										
Nongoal-directed activities								—.41*		
Activity scope	—.62**	(—.35)	—.45*	.56*		(.34)	(—.32)	(—.31)		
Self-criticism					—.41*				—.33**	—.23*
Respondent-interviewer agreement	(.38)		(.37)	.40*					.39**	.24*
AFFECT BALANCE AND:										
Familial roles										
Occupational roles										
Total role scope							—.39*		.24*	
Instrumental activities		.43*							(—.18)	
Expressive activities					(.37)				.27**	
Philosophical activities		(.34)							(.17)	
Social-service activities		.62**						—.42*		
Ease-contentment activities										
Hedonistic activities				(.38)						
Growth activities		(.38)							.20*	
Nongoal-directed activities		.43*								
Activity scope				.52*			(—.36)			
Self-criticism		(—.33)		—.36				(—.33)	—.26**	
Respondent-interviewer agreement				.50*					.29**	—.20*

a Parenthesized correlations attain a probability between .10 and .05; correlations with one asterisk have a probability between .05 and .01; correlations with two asterisks have a probability of less than .01.

b For all measures, a higher score indicates more of the assessed construct.

selective and self-serving in their activities and relationships. For
example, the only exceptions to the general statement that activity is
unrelated to satisfaction were found among those facing retirement.
In this oldest group, social service (activities involving helping others
in the community) was dissatisfying to the men, and, as might be
expected on the basis of the discussion in Chapter Four, the day-to-
day routine of shopping and housework was dissatisfying to the
women. Further support for this conjecture of greater selectivity in
activities is provided by Lemon, Bengtson, and Peterson (1972)
and by Edwards and Klemmack (1973), who report that it is not
the quantity of activity so much as its quality that determines
whether an association with satisfaction exists.

Affect balance was associated with several activities and
roles among the younger men and women. Those higher in affect
balance participated more fully in familial roles, in both instrumental
and expressive activities, and in activities promoting personal growth.
Activity and affect balance were most widely associated among the
high school girls; the boys, as was the case for satisfaction, were the
primary contributors toward the single instance where role performance (more specifically, performance in the worker role) was
associated with a lower proportion of positive emotional experiences.
Similarly, no association between activity and affect was found for
the older people as a group, but only among those facing retirement:
the worker role was associated with lower affect balance among the
men, and expressive activities were associated with lower affect
balance among the women. No associations between social interaction and affect balance existed for the two older stages.

Looking at the positive and negative components of the
affect balance score separately, we found that breadth of social
activities was generally associated with positive experiences among
both the younger and the older groups. Among the older groups,
however, such social breadth was also associated with more negative
experiences, a finding which lends further support to our inference
that the quality rather than the scope of interpersonal relationships
becomes increasingly critical as one moves through the adult life
course.

In the intrapersonal sphere, we selected two components of
self-concept, self-criticism and the discrepancy between public and

private self-image, to compare with life satisfaction.[2] Especially among men, those less disposed to self-criticism were the more satisfied, with significant relationships holding for the high school, newlywed, and middle-aged men, and reaching trend proportions among the preretired (Table 9). Among the women there was merely a trend, and that only for the earliest and the latest stages. This is only one of several indications in our findings of the greater tolerance of the women in our sample for intrapersonal and interpersonal complexities and ambiguities.

The relationship between public and private self-images, as we saw in Chapter Four, is associated with the individual's "fit" with his interpersonal world. For example, those men who saw themselves quite differently from the way others perceived them also had discomforting relationships with members of their family, and were lonelier. The causality involved in such an association is impossible to derive from this cross-sectional phase of our research. In the related area of self-disclosure, however, Jourard (1959, 1971) suggests that the inability to disclose personal aspects of one's self to others may hinder interpersonal relations and lead to severe problems of adjustment. One might assume, then, that the individual who wittingly or unwittingly projects a self-image at odds with his own would be less satisfied than the one who tends to be seen as he sees himself. This proved to be the case for the younger people and, to a lesser extent, the older people as well.

The fit between public and private self-image had less connection with the quality of recent emotional experience (affect balance) than it did with satisfaction in general. Only among the newlywed women were those who revealed considerable discrepancy likely to report more negative than positive experiences. Self-criticism, on the other hand, was associated with recent negative experiences among all women except the middle-aged. Among men it was true only for those facing retirement. Among men, moreover, we have seen that self-criticism was strongly related to the presumably

---

[2] Self-diffusion and the indexes of masculine and feminine self-concept (discussed in Chapter Four) generally were not associated with either life satisfaction or affect balance. Two groups were exceptions: high school women and preretirement men. Among both, those low on diffusion and high on masculinity were more satisfied.

less transient level of life satisfaction. Since this was not true for women, one might conclude that the self-concept of women is more influenced by immediate interpersonal feedback than is that of men, a finding which further hints at the possibility (suggested in Chapter Four) of developmental differences between the sexes.

Affect Typology

Bradburn's (1969) measure of balance between recent positive and negative experiences does not take into account the frequency of such experiences. That is, the person with one positive and one negative experience falls into the same category as the one with four of each. Since, as we have seen, older groups report fewer recent emotional experiences, frequency is a component of importance for a study across the life course. To correct this deficiency for our purposes, we compared those high and low on negative experiences with those high and low on positive experiences. The result is a fourfold typology. For convenience, we have labeled those with more negative than positive experiences the "beset" and those with more positive experiences the "exultant." The "balanced," in Bradburn's terms, are of two extremes: those with many positive and many negative experiences, the "volatile," and those with few of each, whom we call "bland."

The distribution of affect types varies markedly across the four stages. Some of this variation is attributable to the significantly greater frequency of emotional experiences reported by the younger respondents. When the two younger groups are compared with the two older, 44 percent of the younger fall into the volatile category, as compared to only 12 percent of the older. Conversely, fewer than one tenth of the younger respondents were of the bland type, as compared to fully half of the older.

Stage differences in the beset and exultant types reflect the higher number of negative experiences among the young. The younger people were more likely to be beset than exultant, while the reverse was true for the older. High school seniors contributed disproportionately to the predominance of the beset among the young: 39 percent of them fell into this category, as compared to 11 percent who were of the exultant type. There were also relatively few of the exultant type among the newlyweds, despite the fact that they rated themselves happiest; the majority were volatile, reporting many positive and many negative experiences.

Among older subjects there were no dramatic differences between the middle-aged and the preretirement stages, but there was an interesting sex difference: of the sixteen people categorized as beset, eleven, or over two thirds, were men. Here, then, is one of the few instances where men report more negatively than women. This may well be due to the inclusion of items, such as boredom and restlessness, which may not conflict with the masculine self-image.

For the sample as a whole, the association between our typology and measures of the sense of well-being support Bradburn's balance thesis to some extent: the exultant scored highest on life satisfaction; the beset were lowest; the bland and the volatile fell in between. Trends in this direction were found in both older and younger groups. There were, however, significant differences between men and women. Men reflected the pattern of the sample as a whole. The volatile were significantly lower in satisfaction than either the bland or the exultant; the volatile, indeed, averaged lower scores on satisfaction than the beset, although the difference was not significant. Among women the volatile were as happy as the bland and the exultant, and significantly more so than the beset. This again suggests a greater complexity among women, who can apparently integrate many and diverse emotional experiences. Men seem more distressed by the ups and downs of emotional life; they apparently thrive either on a preponderance of positive emotional experiences or a relative lack of any kind. These sex differences become most evident among those facing retirement, where we found volatile men to be the least happy—less so even than those whose negative experiences outweigh the positive. The volatile pre-retired women, on the other hand, ranked highest in satisfaction, although the differences between the volatile, the bland, and the exultant were not statistically significant; only the beset type was noticeably more dissatisfied than the others.

The typology is particularly useful in assessing the relationship between affect and social interaction. Since the typology is based primarily on affect arising from interpersonal experiences, one might expect the exultant to be more active socially than the beset, the volatile highest and the bland the lowest. From the perspective afforded us thus far in this chapter, however, morale has been less associated with activity among the older groups. Considering just the breadth of activities, we found that among both men and women the volatile ranked highest, followed by the exultant, the beset, and, finally, the bland. There were, however, distinct differences between the two younger and the two older stages. Among the older people, the volatile, followed by the beset, were highest in their scope of activities; the exultant and the bland, who also scored higher on life satisfaction, were lower in activity scope. Among the younger people, the exultant and the volatile ranked highest on satisfaction, while the bland and the beset were almost exactly equivalent.

There is, in other words, some cross-sectional evidence that the relationship with activities may shift over the life course, and that among older people a greater breadth of activities actually weighs against life satisfaction. Our measure of the breadth of activities, of course, included such pursuits as outdoor hobbies, travel, social life and parties, shopping, and listening to the radio. A high score on such an admixture of activities would indicate that the individual maintains a highly diversified or complex life style. Among older people, such a complexity of activity may represent a lifelong accumulation of activities, some of which may come to be viewed as unwanted or unimportant. As is shown in the chapters on time perspective and values (Chapters Seven and Ten), getting rid of unwanted duties and obligations and settling for ease and contentment (but not necessarily inactivity) as a way of life may represent one of the major adaptive tasks for older people in the sociocultural group we are studying. Among the younger people, on the other hand, there is a suggestion that greater breadth of activities is associated with greater life satisfaction. It may be that younger people are better able to assimilate or to accept the diversity of experience that an active life style often generates.

VI

Complexities of Adaptation

In the previous chapter, we found that most of our subjects considered themselves happy; this was true of older persons facing changes that might be considered decremental, involving role losses, as well as of the young who confronted incremental transitions. The men who considered themselves happiest were those with predominantly positive emotional experiences in the recent past, while the happiest women tended to be those with both positive and negative experiences. In this chapter we carry the "balance" concept a step further. Earlier studies have shown that persons psychologically incapable of coping with the problems of their day-to-day lives may be happy (Lowenthal, Berkman, and Associates, 1967). On a more theoretical level, Rosow (1963) has criticized the usefulness of the concept of happiness because of its cultural relativism and its uncertain relationship to level of functioning. Mark Twain portrays the relativism, and perhaps the ambiguities, of the concept more dramatically in *The Mysterious Stranger,* where an angel promises happiness to an old man. The angel fulfills his promise by making the man insane, and he spends the remainder of his life in an institution, receiving illusionary old friends and dispensing imaginary largesse.

We first assess the adaptive level of our subjects along two dimensions: a traditional one focusing on degree of impairment, and a more innovative one growing out of a long-standing collaborative effort to operationalize concepts relating to psychological resources or "positive" mental health. We then turn to a brief summary of the relationship between physical and psychological status, which, as will be further documented in Chapter Eight, is becoming an increasingly challenging field for research on adaptation in adulthood. Finally, we discuss the merits of a suggested "dual model" of adaptation—a model that combines psychological resources and deficits.

Psychological Deficits

The impairment dimension of psychological adaptation has been utilized in several large surveys of community-resident populations (for example, Gurin, Veroff and Feld, 1960; Langner and Michael, 1963; Leighton, 1959). These studies were designed to measure the prevalence of mental disorder and to relate it to a variety of demographic characteristics. The second or "positive" dimension has been often proposed (Jahoda, 1958; Clausen, 1969; Smith, 1969) but rarely applied in empirical studies. Through a long-sustained collaborative effort involving a review of theories of adaptation and detailed analyses of life-history protocols collected in pretest interviews, we have been able to operationalize some of the concepts that the multidisciplinary team (which included psychoanalysts Robert Butler and Leonard Micon) considered most pertinent. (These concepts are listed in Appendix B, Adaptive Ratings.)

While several measures contribute to the negative dimension of the model (see Table 10, under "Deficits"), we shall here draw on two which provide an overview of the extent of psychological malfunctioning in our sample. The first is the subject's own assessment of emotional problems that have occurred thus far in his life;

the second is a series of questions about psychological symptoms. In addition to these measures, we also used the Gottschalk, Winget, and Gleser (1969) anxiety and hostility scores, which were derived from TAT cards; the self-criticism measure from the Adjective Rating List (described in Chapter Four); and degree of impairment and prognosticated outcome as rated by the interdisciplinary team of social scientists.

In response to the question "Do you have or have you ever had any emotional problems which interfered with what you were doing or wanted to do?" slightly over one fourth of our subjects reported positively, approximating the 23 percent in the nationwide survey conducted by Gurin, Veroff, and Feld (1960). Although the question covered the life span, it was not the older subjects, who of course had the greater number of years at risk, but the newlyweds who reported the most emotional problems (nearly half, as compared with fewer than one fourth of those facing retirement). Gurin, Veroff, and Feld (1960), who also found that those in their late fifties and early sixties reported fewer problems, suggest that there may be a generational difference in the willingness to acknowledge such "shortcomings," younger people being more socialized in school and through the mass media to accept them as part of the human condition. In our sample the problems reported by the newlyweds may also be associated with marriage; fully half of those reporting problems mentioned that they had occurred in the past year, which also was the year in which their marriages took place. In other stages, women consistently reported more problems than men. Newlyweds excluded, one tenth of the men and nearly one third of the women reported problems. Among newlyweds, the men were just as likely to report them as women.

Depression was the most common problem (accounting for about one fifth of the problems reported); family problems, phobias, "nervous breakdowns," and feelings of inferiority also received frequent mention. Nearly half of those reporting problems had sought professional help. This amounts to 13 percent of the entire sample, a proportion again very close to that reported by Gurin, Veroff, and Feld (1960). If we add men and women who turned to nonprofessional resources such as friends and relatives, over half of those who reported problems had sought help. We are left with the

Table 10.

PSYCHOLOGICAL DEFICITS, PSYCHOLOGICAL RESOURCES, PHYSICAL HEALTH[a]
(averages, except as noted)

	High School		Newlywed		Middle-Aged		Preretirement	
	Men	Women	Men	Women	Men	Women	Men	Women
Deficits								
Psychological symptoms[b,d]	9.1	11.1	11.8	10.9	7.6	11.3	7.4	10.6
Psychiatric rating[d]	9.4	8.3	8.6	7.7	9.4	8.0	9.5	7.8
Gottschalk anxiety (TAT)[b]	2.0	1.9	1.8	1.9	1.9	2.1	2.2	2.2
Gottschalk hostility (TAT)[b]	1.8	1.8	1.8	1.7	1.6	1.9	1.7	1.7
Self-criticism[b,d]	4.1	7.1	4.8	6.9	5.0	7.6	5.4	6.3
Degree of psychological impairment	8.7	9.1	9.4	8.8	9.3	8.9	9.6	9.4
Direction of psychological impairment[c]	9.1	5.6	11.8	5.2	4.7	4.7	4.8	4.6
No reported emotional problems (%)[c,d]	96	70	56	52	89	70	87	67
Never sought professional help (%)	100	89	88	64	100	85	93	80
No major childhood upsets (%)	56	56	56	40	70	70	57	53
Resources								
Contextual perspective[e]	7.1	7.1	8.6	7.4	8.1	7.7	8.1	8.0
Life-cycle perspective[e]	7.5	7.6	8.0	7.8	8.4	7.9	8.2	8.6

Familial mutuality[c]	6.9	7.9	8.9	8.1	8.0	7.7	7.6	8.3
Extrafamilial mutuality[d,c]	5.9	7.8	7.3	6.9	7.4	7.3	6.5	7.7
Growth[c]	8.0	7.7	8.8	7.9	6.9	7.1	7.0	6.9
Intrapersonal competence[c,d]	8.0	7.7	9.3	8.4	9.3	8.1	9.1	8.9
Insight[c]	7.0	7.4	7.7	7.6	7.5	7.4	7.5	7.7
Hope[c]	9.1	9.0	9.6	8.9	8.1	8.0	8.5	8.1
Satisfaction with competence[d]	8.7	8.1	9.4	8.1	9.1	8.0	9.3	8.9
Satisfaction: interpersonal[c]	7.2	8.5	9.1	7.7	8.6	7.8	8.9	8.6
Satisfaction: self[c,d]	8.3	8.2	9.0	7.7	8.0	7.2	9.1	8.1
Perceived accommodation (% high)[c,d]	52	70	48	100	41	74	57	83
Judged accommodation (% high)[c,d]	60	59	40	80	30	56	40	57
WAIS Vocabulary[c,f]	48.0	41.7	62.5	61.3	63.1	61.7	64.8	62.2
WAIS Block Design[c,d,f]	37.0	33.2	39.9	37.1	34.5	32.4	31.4	30.5
Physical Health								
Above-average energy (%)[c]	52	26	29	20	48	33	47	53
No physical problems (%)[c]	68	70	40	56	52	30	30	20
One or no visits to the doctor (%)[c]	60	70	36	25	70	41	43	37

[a] For explanations of scoring systems, see separate listings in Appendix B.
[b] High scores imply greater deficit.
[c] Differences between the stages are significant at $p < .05$.
[d] Differences between men and women are significant at $p < .05$.
[e] Interaction between sex and stage is significant at $p < .05$.
[f] Uncorrected for age.

impression that the quiet, stable, middle-class community which we studied—with few serious economic, ethnic, or intergenerational problems—is no better off than the population at large in terms of the frequency of psychological difficulties.

A forty-two-item Symptoms Checklist recorded not only the presence or absence of particular symptoms but a description of the behavior or feelings involved as well. We introduced the latter specification on the grounds that it is often the context in which the symptoms occur which ultimately determines their significance for psychological well-being (Vaillant, 1971; Michaels, 1959; Fried and Lindemann, 1961; Coleman, 1971). Items in the checklist were those that a team of psychiatrists (Robert Butler, Leon Epstein, Leonard Micon, and Alexander Simon) considered, on the basis of clinical evidence, to be most often associated with psychological dysfunction. The sample as a whole averaged ten such symptoms. No stage differences were apparent, but women reported more symptoms than men (they averaged eleven, as opposed to nine for the men). Sex differences were most marked among the two older groups, whereas among the newlyweds men averaged slightly higher rates of reported symptoms than did women, although the difference was not significant.

A psychiatrist (Hal Goldberg, of the Langley Porter Neuropsychiatric Institute) subsequently evaluated the descriptions of context and feelings associated with each symptom. The one-month Pearson correlation coefficient for individual symptom responses was .90 ($N = 407$); for the global rating, .85. Some descriptions contained evidence of psychopathology; others did not. Compare, for example, the following reactions by two newlywed men to the question "Have you felt that different parts of your body were not under your control or have become disconnected somewhat?" One man, evasive and troubled, received a rating of moderate impairment on this symptom: "Oh, I don't know, that's just sort of difficult to talk about. I sometimes feel that way, but I don't know just exactly what I mean by it. It's sort of strange. I'd rather not talk about it." Another response contained minimal evidence of pathology: "Occasionally I wake up with my arm gone utterly to sleep. I usually have lain on it." As with the simple symptom count, the number of responses with a high probability of being associated with underlying pathology differed little across the life stages, but there were fewer of them—an average of six. Sex differences were more pronounced with this psychiatrically evaluated count, and high school women joined middle-aged and preretirement women in having more symptomatology than their male counterparts. (The psychiatrist also made a global rating of the implications of the total response set per respondent, with similar results: no stage differences, but women, on the average, were judged to exhibit greater evidence of pathology than the men.)

Over half of the sample reported feeling at times "moody and blue for no reason"; nearly half reported that their feelings are easily hurt and that specific objects or circumstances, such as the dark, heights, or snakes, frightened them. Contrary to clinical reports, which suggest that such states are more common in later life (Goldfarb, 1963; Zinberg and Kaufman, 1963), depression severe enough to interfere with daily affairs was more common among the two younger stages: nearly half reported feeling severely depressed at some point in their lives, resembling the middle-aged women in this respect. Together, the two younger groups and the women about to enter the postparental stage make up four fifths of those reporting depression. Among the older subjects in general, problems relating to social interaction were most pertinent. Nearly two fifths of them, as compared with one fifth of the younger respondents, reported that people often annoy or irritate them. Two fifths of the oldest group also reported that criticism always upsets them.

There is a curious parallel between older women and newlyweds in terms of existential despair, with both groups having felt that life is meaningless. Two thirds of those who reported such feelings were either older women or newlywed men. Middle-aged and newlywed women were the most likely to have contemplated suicide. Men and women in both stages, of course, were confronted with the necessity for restructuring their lives around the presence or absence of other people. Marriage involves a maximum demand for social readjustment (Holmes and Rahe, 1967) and can be construed as being accompanied by a kind of "death" of the former social self, perhaps especially for women who have no major commitments other than marriage and a family. For the older women, the imminent empty-nest period may have had similar connotations.

Since on the verbal level these women profess to look forward to the departure of their youngest child (Lowenthal and Chiriboga, 1972a), obviously their anxiety exists on a deeper level of consciousness. Older men, on the other hand, may be escaping from similar anxieties by becoming dependent on alcohol: twice as many older men as women reported that drinking was or had been a problem.

Another characteristic differentiating men from women is the need to maintain a strict schedule, which was reported by nearly half of the men in the two later stages. We saw in Chapter One that many of the middle-aged men are of the focused type, with their activities—and, as will be shown in subsequent chapters, their anxieties as well—centering on work. A certain rigidity of scheduling may be of service in allaying these anxieties or in keeping them well below the level of consciousness. Of the ten middle-aged men who noted a need for strict scheduling in their lives, eight fell into the focused category. Such a distribution, found in no other group, emphasizes a need for order and control, which may reflect the peaking of responsibility and obligations reported by Neugarten (1968b) as typifying the middle years.

Older women reported more psychophysiological disturbances, which the majority of them attributed to the menopause. For example, in discussing the sleep disturbances common to many older women, one fifty-seven-year-old housewife reported: "[Sleeping] is the worst problem that I have. I think it is caused by the menopause, although I've never had any flashes with it. I think I should have been a nightwatchman, I can stay awake all night. I don't take pills. Luckily, I need relatively little sleep."

Psychological Resources

While the need to take psychological resources as well as degree of impairment into account has been marked by many researchers and theoreticians, the characteristics advocated for study (characteristics such as "emotional maturity," "strength of character," or a "happy disposition") are often highly generalized or abstract. It is small wonder that some workers have expressed skepticism about the feasibility of assessing psychological health.

Lewis (1958, p. 173) offers a particularly telling—albeit one-sided—critique:

> *A rather silly but often repeated truism says that the aim of psychiatric treatment is to promote mental health. It is hard to tell what the latter phrase means. Mental health is an invincibly obscure concept. Those who have attempted to define it in positive terms have twisted ropes of sand, telling us, for example, that a man's mental health consists in: (a) active adjustment or attempts at mastery of his environment as distinct both from his inability to adjust and from his indiscriminate adjustment through passive acceptance of environmental conditions; (b) unity of his personality, the maintenance of a stable, internal integration which remains intact notwithstanding the flexibility of behavior which derives from active adjustment; and (c) ability to perceive correctly the world and himself. This clutter of words is groping toward an ideal, a sociobiological ideal, but much of it can have no operational referents and it abounds in terms which are undefined and at present undefinable.*

Although perhaps more outspoken than most, Lewis is not atypical. As Leighton (1959, p. 6) has commented, "Grappling with illness is difficult enough." More recently, Shakow (1972, p. 21) has complained that positive aspects of mental health are overemphasized: "We have had dinned into our ears a Madison Avenue type slogan of 'positive mental health' as if there was a negative mental health—as if being healthy wasn't good enough. And in recent days this trend has had hitched onto it a bandwagon, a fad of sentience and 'groupiness' onto which so many have leaped." On the other hand, those who believe that a more complex approach to the issue is desirable (Jahoda, 1958; Smith, 1969; Clausen, 1969; Haan, 1969) also think that it is feasible. The most common position is that mental health represents an averaging of an individual's resources and deficits. Beiser (1971, p. 250), for example, asks us to imagine a situation in which "Maladaptive patterns may be seen as a series of black dots and positive patterns as a series of white dots. If one were to think of capacities as occupying the left hand of the continuum, then, as one moves from left to right, there would be a gradual transition from a picture in which white dots predominated to a central position in which there was more or less mixing of the two to the right-hand position where there are more black dots than white."

In our systematic searches of the literature and in a year-long seminar devoted to interdisciplinary assessment of life-history interviews, we endeavored to operationalize some of the "white dots." After several sessions devoted to the selection and definition of such resources, two sociologists, one anthropologist, one psychoanalyst, and two psychologists independently analyzed and rated respondents on thirteen characteristics (see also Adaptive Ratings, Appendix B). These variables, and two subtests from the Wechsler Adult Intelligence Scale (WAIS), make up the positive dimension of the model (see Table 10, under "Resources"). Here we shall report on the results of five of them, as applied to the total sample: accommodation (judged), growth, hope, mutuality (familial and extrafamilial), and intelligence.

Accommodation is a concept adapted in part from Goldstein (1963), who believes that man alternates between submissive and assertive tendencies in coming to terms with his milieu. When an individual resorts primarily to one of the two tendencies, "something has gone wrong in the relationship between the individual and the surrounding world" (p. 205). In operationalizing this concept, we attempted to measure what the individual at that time considered his or her customary stance: whether he or she usually dominated others or accommodated to them. As shown in Table 10, there are stage differences in interpersonal accommodation among both men and women. Among the men, three fifths of the high school seniors were prone to give in to the demands or needs of others; among the middle-aged parents and those facing retirement, the proportion drops to approximately one third. This is contrary to the age-linked decline in mastery reported among men by Gutmann (1964) on the basis of projective data, but his (cross-cultural) samples included only older people (from middle age to advanced old age).

Among women, the newlyweds were most accommodating: four fifths ranked high on this tendency, as compared with slightly more than half in both the younger and older stages. We saw in

Chapter Two that these young women were far more likely than older married women to report their husbands as the "bosses" of the family and to rate themselves high on submissive qualities in the Femininity Index. We thus have reinforcement for the possibility that as women begin to face parenthood their need to be submissive and taken care of is greatest. Conversely, when their practical responsibilities may seem most pressing, in the newlywed and middle-aged stages, men are significantly less accommodating than women. At the high school and the preretirement stages, men and women did not differ in their levels of accommodation.

The *growth* dimension is akin to, and has its theoretical roots in, the concepts of development and self-realization postulated by Allport, ([1937], 1961), Maslow ([1962], 1968), Rogers (1954), Erikson (1963), and Bühler (1962), among others. People rated high on our measure revealed openness, curiosity, and the willingness and courage to experiment and change. Those rated low seemed restricted and resistant to change. In our middle- and lower-middle-class sample, selected in part to test the general applicability of concepts of self-actualization developed primarily from rather elite subjects or patients, almost twice as many people had a circumscribed rather than a growth-motivated approach to life. About one fifth of the men and only half that many women proved to be growth-oriented. People in the two younger stages were significantly more growth-oriented than those in the two later stages, with the newlyweds proving to be the most open to new experiences.

Absence of growth motivation in this sample, however, does not have an adverse effect on well-being. Indeed, several studies (Beiser, 1971; Grinker, 1962) have found that individuals who appear anything but "self-actualizing" are happy and content. Moreover, as the findings on time perspective and values reported in Chapters Seven and Ten indicate, our older respondents seek a relatively restricted life style. A potential problem for such people would be the development of a situation requiring a new life style, such as widowhood, divorce, or an illness or disability. Beiser (1971), for example, has reported that individuals with a circumscribed or self-protective approach to life experience more difficulties in adjustment if faced with the need to make major changes than do those who have lived more adventurous and perhaps more stressful lives. Regardless of former life style, most people as they move into their seventies and eighties tend to become more circumscribed in their behavior.

Hope is a psychological resource in part because of its relationships to goal-directed striving (French, 1952; Lewin, 1951). Stotland (1969, p. 7), for example, maintains that "hopefulness is a necessary condition for action." Among people who are not growth-oriented, hope may be merely directed toward the goal of maintaining the status quo. We defined hope as the feeling that what is desired is also viewed as possible. People's expectations for the next ten years were used as the basis for evaluating this dimension. Although at least one study (Haberland and Lieberman, 1969) reports that an unrealistic degree of hope (as well as the lack of it) may be associated with maladaptation, our rating instrument was not sufficiently refined to detect such nuances.

Three fifths of the sample clustered in one of the three middle categories of the scale; nearly one third were very hopeful; and one tenth were altogether lacking in hope. While there were no differences between the sexes, those across the four stages were clear— the two younger groups being more hopeful than the two older. Stage differences appear to be rather gross, for the high school students did not differ from the newlyweds, nor did the middle-aged differ significantly from those facing retirement. There were, however, trends between the two older groups, in a direction opposite to what might be expected. Men and women at the preretirement stage included only four people in the hopeless category. The middle-aged were most likely to be lacking in this characteristic: nearly one fourth felt that they could not achieve what they wanted to, or generally had low expectations for the future. Their hopelessness reflects a kind of anomie dramatized by conscious or unconscious apprehension about the postparental phase of life, which they are about to enter. The men, often struggling against a career plateau, and the women in the final period of child rearing were perhaps lacking in hope because they had not yet established goals for the new life stage. One middle-aged man, acutely aware of eventual retirement, was very pessimistic and had no plans for it. His comments are typical of men and women at this stage of life: "It's just an unknown quantity. I can't see anything ahead. I suppose

I could consider traveling, but that doesn't appeal to me too much now. More grandchildren? We have more than enough now. Just waiting to pass time before you die. Not knowing what to do. But age is the first thing against you in trying to do anything big or spectacular. Even if you decide on something, you may not have time to do it. I guess you have to be realistic about things. When you are young you have all of life ahead of you." In the following comments by a middle-aged mother, the departure of the family is perceived as a mere punctuation mark in a drab and unrewarding life: "I just live from day to day. I'll just see what happens. We may just coast along like this or everything might blow up. There's just kind of an undercurrent all the time here. Maybe after the family are gone, I'll make my own plans. But I don't know how long I can continue like this. . . . After Joyce [daughter] leaves, I don't care what happens to me any more because my life is just not that important."

In previous chapters several dimensions of social interaction have been reported, including scope and complexity. Among other functions, interpersonal relationships may serve to mediate the effects of stressful events. Rosow (1967), for example, has shown that elderly persons, particularly when living in areas with a high proportion of age peers, provide support for each other in times of illness or need. Lowenthal and Haven (1968) underscore the importance of at least one person who is considered a confidant (a role sometimes filled by a grocery or room clerk) in helping older people cope with the multiple stresses of aging. Not only the breadth of one's social networks but the perceived closeness is evidently crucial, even though individual concepts of intimacy or mutuality obviously cover a very broad range.

We defined *mutuality* as the capacity for relationships characterized by respect, trust, support, empathy, and responsibility, as well as the capacity to give as well as to receive. Relationships with family members and with friends were assessed separately. Here we shall draw upon scores combining the two.

There were no systematic differences among the four life stages in the capacity for mutuality. Highest among the women were the oldest, but stage variations were relatively slight; among men, the teenagers and those facing retirement ranked lowest, while the newlyweds manifested the greatest capacity for mutuality. In contrast to the older women, men at the preretirement stage had a relatively low level of mutuality. This finding is somewhat puzzling, since, as was shown in Chapter Four, these men are the most likely to rate themselves as having warm interpersonal relationships. Not yet quite recovered from the economic strains and preoccupation involved in providing for retirement (which are already manifest in the middle-aged men), they may perhaps be indulging in wishful thinking or hopes for change in the future. Such an interpretation finds some reinforcement in the increased discrepancy between real and ideal friends as described by these men (Chapter Three).

Among high school seniors, women scored higher than men— more because of the low standing of the men than because of any particularly strong indications of mutuality among the women. Among the newlyweds and the middle-aged parents, men if anything ranked higher on mutuality than women, although the differences were not significant. In short, though a wide range of studies indicate the stronger focus of women on interpersonal relationships, their interest in, or capacity for, mutuality in comparison with that of men appears to vary considerably across the life course.

Since *mental capacity* is a critical component of the individual's psychological resources, we conclude this review by summarizing findings from two subtests of the Wechsler Adult Intelligence Scale, the Vocabulary and the Block Design tests. While the usefulness of such tests has been sharply questioned in recent years, largely because of the cultural biases inherent in most of them, we believe that they are appropriate measures for the culturally and economically homogeneous group which makes up our sample.

While some differences were found in the raw scores, it seems reasonable to rely on those standardized for age, as established by Wechsler (1955). We compared the proportion of persons whose scores on either the Vocabulary or the Block Design test were more than one standard deviation from the mean. There were no sex differences in any stage with respect to Vocabulary. Compared with other stages, however, proportionately fewer of the high school seniors scored high. As was the case for Vocabulary, only stage differences were found with Block Design. Preretirement men and women scored highest: 42 percent of them were more than one standard deviation higher than the mean of their age group, as compared to approximately 30 percent of the newlyweds and middle-aged parents, and 16 percent of the high school seniors. In short, on both the Vocabulary and the Block Design subtests, the high school seniors ranked low, whereas those facing retirement ranked high in terms of age-adjusted scores.[1] Scores for all groups, however, fell within what Wechsler (1955) established as the normal range.[2]

Whatever the trends in the general population, variations within our sample proved to have relevance for other aspects of our subjects' lives—such as, for example, exposure to presumptive stress (discussed in Chapter Eight).

Physical Status

To round out our assessment of the adaptive levels of these respondents who are about to enter a new life stage, we shall briefly summarize their physical condition as revealed by self-reports. Three measures were used: enumeration of current physical problems, number of visits to a physician in the past year, and energy level (see Table 10, under "Physical Health").

As is no doubt inevitable, older people reported more health problems and medical appointments. As shown in Table 10, well over two thirds of the high school students said that they had no physical health problems, compared with only one fourth of the pre-retirement men and women. Physicians were visited more often by women than men, especially among the middle-aged, and stage differences were again strong. Only one third of the high school

---

[1] The lower proportion of high school seniors falling within the superior range of the Vocabulary and Block Design subtests is most probably a result of the selection procedures followed by the high school system from which the sample was drawn. Students with above-average academic records are given the option of attending a school designed to prepare them for the more prestigious colleges. Our seniors attended a high school whose student body represents an admixture of those with average or below-average academic records and those few who opt not to attend the more elite school.

[2] Standardization of WAIS subtests, including both the Vocabulary and the Block Design, was last done in the early 1950s (Wechsler, 1955). There is, therefore, some doubt about the applicability of such standards to our data; in the absence of alternatives, however, we have chosen to utilize them.

seniors consulted a physician more than once, compared with 60 percent of the oldest group. Newlyweds did average more such consultations than the preretirement men and women, but their higher incidence was due primarily to premarital examinations and to physical examinations in connection with job applications.

Since the self-reports on energy level were in comparison with age peers, it is not surprising that we did not find the age-related decline in energy reported in many studies (for example, Lowenthal, Berkman, and Associates, 1967; Neugarten, 1968b; Kuhlen, 1968). Despite reporting the most health problems, pre-retirement men and women felt that they were in the best shape in this respect: nearly half felt that they had more energy than the average person their age. Newlyweds as a group ranked lowest: fewer than one fourth felt that they had more energy than their age peers. This was true of the newlywed men as well as the women, despite the fact that in the self-concept material (Chapter Four) the men were the most energetic and buoyant of all male groups.

In this comparatively healthy sample, the relationship between physical health and morale is not very strong. The presence of physical problems, for example, was not associated with dissatisfaction in any life stage or for either sex. There was a relationship, however, between affect balance and self-reported physical status among newlywed and preretirement women: those with fewer health problems also had had fewer negative (relative to positive) emotional experiences in the past week. Among women, too, there was some relationship between self-evaluated health status and psychological adaptation. Preretirement women with fewer health problems were rated high on mutuality and had fewer psychological deficits and a broader perspective on their lives. Healthier middle-aged and newlywed women also had fewer psychological deficits than those considering themselves less healthy.

Among men, the association between physical problems and psychological well-being is weaker, and tends to be in a direction opposite to that found among the women. For example, the oldest men with the fewest physical health problems were rated as deteriorating in psychological health. Similarly, high school boys reporting few physical problems ranked lower on certain psychological resources than their age peers who felt themselves to be less healthy.

These differences between men and women may be due to variations in response styles. Evidence for the reluctance of many men to discuss any kinds of problems has been reported in this chapter and in earlier ones as well. Gurin, Veroff, and Feld (1960) found a similar trend in their national survey of how Americans view their psychological problems. Shanas and others (1968), in a cross-national prevalence study of physical health among older subjects, also found that men consistently report fewer problems than women. Further evidence for the existence of a group of strong deniers among the men, and of the possible consequences of this denial for their physical health status, will be offered in Chapter Eight.

There is no relationship between reported energy level and life satisfaction in any groups. Older men reporting the most energy, however, also reported more positive than negative emotional experiences. Curiously enough, among the newlywed men this association was reversed, those with high energy tending to have a low affect-balance score. Perhaps the rather frenetic pace of these younger men, as reflected in their self-image, leads them to exhausting extremes. In fact, those newlywed men reporting more energy than their age peers seemed possessed by a driving need for physical exertion. Heavy labor and fast cars were recurrently mentioned as providing great satisfaction. In talking about what frustrates him, one newlywed illustrates this frenetic behavior: "There is so much to do and such limited time to do it. I am probably the only person you have met who has a hundred hobbies." In spite of overextension, the idea of cutting down on their activities was abhorrent to these young men. Another newlywed rejected the idea outright. Asked what activities he would eliminate if time pressures so required, he suggested the strategy of just speeding up. And yet, as exemplified by the inverse correlation of affect balance with energy among these men, as well as by their own comments, they are aware that their restlessness creates a tension. Just as disengagement may become a critical issue for those in the later stages of life, for these newlywed men overengagement—with its attendant possibilities of diffusion and conflict—may be interfering with (or providing an escape from) the establishment of psychic equilibrium.

Among women greater energy was associated with more

psychological resources. Highly energetic high school girls had more capacity for mutuality, more insight, a better perspective on themselves, more competence, and a greater tendency to assert themselves than did their less energetic counterparts. Similar patterns, though with somewhat fewer significant correlations, held for women in the three later life stages. Among men the only psychological resource associated with a high energy level was a *low* ranking on mutuality. This was true for all men except high school seniors. One inference to be drawn from these differences between the sexes is that middle- and lower-middle-class men in our culture focus on involvements other than the interpersonal, which they may construe as women's business.

Toward a Dual Model

It is a truism that every individual harbors both deficits and resources within his psychic makeup. Some degree of psychopathology exists, for example, in seemingly well-adapted individuals (see Barron, 1963; Singer, 1963; Lowenthal, Berkman, and Associates, 1967). There is also some evidence that the incidence of conventional indicators of psychopathology in "normal" populations increases with age (Neugarten and Miller, 1964). One obvious explanation for the adaptive coexistence of deficits and resources is that one or more "strong" resources may offset or counterbalance a given deficit. As noted in the previous chapter, Bradburn (1969) has found that the ratio, or balance, between recent positive and negative affective experiences predicts the subjective sense of psychological well-being more effectively than either type of experience alone.

Here we extend this bilateral approach one step further, tracing the balance between psychological weaknesses and strengths among men and women at different stages of the life course, and the relationship between these patterns and the sense of well-being. (Correlations between attributes representing resources and those representing deficits ranged from .00 to .30, with the majority falling below .10.) In the longitudinal phase of the research, we shall evaluate the relationship between these configurations and restrictive or expansive changes in behavior that may have occurred in the course of the transition.

In order to contrast psychological resources and deficits, we summated the scores on all measures subsumed under each dimension. On the basis of their summated scores, respondents then were ranked in the top, middle, or bottom third of the distribution of resources and deficits, respectively. The result was a nine-cell typology. Individuals in the top third for both resources and deficits were called "complex"; those in the bottom third on both were called "simple."

The separate dimensions are related to life satisfaction in a completely expectable fashion. Among men and women, young and old, those high in resources ranked higher in life satisfaction than the intermediates did; and the intermediates in turn ranked higher than those who were low in resources. Conversely, those who ranked high in deficits ranked lower in life satisfaction than those who ranked intermediate or low in deficits. The interrelationship among deficits and resources, however, is best illustrated by looking at the proportion of individuals who fall into categories of the typology that would be expected (a) if resources and deficits simply represented opposite ends of the same continuum (that is, convergent categories) or (b) if they represented relatively distinct dimensions (that is, divergent categories).[3] Approximately 36 percent fell into convergent categories, with 16 percent low in resources and high in deficits, and another 20 percent high in resources and low in deficits. Of the divergent categories, 7 percent were high in both resources and deficits, and another 39 percent were moderately divergent (being, for example, intermediate in resources and low in deficits, or intermediate in resources and high in deficits). The remaining 18 percent of the respondents fell into categories that could not be readily classified as either convergent or divergent: those low or intermediate in both resources and deficits.

Correlates of Balance Typology

In assessing the relationship between psychic equilibrium (as reflected in the typology) and the subjective sense of well-being, we used the Bradburn overall happiness measure. (We could not use the presumably more stable Life Satisfaction Index because it in-

---

[3] Kendall Tau rank correlation coefficients computed between the psychological resource and deficit dimensions for men, women, and older and younger respondents were all significant, ranging from $-.10$ (men) to $-.32$ (women).

cludes self-concept data also present in the dual model.) For the sample as a whole, the happiest people were at the extremes (among the psychologically simple and the psychologically complex) and in one intermediate group (those moderate in resources and low in deficits). Of the three least happy groups, two ranked high in deficits and intermediate and low, respectively, in resources; the third is the one we have called bland, being intermediate in both. Eventually, and with, of course, larger samples, it will be of interest to see how these groups differ in such characteristics as cognitive complexity.

Our original impetus to work toward a more complex model than the degree-of-impairment one stemmed from insights gained from aging studies, where life-history analyses prompted the conclusion that one resource may offset a number of deficits and that a resource at one life stage may not prove to be a resource at another stage. Because there are nine cells in our typology (which we found difficult to condense further) and because we are dealing with small subgroups, we can here only suggest its potential usefulness for studies across the adult life course. Again using the subjective sense of happiness as the criterion, we found that the psychic configurations represented by the typology do indeed have different implications at successive life stages. In line with the findings for the sample as a whole, as reported above, among the high school seniors the happiest were those who were high in both resources and deficits. The significance of such psychic complexity for well-being decreases regularly and progressively through the successive life stages. The happiest newlyweds were those with many resources and few deficits. The happiest middle-aged people also had few deficits, but they were intermediate in resources. In the preretirement stage, the happiest were those who ranked low in both dimensions of the typology. Possibly because of the closing off of avenues for self-expression for older people in our society, psychic complexity becomes increasingly maladaptive. Indeed, in the oldest group the most unhappy people (unhappier even than those with many deficits and few resources) were those who ranked high in both resources and deficits.

The potential usefulness of an adaptive-balance typology may be illustrated by comparing the simple with the complex types on a few other characteristics. Although both types say that they are happy, their sense of well-being seems to be achieved by quite different routes. In comparison with the other eight types, the psychically complex were buoyant and expansive. At all stages, they engaged in a broader range of activities, maintained a more complex goal structure, reported more turning points across the life course, as well as more recently experienced important events, experienced greater social stress, and perceived more stress in their lives. The complex types, at least among the two younger groups, also tended to rank high on the number of years projected in the future. (Turning points, important events, time perspective, social and perceived stress, and the complexity of goal structure are discussed in detail in Chapters Seven, Eight, and Eleven.) Further indication of the marked change across the life course in the adaptive function of psychic complexity is found in the fact that the complex high school seniors had the highest ratio of positive to negative emotional experiences in the week prior to the interview, while the complex in the preretirement stage had the lowest.

By way of contrast, those with a simple psychic structure displayed constriction in many areas. Across their life spans they had experienced few major turning points and, more recently, few significant events. At all stages the simple projected minimally into the future, and older men and women also displayed little complexity in their goals for the next few years. Current emotional experiences, both positive and negative, were few. Interestingly, the activity pattern of the simple type varied markedly by life stage: activity scope was low among the high school seniors of this type, intermediate for the newlyweds and the middle-aged, and high among those facing retirement. We have also seen that the simple types are the happiest among the oldest groups. It may be, as we suggested in an earlier paper, that these are the people for whom the maintenance of an accustomed and, in this instance, varied behavioral pattern becomes in itself a source of satisfaction (Lowenthal, 1972).

Implications of Dual Model

While this model is a very preliminary one and not yet translated into terms which are applicable to large-scale structured studies, our findings suggest that further refinement may well prove rewarding. The two dimensions were independently relevant to the sense of well-being. Consideration of the relationship between resources and deficits, however, added to predictive efficiency: a positive status on either dimension (that is, either high resources or low deficits) was found to compensate for, or balance, negative status on the other. Moreover, the coexistence of generally positive and generally negative attributes within the same individual may actually enhance the sense of well-being; in at least one stage, those with an admixture were happier than those who were high in resources and low in deficits. This suggests that continuum models of mental health, as exemplified both by the medical model and by models positing extreme illness and robust mental health as opposite poles, may inadequately reflect the dynamics of adaptation. Several studies comment on groups of individuals who have made a seemingly successful—albeit rigid—adaptation by means of a circumscribed life. These people appear to maintain a comfortable life during times of stability; however, they react to social or economic stresses, or environmental change, with acute stress, and coping strategies involve primarily attempts to reestablish the former life style.

In our sample, the complex demonstrated an ability to penetrate into their social worlds and to cope with the diversity of stimuli such penetration involves. In this respect, they resembled descriptions of creative individuals. Rothenberg (1971), for example, suggests that "Janusian thinking," or the ability to conceive and use opposing ideas simultaneously, is central to the creative process. Similarly, Weisberg and Springer (1961) found that a group of healthy "gifted" children exhibited a combination of anxiety, open conflict, ease of regression, security, and a strong self-image. Perhaps, as Klein (1960) theorizes, qualities such as insight allow for a more successful—and perhaps creative—integration of anxieties and impulses into the psychic structure. And in our middle- and lower-middle-class sample, the complex type did prove most adaptive for younger people. For the preretired, however, the simple type (with few resources and few deficits) was associated with the highest sense of psychological well-being. This finding suggests that the more complex can grow old gracefully and happily in our society only if they belong to a more privileged class, where life-style options remain more open. The characteristics of the simple, indeed, are not unlike stereotypes of the aged, while the complex resemble stereotypes of younger people. This convergence of optimum balance style and cultural stereotypes may not be coincidental.

VII

Perspectives on Life Course

The stance toward time, investigators have found, significantly differentiates such diverse sample populations as schizophrenics from nonschizophrenics, high achievers from low achievers, and alcoholics from "social" drinkers. The most common finding is that those who in some social or psychological sense are less "healthy" dwell more on the past and have a more limited perspective on the future. That such a variety of groups differ markedly in time perspective suggests that it may be a personal characteristic of some importance (see Lewin, 1939; Kastenbaum, 1964; Piaget, 1966; Kluckhohn, 1953). Little is known, however, about the importance of time perspectives in everyday life, and even less about variations across the life course. Results from the few cross-sectional studies that do exist are provocative and point to substantial age differences in time perspective. Cameron (1972), for example, in a large-scale survey, found evidence, contrary to the popular stereotype, that older people do not think more about the past than do others. On the other hand,

Bortner and Hultsch (1972) and Lieberman (1970) found that evaluations of the past are more positive and satisfying for older people. In other words, older people may not think more about the past, but their feelings about it may differ from those of younger people.

The individual's perspective on his life course and its conclusion constitutes the subject not only of this chapter but of the succeeding chapters as well. Here we will first discuss three dimensions of the sense of time: density, direction, and extension. Density reflects the individual's perceptions of the "fullness" of his time; direction has to do with where he places himself in time, whether he sees it as before him or behind him; extension documents his view of where the "river of time" will end for him. Our informants' attitudes toward death are explored in the final section.

Density of Time

The eventfulness of time has been recognized as a potentially important variable in research for some time (see Kastenbaum, 1964). It may reflect the individual's sense of movement through life. Piaget (1966), in discussing the sense of time in children, for example, states that "psychological time" reflects both the quantity and the pace of activity. In our own study we have found that fewer events seem to impinge on our respondents who are in the later two of the adult life stages. In the first chapter, for example, we saw that the activities of older people were both less diversified and less intensely pursued than those of younger respondents. In Chapter Five, middle-aged parents and preretirement men and women were reported to experience fewer emotions, either positive or negative. Such findings suggest that our respondents were experiencing some lessening in the eventfulness of their lives, and perhaps some lessening in the perceived eventfulness, or density, of time.

We explored perceptions of temporal density through a series of five questions dealing with the timing of specific events in a person's life, as well as through the Life Evaluation Chart, wherein respondents rated each year of their past, present, and expected future according to a nine-point scale of satisfaction. The five questions bore on the timing of major turning points, frustrations, the

Table 11.

MEASURES RELATED TO TIME AND TO DEATH

	High School		Newlywed		Middle-Aged		Preretirement	
	Men	Women	Men	Women	Men	Women	Men	Women
Turning Point Within 5 Years (%)[a]	96	77	72	92	27	35	25	14
Major Frustration Within 5 Years (%)[a]	83	84	61	72	42	35	4	31
Last Important Event Within 1 Year (%)[a]	84	80	100	100	56	81	54	69
Next Important Event Within 3 Months (%)	29	32	36	50	20	52	33	21
Rarely or Never Engrossed (%)[a]	8	46	24	17	48	27	41	41
Average Scores for Density:								
Past 5 years [a,c]	2.4	2.5	2.6	2.6	0.9	2.1	1.4	1.4
Past 6-10 years [a,b]	2.0	2.4	2.4	3.0	0.9	1.8	1.3	1.2
Past 11-20 years [a,c]	1.2	1.2	3.7	3.2	1.6	3.5	3.0	2.2
Future 5 years [a]	2.0	1.8	1.8	1.8	0.4	0.6	0.6	0.8

Future 6-10 years[a]	1.2	1.2	0.9	0.7	0.2	0.4	0.3	0.2
Future 11-20 years[a]	1.6	1.9	1.3	1.2	0.4	0.6	0.9	0.4
Time Extension[a]	59.6	66.8	43.7	60.0	28.1	27.3	19.4	16.1
Oriented to Future (%)	60	42	52	52	38	44	43	59
Active Reconstruction of Past (%)[a]	33	00	43	25	50	38	11	11
The Best Age to Be Is:[a]								
Adolescence/twenties (%)	92	92	70	76	50	35	33	21
Middle age (%)	00	00	00	4	19	31	41	59
The Worst Age to Be Is:[a]								
Adolescence (%)	20	46	45	50	33	44	46	57
Old age (%)	56	27	45	38	37	22	24	17
Often Think of Death (%)	24	38	12	50	26	28	41	31
Complex Thoughts About Death (%)	9	8	24	28	11	30	23	24

[a] Differences between the stages are significant at $p < .05$.
[b] Differences between men and women are significant at $p < .05$.
[c] Interaction between stage and sex is significant at $p < .05$.

last important event experienced, the next important event expected, and periods of engrossment. As shown in Table 11, younger people reported more major turning points within the recent past: over four fifths of them, compared with one fourth of the older informants, reported turning points within the past five years. Older respondents were not only more distant from their last major turning point, but they were also twice as likely to perceive the turning point negatively.

In response to the question about the timing of major frustrations, a similar pattern emerges: nearly three fourths of the younger people reported frustrations within the past five years, compared with only one fourth of the older people. While these findings support the conjecture that time is less filled for older people, there are some complexities. When we look at the actual number of frustrations reported, older people mentioned multiple frustrations more often. Among older people, too, recent frustrations were much more likely to be multiple than were those in the more distant past. In other words, although older people reported fewer recent frustrations, when frustrations did occur they tended to occur in clusters.

Answers to the question bearing on the last important or interesting event again indicate that older subjects experienced fewer recent events. Two thirds of them reported that such an event had occurred in the past year, compared with more than nine tenths of the younger subjects. There were, however, no stage or sex differences in terms of the positive or negative quality of the last important event; the majority, perhaps because of our use of the word *interesting,* reported it as a positive one.

As to the next important or interesting event anticipated, there was little difference in timing between the two older and the two younger stages, the majority expecting it to occur more than three months in the future. Although this finding does not support the hypothesis that time is less "filled" for older people, the relationship of distance from the last event to distance from the next important event does suggest that a single underlying sense of timing may be operating. Those who reported that their last important event had occurred further in the past were more likely to expect the next important event to occur further in the future; those who reported that their last important event had occurred recently expected the next event relatively soon. This was true for the younger as well as the older groups, suggesting the possibility, which can be tested only in the longitudinal phase, of a certain consistency in the timing, or in the perception of timing, of life events.

Finally, we asked our subjects how often they became "so involved in something that you lose all track of time and place." Two fifths of the older subjects reported rarely or never becoming thus involved, compared to one fourth of the younger subjects. The self-reports of older people, then, suggest both a more restricted perception of things happening in their lives and also less involvement in the circumstances that do occur.

As an additional check on perceptions of the density of life events and circumstances, the number of yearly changes in satisfaction with life was tabulated on the Life Evaluation Chart for periods of varying distance from each subject's present age. (Figure 2 gives examples of the kinds of changes depicted on these charts.) Within the past five years, high school seniors and newlyweds reported a markedly higher proportion of the life events or circumstances linked with changes in life satisfaction than did people in the two older stages. While high school and empty-nest women reported more changes than their male stage peers, newlywed men reported more changes than newlywed women, and preretired men and women were essentially alike in this respect. For Life Evaluation Chart changes from six to ten years in the past, the younger people and women again reported more changes. After ten years, the pattern begins to change, with middle-aged women and preretirement men also exhibiting greater density.

As to changes projected for the future, the two younger groups expected more change in the next five-, ten-, and twenty-year periods than did the two older. In short, their records on the Life Evaluation Chart support findings resulting from the more concrete questions about change, indicating that time is much less "busy" for older subjects, whether they are looking at the recent past or at the future. In some sense the tempo of life, as these older subjects perceive it, seems to have slowed down. The possibility exists, of course, that the differences by stage are a result of cohort effects. In order to check on such a possibility, we compared mean density scores by decade for each stage/sex grouping. The prior decades with the most reported change for the preretired were the past third to fifth

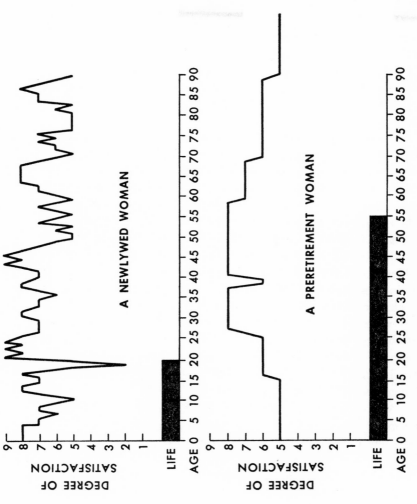

FIGURE 2. Sample Life-Evaluation Charts. On these charts, subjects rated each year of their past life (as well as their estimates of their future life) on a nine-point scale of satisfaction/dissatisfaction.

(the teens through the early thirties); for the middle-aged they were the third and fourth (the teens and twenties); for the newlyweds, scores are generally high, but the second decade (the teens) is most dense; while for the teenager the first decade, particularly the past five years, was most changeable. In other words, young adulthood is unanimously subscribed to as the most changeable period of the life course.

Direction

In studying the directional dimension of time perspective, we were interested in whether our informants looked primarily forward or backward. Direction was examined from two perspectives: First, does the past or the future seem more important to respondents? Second, when in time do they place the best and worst ages of life? In response to the question "When you have the chance to think about yourself and your life, would you say that you tend to think or daydream more about the past or the future?" nearly half of our respondents said that they thought about the future, one fourth said they thought about the past, and one fourth reported that they did not think about any one period more than another. Very few (3 percent) focused on the present, probably because the question asked only about the past and the future. Like Cameron (1972), we found no significant differences in the frequency of past versus future *time orientations* among younger and older respondents, but a somewhat larger proportion of the older (32 percent) than the younger (22 percent) respondents did think more about the past.

The quality of reminiscing about the past showed far more variation across the four life stages. Ratings were made on degree of involvement; that is, whether there was an active reconstruction or reliving of the past events or a more passive viewing as though of a motion picture. This dimension might be seen as akin to engaging or not engaging in a life-review process (Butler, 1963).

Active reconstruction of the past, characterized by a concern with "rehashing" specific past decisions or behavior, shifted by stage, peaking at middle age: 14 percent of the students, 33 percent of the newlyweds, 44 percent of the middle-aged parents, and 12 percent of those facing retirement manifested such concerns. Sex differences were not significant, although it is interesting that, for the sample as a whole, nearly twice as many men as women were still concerned with whether they had made the right decisions in the past.

To the extent that such an active reliving of the past (in contrast to a more passive style of reminiscing) reflects a life-review process, the preretired, as the oldest group, should exhibit the highest incidence. Butler's (1963) provocative analysis of the significance of the life review for the elderly, for example, suggests that it is a way of putting one's house in order: coming to terms with past inconsistencies or "mistakes" and preparing for the final haul. On the other hand, Butler (personal communication, 1970) has subsequently extended his view of the applicability of the life-review process to any period of crisis or transition, and it is this later observation that provides a possible explanation for our results.

Among the preretirement men and women, there is evidence, as we shall see in the next section, that any reevaluation of the past involved in preparing for the retirement transition had already taken place. The high school seniors, for their part, could look to the past for scant assistance because of the relative brevity of their personal histories. Of the two groups with the highest levels of reconstruction, the newlyweds and the middle-aged, the former were facing the consequences of one major life-course transition (marriage) and preparing for another (parenthood), while the latter were concerned both with the imminent postparental phase and (the men, in particular) with eventual retirement, despite its relative remoteness.

One woman captured the preoccupation many newlyweds continued to have in regard to the decision to marry:

> *I daydream about the past. [What kinds of things?] It's hard not to daydream about [former boyfriend] because I went with him for two years—passing someplace we would have gone. . . . I always do and I think [husband] knows it. . . . Lots of times I'll daydream about him and maybe sometimes I'll think, "What if I married him or decided not to marry him," but then in two minutes [husband] will give me, just by talking to me or something, a thousand reasons why I was right in marrying him. That's mainly the only thing I daydream about because I don't think I've been married long*

enough. . . . You know, I think maybe after I've been married a year—that seems like a long time—then I would be completely free so that I wouldn't even day-dream about the past, but only the future. But it would probably take that long to adjust [laughs].

Among the middle-aged, while the prospects of the last child's leaving home may have prompted a life-review process in both men and women, men seemed to focus rather more closely on their closing career options, reviewing past career choices and their implications for the present. One man, for example, not only had thought about the implications of past career choices but also was attempting to work through his doubts about the proper career path: "I think about what would have happened if I had gone into another business, if I had worked strictly as an accountant or if I had gone into the real estate business with a friend of mine. I knew a great deal about real estate and he had a great deal of money. I'm sure we would have made a successful venture. I may still do that, of course. But I keep on wondering if I would have made more money at that type of work or been happier. I don't think I would have been as happy: accountants die young and real estate is dreary." Middle-aged women were less specific in their reworkings of the past. As one woman expressed it: "I think of the past quite a bit, I do. You think of what you did or if you could have done things differently. I can't see many changes for us in the future." Often, for these women, a vague discontent with the present and perhaps the future reveals itself, as if they were wondering: "Where did I go wrong?"

An active review of the past, then, may follow from the need to resolve present life problems. In the majority of cases, however, the process was relatively passive. The older respondents in particular reminisced almost as though they were spectators at a relatively pleasing event. Few at either the youngest or the oldest stage were interested in reworking or learning from the past: perhaps for the teenagers it was too early; for the preretirees, too late. The following comment by a preretirement man typifies those given by respondents who engaged in reminiscing for its own sake: "Oh, the past, that's for sure [said with a smile, suggesting that this was an enjoyable activity]. Oh, possibly the way I could have improved things. But I don't daydream that much. I think about it when I hear people talking about their past, like my buddies who talk about the good old days. I guess when you reach a certain age you start daydreaming backwards. When you are young you daydream forward." On the other hand, it is possible that when the anticipated transition actually takes place and these people begin actively to adjust to a new stage of life, a more purposive review process may develop.

In general, our review of time orientations suggests that one's stance toward the past and future is closely linked with engagement or involvement in life. To explore this latter possibility further, we compared time orientations with the timing of the next expected event and with our measure of engrossment. Among both younger and older people, a past orientation was associated with a greater likelihood that the next event would be removed in time; the future-oriented were more apt to expect the next event within the next two or three months. Time orientations were also associated with the degree of engrossment in activities, but only among the two older groups. We found that those older persons with a future orientation were more likely to report getting so absorbed in something they were doing that they lost track of time. The converse of this association, that past orientation is linked with lack of present engrossment, suggests that some of our older subjects may have been going through a process of life review.

To elaborate on past versus future orientations, we determined the point on the life course which our subjects considered to be the best. Most studies dealing with the best or happiest period of life indicate that young adulthood, particularly the twenties, is the most favored period, and ours is no exception. The periods of adolescence and the twenties were chosen by about three fifths of our informants, but there were marked differences among the stages. For example, while more than four fifths of the high school seniors and newlyweds subscribed to the notion that the early years are best, this was true of only a third of the middle-aged parents and the preretirement men and women. Those in the two later stages, indeed, were more apt to favor the middle years of life, the period extending from the forties through sixty-five: nearly 40 percent of them felt this way (as compared to only one younger person, a newlywed woman).

Interestingly, the appraisals of any particular period as best were similar for men and women in all stages.

Apparently there is a basic tendency among those at the several life stages to view most favorably the period currently being experienced. In fact, nearly half of our respondents selected a period within five years of, or including, the present. Of the thirty who gave the present itself as best, moreover, nearly all indicated that they probably would have selected an earlier period when they were younger. Although the focus on present or recent past as the best period is common to both earlier and later stages, the reasons given for this selection are markedly different. Those emphasizing the early years (mainly the younger people) spoke of a time of discovery and newly won independence, and the satisfaction of finally becoming an adult in the eyes of society. Those choosing later periods (almost exclusively the older subjects) were mainly concerned with the increased potential for ease and contentment. Child-rearing responsibilities were on the decline, financial pressures were easing, and many of the uncertainties of life were past. One fifty-year-old housewife reflected the opinion of many when she said: [Best age?] "Oh dear, that's a hard question. Oh, I would say in your forties, when your children are practically grown; then you don't have many responsibilities. You are set in life and you have enough to be comfortable."

Although a "present" orientation prevailed in the reports on the best age to be, there was a marked stage difference among those informants who placed the best age either in the past or in the future: none of the middle-aged or preretirement groups were future-oriented, while over three quarters of the high school seniors and newlyweds saw the best time as yet to come.

There was considerable agreement on the periods of life considered the worst: over three quarters chose either adolescence or old age. Altogether, more than two fifths viewed adolescence as the worst. In keeping with the tendency to upgrade the present, only one third of the teenagers themselves perceived their stage as the worst. The proportion rose to over half among those who had progressed furthest from adolescence: the preretirement men and women.

On the face of it, the choice of adolescence would seem to clash with the results reported in the section immediately preceding this one, where we saw that adolescence was often chosen as a "best age." In most cases, however, a distinction was drawn between early and later adolescence, the former being portrayed as a period with many conflicts and few compensating satisfactions. For example, only three of the high school seniors saw themselves as currently being in the worst age; another 13, or one quarter of the high school sample, felt that the worst age was from two to five years in the past.

Considering the low esteem in which old age is supposedly held by people in the United States, it is surprising that only one third of our respondents mentioned old age—with its attendant loneliness, dependencies, and physical debilitation—as the worst age to be. Stage differences were clear: only one quarter of those in the later stages reported old age to be worst, as compared with more than two fifths of the high school seniors and newlyweds. By way of contrast, we have already noted that those individuals more distant from adolescence saw the latter period more often as worst. Such results suggest that there may be a tendency to place bad times far from the present—paralleling the tendency, noted in the previous section, for the best age to be placed near to the present.

Differences between the sexes suggest that women of all ages felt that they had already gone through the most troubled times of their lives, while the majority of men felt that the worst was yet to come. If we consider just those who mentioned either adolescence or old age, more than half of the men chose old age as worst, while two thirds of the women chose adolescence. Sex differences were most evident among high school seniors and newlyweds, where more than three fifths of the men chose the later period and an equal proportion of the women chose adolescence. This optimism of women stands in intriguing contrast to their greater tendency to complain or hold negative views of such specific aspects of life as family conflicts, self-concept, and health.

Extension

We assessed our subjects' sense of time extension by counting the number of years projected into the future on the Life Evaluation Chart. A sizable minority of people—approximately 16 percent—

refused to project at all on this instrument, with those in later stages refusing more often than high school seniors and newlyweds. Those most resistant were the preretirement women, which is somewhat surprising when we consider that they were far less likely than their male cohorts to select old age as the worst period. One third of these older women refused to project, whereas high school girls were least likely to resist. Similarly, if we combine into a resisters category all men and women who either refused or who projected a maximum of only ten years into the future, we find that resisters accounted for 14 percent of the high school seniors and newlyweds but for more than one third of those in the later two stages.

Newlyweds and high school seniors generally projected further into the future than did middle-aged and preretirement people. No sex differences were evident. The shorter projections into the future evident among the middle-aged parents and the preretirement men and women might be explained away simply on the basis of the sizable age differences between those in the earlier and the later stages. On the other hand, if we look only at those whose projections extended either into the sixties and seventies or into the eighties and above, older respondents continued to be much more likely to make attenuated projections: three fourths of the younger subjects projected at least to the eighties, compared with somewhat more than half of the middle-aged and the preretirement men and women. Those in the preretirement stage, who on an actuarial basis were closest to death, were also the most pessimistic about their life extension: only 46 percent projected to the eighties or above, compared with 66 percent of the middle-aged.

Time Perspective and Adaptation

Direction (here represented by orientation to the past or future) and projections of one's life span, although seemingly highly interrelated concepts, proved not to be significantly related in this study. While nearly two thirds of the respondents oriented to the past exhibited a limited extension into the future, those who were primarily future-oriented were evenly divided between curtailed and long extensions into the future. Only among older respondents was there a significant association: those with a future orientation expected to die at a later date than those who were past- or present-oriented.

Because of its obvious connection with expectations concerning length of life remaining, physical health status might be expected to exhibit a strong relationship with projection of the life span, and perhaps with time orientation in general. We used two measures of health in this analysis: (1) the presence or absence of physical problems which influence activities; (2) subjective evaluations of health status. For neither were relationships with measures of time any different than might be expected by chance. The general conclusion, then, is that, among a basically healthy group, little relationship will be found between one's perception of health status and one's characteristic stance toward time. One difference between the older and younger groups, however, warrants attention. Looking just at those subjects who saw their health status as good to poor (as opposed to very good), the younger people tended to be future-oriented, while the older were split approximately equally, with 52 percent being past-oriented. An obvious interpretation of this trend is that the young are more likely to anticipate improvement in their general health status.

Perhaps the most common finding in the literature is that individuals with a disturbed time perspective (usually limited extensionality) are *psychologically* maladjusted. Our data support this finding. We first looked at the relationships between a psychiatrist's rating of psychiatric impairment (based on evaluation of symptoms lists) and projections of the life course. The two measures were not significantly related among the two younger groups. Among the older, however, nearly two thirds of those rated as considerably impaired had a limited time extension. A trend in this direction was found among women. Psychiatric impairment was not associated with directionality; that is, with whether the subject was preoccupied mainly with the past or with the future.

If we take into account not only degree of impairment but psychological resources, as presented in Chapter Six, we find a more marked association between time perspectives and adaptation. For the sake of brevity, we will here consider only intrapersonal competence and hope, although many of the other resources were also significantly interrelated with time. Life-stage differences proved to be especially notable. For example, younger persons rated high in time extension ranked lower in competence, while older people with similar projections ranked high in competence. Similarly, among people who were future-oriented, the younger were more often rated as incompetent and the older as competent. One conclusion to be derived from these findings is that time perspectives may have different functional significance at different points along the life course. More specifically, young people lacking in psychological resources may look to the future for alleviation, whereas older people with such deficiencies focus on the past, when they had—or have convinced themselves that they had—more such resources.

It seems reasonable to expect that a future-oriented individual will be hopeful or optimistic about the future, whereas a past-oriented person will see the future more pessimistically. Indeed, our findings generally supported this common-sense conjecture, but only among informants in the two later stages. Among these older individuals, especially the women, more than two thirds who were past-oriented felt hopeless about the future, whereas most of the future-oriented ranked moderate to high on hopefulness. The relationship between life-span projections and hope, however, was not statistically significant, although there is a suggestion, when all respondents are considered together, that those with a limited extension were somewhat less hopeful: 43 percent of those with limited life-span projections ranked low on hope, 35 percent were of average hopefulness, and 26 percent were very hopeful. Among men, those with a broad extension in time were hopeful. Among women, conversely, those with limited life-course projections were at least moderately hopeful.

We next compared time projections and orientations with affect-balance scores, which measure recent emotional states, and Bradburn's (1969) overall happiness measure, which reflects the individual's prevailing mood. (Because our measure of life satisfaction includes data extracted from the Life Evaluation Chart, we used overall happiness in order to avoid possible contamination.) Projected duration of the life course had no bearing on either affect balance or happiness among the young, but it did among the two older groups. Two thirds of the older subjects who had relatively

long life-course projections scored high on affect balance, while
nearly half of those with limited projections scored low. Among
those in our older stages, longer projections were also associated with
greater happiness. Time orientation, as reflected by a focus primarily
on the past or future, was also significantly related to affect balance
among only older subjects. Over two thirds of the happier older
people were future-oriented, while over half of the less happy were
past-oriented. Overall, then, our results suggest that time projections
and orientations have a greater significance for the sense of emotional
well-being among older people.

Concern with Death

One's attitude toward death might well be viewed as complementary to one's perspective on life. This section explores some
rather elementary questions bearing on the human experience. It
has, for example, been suggested that conceptions of death change
with age (Lidz, 1968; Feifel, 1959), but no empirical evidence has
been offered either to confirm or to deny this possibility, perhaps
because the concept of death is scarcely comprehensible to many
people. Freud (1957, p. 289) posed the problem well when he
declared, "It is indeed impossible to imagine our own death; and
whenever we attempt to do so, we can perceive that we are in fact
still present as spectators." There may be a Huck Finn in all of us,
a child who craves to attend his own funeral and hence to reaffirm
personal immortality. We were therefore somewhat surprised to find
that our potentially disturbing questions about death evoked rich
and diverse responses. Many of our informants seemed to welcome
the opportunity to express their thoughts on the subject, and none
refused or seemed to find them offensive. This openness is similar to
that reported by several researchers (Kübler-Ross, 1969; Cappon,
1970; Hinton, 1967).

The questions put to our subjects were "Do you ever find
yourself thinking of death and dying?" and "When are such thoughts
likely to occur?" Analysis of the responses yielded four dimensions:
the frequency with which the respondent thinks of death or dying,
the times when these thoughts are most likely to occur, the sub-

jective meaning of death, and the degree of complexity of the concept of death. (See Table 12.)

There was no evidence of stage or sex differences in the frequency with which our subjects thought about death. Approximately one third, respectively, reported thinking infrequently, sometimes, and often about death. Here, then, is some information which seems to contradict the common assumption that older people think more of death. The lack of a sex difference also goes contrary to the trend established in several of the preceding chapters, as well as in other studies (for example, Gurin, Veroff, and Feld, 1960; Shanas and others, 1968), for men to deny and women readily to verbalize' about problems and emotions.

The contexts in which people thought of death, however, did vary according to stage and to sex. For example, while only 8 percent of the total sample reported that they thought about death during times of strain, 17 percent of the newlywed women did so. The following is a typical example: [Think of death?] "Oh yes." [When?] "Not often, but especially when I'm frustrated or tired. I get tired of all this and I'll think about how it would be to die. Not to kill myself, just to die. It's only a mood change, when I'm depressed." High school girls were most likely to be reminded of death when they saw accidents or reports of wars or catastrophes; high school boys were prompted by personal involvement in dangerous situations such as potential auto accidents. The newlywed men were most likely to report that they did not associate their thoughts of death with any particular time or circumstance. People in the middle-aged group (both sexes) were most likely to think about death when they were ill, as did men in the preretirement stage. Women in this oldest group, however, were most likely to think about death when close contemporaries died.

Though they were not specifically asked to do so, more than half of the respondents also volunteered their ideas about what death means to them. High school seniors and newlywed men thought of death as frightening. As one high school girl put it: [Think of death?] "Yes, when I get scared and if I watch a movie about dying or if somebody dies. If it is a beautiful death, I don't think about it. One death that kind of affected me was when the last pope died. That is when I started getting scared of dying and when I think

Table 12.

THOUGHTS OF DEATH COMPARED WITH PHYSICAL AND PSYCHOLOGICAL ADAPTATION (percentages)

FREQUENCY OF THOUGHTS OF DEATH

	Younger[a] Men			Younger Women			Older[b] Men			Older Women		
	Seldom	Some	Often	Seldom	Some	Often	Seldom	Some	Often	Seldom	Some	Often
Religious Affiliation												
None	7	12	0	7	0	0	4	0	0	5	0	0
Jewish	7	12	0	7	0	14	9	7	22	10	17	25
Christian	78	71	77	73	100	76	82	71	78	85	84	75
Other	7	4	22	13	0	9	4	21	0	0	0	0
Religious Participation (more than once per month)	40	42	67	40	54	45	33	50	50	55	56	56
Reported Self as Religious	40	46	56	47	50	68	27	86	56	55	56	56
Good Health Status	53	58	44	60	62	64	36	29	50	25	22	25
Low Psychiatric Impairment	67	81	56	73	85	54	68	71	72	60	39	56
High Life Satisfaction	40	50	44	67	62	27	36	57	61	65	72	56
Very Happy	47	68	78	53	46	23	36	43	56	35	28	50
High Activity Scope	53	69	67	67	77	68	9	57	28	45	22	50

COMPLEXITY OF THOUGHTS OF DEATH

	Younger Men[a]			Younger Women			Older Men[b]			Older Women		
	Simple	Average	Complex	Simple	Average	Complex	Simple	Average	Complex	Simple	Average	Complex
Religious Affiliation												
None	0	11	0	10	0	0	0	4	0	6	0	0
Jewish	12	11	0	0	7	17	15	14	12	6	10	36
Christian	75	75	66	80	81	83	77	71	88	89	90	64
Other	12	4	33	10	11	0	8	11	0	0	0	0
Religious Participation												
(more than once per month)	50	48	28	60	44	43	23	46	50	67	55	43
Reported Self as Religious	50	48	43	60	58	57	54	54	75	61	55	50
Good Health Status	62	59	43	60	67	57	38	50	12	22	35	14
Low Psychiatric Impairment	100	72	57	70	74	29	62	79	62	56	60	36
High Life Satisfaction	50	48	29	50	44	29	62	39	75	67	70	57
Very Happy	38	29	43	30	37	14	54	32	88	44	35	36
High Activity Scope	50	76	57	90	74	43	31	36	12	33	35	50

[a] High school and newlywed.
[b] Middle-aged and preretirement.

about someday I will have to die, it scares me so much. I don't like to talk about it or even mention it at all." [What is it that usually scares you?] "Like if I see somebody getting shot in the war and seeing death that is really a tragedy. Seeing graves, that scares me because you are just put in the ground and you turn into bones. There is nothing after that, you know." Two fifths of the newlywed women who elaborated on the subject, on the other hand, thought of death as an escape from earthly problems. The only other people who had this type of association were the middle-aged women, but they also mentioned death as a frightening unknown or worried about their families with equal frequency. Nearly one third of the women in the preretirement stage and considerably more of the middle-aged men shared the middle-aged mothers' worry about their families in the eventuality of their own deaths. This concern with provision for others seems to bear out Lidz's (1968) suggestion that responsibilities stemming from marriage and family lead to an altruistic concern about the fate of survivors.

The richness of the responses to questions about death was interpreted as a measure of the complexity of such thoughts. The following response, for example, was classified as superficial or shallow: [Think of death?] "The only time I think of death is when I have mentioned to the children that I do not want an elaborate funeral." [Past thoughts?] "No." By contrast, answers such as that of a woman in the preretirement stage were classified as complex: [Think of death?] "Quite often. Sometimes when I wake up in the morning. If I've slept very soundly, I wake up and think, 'Oh, that was death.' When I can't remember anything, I think to all intents and purposes that was what death was like. I didn't even know that I existed. I wake up and I'm surprised. I think that's what death is." As was the case with the frequency of thoughts about death, there were no significant differences in complexity among the stage or sex groups, though there was a trend toward greater complexity as one moves across the four stages. Only four high school students, for example, were classified as complex, followed by ten each among the newlyweds and the middle-aged parents, and twelve among those representing the preretirement stage. From a statistical point of view, these figures are insignificant, but an increase in complexity would seem to be logical, and perhaps worthy of further investigation with larger samples.

Many investigators have reported a close relationship between attitudes toward death and various measures of personality and psychological well-being (Templer, 1971; Feifel, 1961; Hutschnecker, 1959; Teahan and Kastenbaum, 1970; Hooper and Spilka, 1970; Clark and Anderson, 1967). In this study we examined the relationship between death attitudes and religiosity, and between death attitudes and measures of physical and mental health, as well as activity scope (discussed in Chapters One and Six).

The religiosity measures included denomination, frequency of participation in religious activities, and perception of oneself as a religious person. The denomination with which the respondent identified was not substantially associated with either the frequency or the complexity of death thoughts except in the case of complexity in females. Catholic and Protestant women of all stages had more simple responses than would be expected by chance, while the Jewish women's thoughts about death were significantly more complex. Perhaps Christianity may provide at least its female followers with a means of coping with, or perhaps denying, the threat of death.[1] Among men and among people of both sexes in the later stages, on the other hand, there was evidence that *involvement* in religion, either through feelings of religiosity or through greater participation, allows for a more direct handling of the prospect of personal death. For these later groups of people, reports of greater religiosity were associated with more frequent thoughts about death. Greater participation by older respondents was also associated with greater complexity and frequency of thoughts about death; this relationship is most pronounced among the men, and suggests that the strong religious bent observed among older men (Gutmann, 1969) may represent a strategy for coping with the threat of death.

---

[1] An alternative hypothesis we entertained was that extraneous factors associated with religious affiliation, as sampled, influenced the complexity of thoughts concerning death. Two prime candidates for explaining differences in complexity were socioeconomic status and verbal intelligence: it was possible that the Jewish women, due either to an enriched social background or to their greater vocabulary, were more comfortable in discussing concepts such as death. However, no differences on either SES or the WAIS Vocabulary subtest were found between Jewish and gentile women.

Our respondents' perceptions of their own health status turned out to be unrelated to either the frequency or the depth of thoughts about death, nor was there any significant association between such thoughts of death and the presence or absence of physical problems which influenced activities. There was, however, a trend among the younger as well as the older subjects, and both sexes, for physical problems to be associated with complex death responses. And there was a stronger association between death thoughts and mental health as assessed by the psychiatrist's rating of psychiatric impairment: the more impaired respondents of both sexes at all stages had more frequent thoughts about death. These thoughts, however, were no more complex than those of the less impaired respondents.

In the preceding section on time perspective, we reported that older people experienced less eventfulness in their lives than did the young, and a growing concern with the development of alternate and more relaxed approaches to life. Some form of psychosocial disengagement was also apparent in attitudes toward death. Among older subjects, those high in complexity were likely to rank lower in the scope of their social activities—reflecting, perhaps, a lesser concern with external affairs. Among these same subjects, moreover, there was a significant association between highly complex thoughts about death and restricted projections into the future; in other words, complexity was associated with limitations both in social activities and in estimated life span.

Review of Findings

In the analysis of questions dealing with the density of time, we found that older people perceived themselves to be more distant from events. They also were less engrossed in those events which did occur and reported fewer changes on the Life Evaluation Chart. The differences in content between those who considered either young adulthood or middle age as best were similarly distinct: themes of ease and contentment characterized the middle years, while themes of challenge, excitement, and active involvement were common to all (including older respondents) who valued the younger years. Such results reinforce the conclusion (reached in the discussion of density and in Chapter Five) that for some older people a different tempo of life becomes increasingly valued. Although such a life style may not represent a "disengaged" life style as much as a push to develop a more rewarding life, the attainment of such a style may be via a selective disengagement from nonrewarding involvements.

The correlates of time perspective yielded much of interest, but here we will discuss only two points. First, our data suggest that an individual's sense of time has a greater implication for well-being in the later stages of life. For example, only among older respondents were the past-oriented more restricted in perspective. Restricted extensionality itself was associated with psychiatric impairment, unhappiness, and more perceived stresses only for older respondents. Similarly, a past orientation was associated with more negative affective experiences and a less hopeful outlook only among the older respondents. Second, the younger and older respondents exhibited opposing correlates of time perspective. For example, future-oriented younger respondents tended to be rated as more incompetent than their age peers; future-oriented older respondents tended to be rated as more competent. Other data suggested that younger respondents who were lower on perceived health tended to be future-oriented; older respondents in poorer health were often past-oriented. In other words, among the aged a future orientation may be a sign of physical and psychological adjustment, whereas for at least some younger people a future orientation may represent a way of escaping from present problems.

☙☙☙☙☙ VIII ☙☙☙☙☙

Responses to Stress

☙☙☙☙☙☙☙☙

In this chapter we provide evidence for a thesis based in part on observations made in an earlier study on normal and abnormal aging (Lowenthal, Berkman, and Associates, 1967) and, almost simultaneously, by researchers working on laboratory studies (Lazarus, Opton, and Averill, 1968): the thesis that preoccupation with stressful events or circumstances does not always bear a direct relationship to exposure to presumed stress.[1] (Additional support for this thesis has been reported in Lowenthal and Chiriboga, 1971, 1972a, 1972b, 1973; Chiriboga and Lowenthal, 1972.)

To develop a typology taking into account both exposure to and preoccupation with stress, we used a slightly expanded version of the Holmes and Rahe (1967) stress scale (see Appendix B, Presumed Stress). This measure—utilizing factual reports from the entire protocol and covering stressful circumstances from early childhood on—is the measure of a respondent's exposure to stressful situations, such as object losses, social discontinuities, and economic and physical changes generally presumed to be stressful. The second

---

[1] In this book we use *stress* and *stressor* interchangeably. We do not use *stress* to refer to the organismic state described by Selye (1956).

146

measure, based on the life-history section of the interview, consists of ratings (made by the interdisciplinary research team) of the respondent's preoccupation with stressful events (see Appendix B, Perceived Stress). These two measures provide the framework for a fourfold typology. The typology, shown in Table 13, includes two styles of response each to (1) relatively severe presumed stress and (2) relatively light or little stress. For convenience, we refer to the four response types as the "overwhelmed" and the "challenged" among the severely stressed, and the "self-defeating" and the "lucky" among the lightly stressed.

Table 13.

STRESS TYPOLOGY

	Preoccupation with Stress	
	Thematic in presentation	Not thematic
Presumed Stress		
Frequent and/or severe	*overwhelmed*	*challenged*
Infrequent and/or mild	*self-defeating*	*lucky*

The overwhelmed, beset by many stressful situations, dwelt on them at length in discussing the ups and downs of their present and past lives; they seemed, in fact, to be reliving the stress. The challenged, similarly beseiged by many stresses or a few severe ones, nevertheless were not excessively preoccupied with them in recounting their histories; they simply reported their stressful experiences and then quickly moved on to other topics. The self-defeating, although reporting little objective stress, weighted their life reviews heavily with themes of loss and deprivation, which they too seemed to be reliving with much of the original affect. Finally, the lucky had few or mild stresses, loss was not a theme in their protocols, and a few reported that they felt mysteriously protected, chosen, or "elect."

Stress Exposure

Exposure to stress inevitably accumulates throughout life; we therefore dichotomized each life stage into heavily and lightly stressed groups in terms of its own norms. The range of exposure to the events in the expanded version of the Holmes and Rahe (1967) scale was 11–84 among high school seniors and 36–183 among those confronting retirement (including multiple exposures to the same type of event). The chronologically closest groups, the high school seniors and the newlyweds, showed the sharpest increase in means (36.4 to 68.8), reflecting, no doubt, the hazards of growing up and leaving home. Despite the fact that the largest gap in chronological age was between the newlyweds and the middle-aged, these two groups reported similar amounts of stress exposure, a mean of 68.8 for the newlyweds and of 72.7 for the middle-aged. In the preretirement stage, the mean stress exposure was 86.4.

In order to trace the characteristics associated with variations in stress exposure (Table 14), we drew on sociostructural, interpersonal, and intrapersonal measures introduced in the previous chapters. (Nearly as many of these measures distinguish between degree of preoccupation as between degree of exposure.) In general, a wider variety of characteristics differentiated between those ranking low and high on exposure than between those ranking low and high on preoccupation, and the differences between young and old and between men and women also were more marked on the exposure measure. (Detailed data on stage and sex differences are available from the authors on request.) Among the heavily stressed, the challenged differed from the overwhelmed mainly in the depth of their interpersonal relationships. Within the lightly stressed group, the lucky differed from the self-defeating primarily in intrapersonal characteristics.

Inasmuch as we deliberately chose to study a lower-middle-class sample, variations in socioeconomic status and education were not great. But even these comparatively slight differences proved to be significantly related to cumulative exposure to stressful circumstances. Among the newlywed men, the highly stressed were significantly better educated. The highly stressed young men were also more involved with the sociopolitical world around them, as measured by the social-horizons score discussed in Chapter One. Among younger women, socioeconomic status rather than education was associated with exposure to stress, and again a high ranking correlated with high exposure. A tendency for higher socioeconomic status to be associated with more exposure to stress also prevailed among the two older groups. Conversely, older women who ranked low on the Wechsler Adult Intelligence Scale Vocabulary score (a measure often associated with educational level) generally had little exposure to stress.

In short, relatively high status, conducive as it is to more varied life experience, by the same token involves more exposure to circumstances which ordinarily would be construed as stressful. Among younger men, such exposure was also associated with a strong masculine self-image, suggesting that an expansive life style may reinforce normative male sex roles.

Among the two older groups, intrapersonal and interpersonal characteristics were also associated with degree of stress exposure. Among older men the more social roles, the higher the exposure. Among these men, too, those with high stress exposure also ranked high on the friendship-complexity score presented in Chapter Three. In short, among younger men the potential for a complex life style (reflected by high educational status and a degree of cognitive complexity) was associated with high stress exposure; among older men the actualities of a more complex life style proved significant. Support for this thesis, in the obverse, was found among older women; here, the lightly stressed emerged as a clearcut type. They were lower in verbal intelligence and revealed a certain flatness about their lives, as reflected by low density in their Life Evaluation Charts (Chapter Seven). At the same time, they were much more family-centered than older women who had experienced more stress. We might conclude that—in contrast to the highly stressed older men, who live extended and complex interpersonal lives—these older women who had comparatively little stress exposure chose, or lapsed into, a restricted (or self-protective) family-centered style, consciously or unconsciously designed to shield them from pressures from the world outside.

About three fifths of the sample had what might be called the expectable reaction to stress, rather evenly subdivided between the lucky and the overwhelmed. The two fifths having "deviant" responses—the challenged and the self-defeating—were also about equally divided. The distribution of the four stress types was remarkably similar across the four life stages, although there was some tendency among lightly stressed newlyweds to be overly pre-

Table 14.

CORRELATES OF STRESS TYPES (percentage of each group above sample median) ≠ ?

	High Presumed Stress			Low Presumed Stress		
	Challenged	Overwhelmed	Total Highly Stressed	Lucky	Self-defeating	Total Lightly Stressed
Sociostructural Variables						
Socioeconomic status	50	42	45	38	41	40
Education (more than high school)	53	57	55	49	54	51
Religion°						
Protestant	58	31	41	46	20	35
Catholic	18	33	27	35	37	36
Jewish	8	13	11	8	15	11
Other	18	22	20	11	28	18
Interpersonal Variables						
Horizons complexity[a]	50	58	55	43	24	35
Marital affect[a]	70	54	60	71	55	64
Familial affect[a]	55	37	43	67	56	63

TAT affect[a,c]	28	35	32	13	38	24
Familial roles	35	36	36	35	37	36
Role scope[a]	70	64	66	55	46	51
Friendship complexity[a]	58	63	59	35	54	44
Familial mutuality[b]	55	39	45	41	43	42
Mutuality	45	42	43	49	49	49
Intrapersonal Variables						
WAIS vocabulary[a]	55	51	53	32	43	37
WAIS block design[a]	49	60	53	48	44	46
WAIS total[a]	60	58	59	41	47	44
Masculine self-concept[a,c]	70	57	62	55	30	44
Feminine self-concept	43	44	44	43	56	49
Positive self-concept	58	47	51	58	44	52
Negative self-concept	45	54	51	38	58	47
Frequent death thoughts[c]	31	40	37	15	40	26
Complex death thoughts[c]	18	24	22	3	24	13
Density of time (past)[c]	48	61	56	33	57	43
Time orientation (future)	43	44	43	68	39	55

[a] Difference between high and low presumed stress is significant at $p < .05$.
[b] Difference between the challenged and the overwhelmed is significant at $p < .05$.
[c] Difference between the lucky and the self-defeating is significant at $p < .05$.

occupied with what little they had, and a converse trend among the heavily stressed facing retirement, who were almost as likely to be challenged as to be overwhelmed.

Within each life stage, however, there were dramatic differences between men and women, who revealed opposite directional shifts between the younger and older groups. (Since the two younger groups on the one hand and the two older on the other tended to resemble each other with respect to sex differences within the stress typology, for purposes of this analysis we generally combine high school seniors with newlyweds, and the middle-aged with the pre-retirement stages.) Among the highly stressed young, as Table 15 indicates, the men were more likely to be overwhelmed than the women. In the two later life stages, these trends were sharply reversed: the highly stressed men were most likely to be challenged, and the highly stressed women were most likely to be overwhelmed. Among the lightly stressed women, there was also a reversal between the stages: young women were overly preoccupied with what little they had had, whereas lightly stressed older women were predominantly of the lucky type. Most of the lightly stressed men in both the younger and the older groups were in the lucky category. Whether these shifts between the life stages reflect developmental trends or generational differences remains to be discerned in the longitudinal phase of the study. At this point, it appears that older women have fewer resources than men with which to counter relatively severe stress, and that older heavily stressed men are less beset by it than younger heavily stressed men. Later in this chapter, support is offered for the thesis that some of the challenged older men may in fact be repressing or denying stressful circumstances.

Stress Preoccupation

With one exception, sociostructural characteristics did not significantly distinguish between those who were and those who were not preoccupied with stress, among either the heavily or the lightly stressed. The exception, as though in support of the stereotyped notion of the Protestant Ethic, was that there were three times more Protestants than Catholics among the challenged. Otherwise, it was intrapersonal and interpersonal characteristics that were associated

Table 15.

STRESS TYPE BY STAGE AND SEX (percentages)

| | Younger[a] | | Older[b] | | Younger and Older Combined | | |
	Men	Women	Men	Women	Men	Women	Total
Considerable Presumed Stress[c]							
Challenged	16	21	30	7	23	14	19
Overwhelmed	36	27	21	40	28	34	31
Light Presumed Stress							
Lucky	32	21	31	32	32	26	29
Self-defeating	16	31	18	21	17	26	21
Total	100	100	100	100	100	100	100

[a] High school seniors and newlyweds.
[b] Middle-aged and preretirement.
[c] Each transition group was dichotomized on presumed stress at the median for that stage for each sex.

with the amount of obsession with stressful experience—interpersonal for the heavily stressed and intrapersonal for the lightly stressed.

Lucky and self-defeating. Among the lightly stressed, lucky men ranked high on masculine self-image, and lucky women tended to do so as well. As Table 14 documents, the lucky tended to be far more future-oriented than were the self-defeating, and they furnished little detail about their past lives. They also gave less thought to death than any other type. In contrast to the self-defeating, they ascribed typical "masculine" adjectives to themselves and seldom acknowledged any negative characteristics at all. Lucky men and women alike tended to rank low on the WAIS Vocabulary test, but they did quite well on the WAIS Block Design.

The interpersonal measure which most sharply distinguished the lucky from the self-defeating was one which reflected minimal involvement with others: the lucky ranked low on the friendship-complexity score (presented in Chapter Three); that is, their friends played interchangeable roles in their lives and were not perceived as having unique or differentiating characteristics. The lucky also revealed little emotional content in their responses to the couple embracing in the TAT card (Chapter Two). Lucky men ranked low on familial mutuality; the younger ones ranked low on familial affect (positive or negative) and also rated themselves low on a mutuality measure drawn from the self-administered Adjective Rating List.

Of the four groups in the stress typology, the lucky were the most sharply delineated. Sex differences within this group were less clearly drawn than was true for the other three types. Their restricted interpersonal relationships and their general flatness of affect suggest minimal involvement with life, perhaps consciously or unconsciously adopted to avoid feedback from others, and a lack of reality testing, which might threaten their positive concepts of themselves and their optimism about the future. To borrow Fromm's (1966) term, the "life plot" of the lucky seemed to be to pursue a stress-avoidant life style, associated with a need to distance themselves from emotional thoughts and relationships.

The most distinguishing characteristic of the self-defeating was excessive preoccupation with death, as assessed by the measures introduced in the preceding chapter. They not only thought about death more often than the lucky, but they also had more complex thoughts about it; and this tended to be true of young and old alike. These self-defeating people included the lowest proportion of Protestants (other than Fundamentalists) and more Jews than the lucky, suggesting that the concept of a vengeful God may have a bearing on their preoccupation with death. They also tended to differ from the lucky in that the self-defeating men, in particular, had a more negative self-concept, and both men and women ranked low on those self-ratings which suggest assertive, or "masculine," traits. Self-defeating women were especially preoccupied with the past.

In addition to the above characteristics common to most of the self-defeating, regardless of stage or sex, the subgroups among them tended to have some distinguishing characteristics. Although, as shown in Chapter One, the sample was purposely selected to avoid the important but complicating issue of minority-group status, or difficulties associated with national origin, many of those who did fall into these categories were of the self-defeating type. Four of the seven self-defeating high school girls reported problems that they associated with ethnic or national origins. A Polish-born girl felt lost without a "homeland"; a Chinese girl born in Trinidad did not know where she "belonged" and was making plans to return; a Filipino girl felt inferior because of her ethnic background. Two of the four self-defeating high school boys also associated their ethnic or national origins with problems of adjustment. Nearly all of these self-defeating young people had difficulty relating to their peers.

Among self-defeating newlyweds, no clear pattern emerged. The middle-aged self-defeating women, however, tended to be depressed over poor marriages, which they experienced as deteriorating—suggesting support for the Freudian hypothesis that many women in midlife reactivate unresolved oedipal problems, with their husbands as foci of the conflict. In the preretirement stage, the term *self-defeating* appears to be an especially apt one, though the label was chosen before the correlates were examined. Among both sexes, there is a strong aura of the introspective, if not of the morbid, about them, especially in contrast to the cheerful, if plastic, nature of the lucky. In many ways, their stress response resembles that characterized by intrusive, repetitive thoughts and emotions noted by Horowitz in his clinical studies of persons who have become psychiatric patients as a consequence of situational stress (Horowitz and Becker, 1972).

Challenged and overwhelmed. Turning next to the stance toward stress among those heavily exposed to it, we find that the intrapersonal characteristics, such as self-image and preoccupation with death, which so clearly distinguished the two lightly stressed groups, do not strongly differentiate between the two heavily stressed groups. In fact, in the face of the reality of considerable stress, resulting from a way of life that they perhaps to some extent deliberately chose, it was close interpersonal relationships—or their absence—that primarily had a significant bearing on whether the individual man or woman was preoccupied with his or her stressful experiences. On the rating of familial mutuality, the challenged ranked the highest among the stress-typology groups, and the overwhelmed the lowest; a strong trend in the same direction appeared in regard to extrafamilial mutuality. The challenged also ranked higher on marital and general familial affect. Among men, this distinction between challenged and overwhelmed was most striking in the high school stage, only somewhat less so among newlyweds. Challenged men at the midlife stage were no longer distinguished by greater mutuality than the overwhelmed; but those in the oldest, the preretirement, group had close interpersonal relationships. This was true of the very few older challenged women as well. That the overwhelmed (women as well as men) rated themselves low on capacity for intimacy supports the proposition that deep interpersonal relationships serve as a resource against stress. These findings support those of an earlier study, in which the existence of a self-defined confidant was found to be an effective buffer against the stressful insults of aging (Lowenthal and Haven, 1968). They run counter, however, to the suggestion of Korchin (1965) that the stress resistant tend to be simple in cognitive style and bland in affect, characteristics which we found to be true of the lucky, who were lightly stressed, but not of the challenged.

The comparative lack of importance of mutuality among middle-aged challenged men prompted a close examination of their protocols in juxtaposition to those of the older men. This analysis revealed that the challenged men in both these life stages were

concerned primarily about retirement, but the nature of their preoccupation with this future life stage differed sharply. Many of the
challenged middle-aged men seemed almost obsessed with ensuring
that they and their wives would have financial security in the retirement phase. The older men, most of whom were much closer to
retirement, were either satisfied with or resigned about their resources for this period. Their preparations were more in the psychological or even the philosophical sphere. They were considerably
more introspective than were their middle-aged counterparts, and
their inner life, both cognitive and affective, was more complex.
Many of the middle-aged, by contrast, seemed anxious, and they
were also less hopeful about the future than were the older men.

It therefore is not surprising that the older men were easier
to recruit for interviewing and that they were more relaxed in the
interview situation, most of them offering rather lengthy discourses
about such matters as the long-range influence of the Depression on
their generation; the significance of parenthood, work, death, and
friendship in their lives; and changes in the educational and sociopolitical scenes. Most of the challenged men in both life stages reported good marriages, but those in the preretirement stage, in sharp
contrast to the middle-aged, were quite articulate about how they
were exploring ways of making this life stage satisfying for their
wives as well as for themselves. This characteristic perhaps contributed to their higher familial-mutuality rating. A city employee
who had had only three years of high school summed up the stance
of these preretirement challenged men aptly, and from a developmental perspective at that: "You don't have much time for thinking
about these angles [what life is all about and what you want out of
life] until you get past middle life. Till the children are off, you don't
have time to think. But when they are out on their own and gone,
then you think of . . . the things you were ready to forgo to support the family."

With the lightly stressed, we saw that the self-defeating were
considerably more prone than the lucky to dwell at length on
thoughts of death. The difference in preoccupation with death between the overwhelmed and the challenged was similar, though it
did not reach significance. As with the self-defeating, the proportion
of Jews and Fundamentalists among the overwhelmed was about

one fourth—considerably higher than among the challenged and the lucky (though not statistically significant.

Since morbid tendencies might also be attributable to the experience of the loss of a close other in childhood or early adolescence, we again looked into the life histories of our subjects, this time to check whether they were more likely to have had an early separation from a parent, through death or otherwise. While this hunch led us up a blind alley in respect to the self-defeating, we discovered that in fact the overwhelmed (considerable stress and very concerned with it) were strikingly likely to have suffered such a loss. Including separation from a parent through divorce as well as loss through bereavement, we found that nearly three times more of the overwhelmed had experienced parental deprivation of this order than had the rest of the sample. Or, from the alternative perspective, of the well over one fourth of the sample as a whole who reported such early losses, nearly half were of the overwhelmed type (the rest were about evenly distributed among the other three groups in the stress typology).

Among the young men and women who had suffered such deprivation, the great majority were overwhelmed, as were the older women. Recalling that the capacity for mutuality was the principal characteristic distinguishing the overwhelmed from the challenged, we see these findings lending some support to the theory that parental deprivation may interfere with the normal progression through development stages—in Erikson's (1968) terms, to the intimacy stage and beyond. The situation was dramatically different among older men, however. Of the eleven who had experienced parental loss early in life, only one was of the overwhelmed type, and five were challenged. We can only speculate about the reasons for this sex difference. One rather obvious interpretation would be that these men, in comparison with their female cohorts, were (through their work involvements and other commitments outside the home) exposed to more ego-strengthening experiences, which served as buffers against the continuing effect of early losses. We have seen that the women in this sample were strikingly family-centered despite their impressive employment histories. Their ego resources may well have been derived from the statuses or achievements of their spouses and children. This reactive, or once-removed, type of resource, however gratifying it may be at some life stages, possibly accounts for the preponderance of older overwhelmed women, and the potential eruption, when facing the empty nest, of any oedipal problems that may remain unresolved. In any event, whatever the reasons for these sex differences in the perpetuation of the effects of childhood losses, the findings in regard to the older men suggest that—traditional analytic theory to the contrary—the adult is not necessarily forever warped by the vicissitudes of infancy and early childhood.

Stress Type and Well-Being

Before comparing the broad indicators of well-being among the stress types, we should recall that the characteristics associated with degree of exposure to presumptive stress were spread over a number of domains. Those associated with degree of stress preoccupation, on the other hand, were more likely to fall in only one sphere—the interpersonal for the heavily stressed, and the intrapersonal for the lightly stressed. By these criteria, the challenged seemed psychologically robust, while the lucky generally exhibited a singular vapidity about their past and projected lives and a kind of detachment from life. The lucky also had inflated self-concepts, suggestive of a narcissism which may well serve as protective armor against emotional involvement with others (Lowenthal, 1972). The second lightly stressed group, the self-defeating, had in common a set of characteristics which reflect a certain weakness in ego strength, such as morbid preoccupation with the past and with death, and restricted social horizons. They also tended to have a negative self-image and thus lacked the shield of self-love which seemed to protect the lucky. The overwhelmed shared some characteristics of the self-defeating, such as concern with the past and frequency of death thoughts. However, the overwhelmed were less restricted than the self-defeating, having more involvement with the outside world, as reflected in the complexity of their social horizons and greater number of social roles.

The indicators of adaptation that we used in analyzing well-being are physical status, psychiatric status, and the Life Satisfaction Index.[2] Pairing off the two heavily stressed groups, the challenged

[2] The Bradburn measure alone, which focuses on current "happi-

and the overwhelmed, we found that they differed significantly in life satisfaction and, though to a lesser extent, in psychiatric status. Comparing the two lightly stressed groups, the lucky and the self-defeating, we found that they too differed on these same measures. Comparisons of the two stress-resistant types, the challenged and the lucky, revealed significant differences on psychiatric and physical status. There were no such differences between the two stress-prone groups, the overwhelmed and the self-defeating; but there were some logically consistent tendencies, which are therefore reported here.

In general, as might have been anticipated, the two stress-preoccupied types were less satisfied with their lives than were the stress-resistant. This difference was most marked among the heavily stressed, except among older women, where half or more of both the challenged and the overwhelmed had little such satisfaction. (The small number of challenged older women makes it unwise even to speculate about the reasons for this.) Among the lightly stressed, there was a rather dramatic reversal among the young, where the lucky were more dissatisfied with their lives than were the self-defeating. Younger lucky women also tended to be more dissatisfied than otherwise. This finding suggests that, as far as life satisfaction goes, the young may thrive better on stress than on the lack of it. Knowing the detachment that characterizes the lucky, one might also interpret this dissatisfaction from a developmental point of view: their incapacity to form close relationships is particularly critical at life stages where the capacity for an intimate heterosexual relationship is the main developmental task (Erikson, 1968). Perhaps the lucky older men and women were not lacking in life satisfaction because of a compensatory trait of wishful thinking, for, as we have noted earlier, a marked future orientation characterized this

---

ness," did not distinguish among the stress types. The other two measures in the Life Satisfaction Index are less time-bound. The one drawn from the self-administered Life Evaluation Chart reflects the mood scale, from "absolute tops" to "rock bottom," prevailing in the year that the interview was conducted. The self-rating from the Adjective Rating List centered on the words *unhappy* and *dissatisfied*. The list itself was administered without reference to time, in a "what kind of person are you" context. Since the addition of measures less restricted in time did produce some significant results, it may well be that stress type relates to broadly prevailing rather than transient affective states.

type, and this orientation was more true of the lucky old than of the lucky young.

Psychiatric impairment was judged by the evaluation of a forty-two-item Symptoms Checklist by psychiatrists (Chapter Five). The overwhelmed were most likely to be considered impaired; at the other extreme, lucky men, especially those in the older groups, were viewed as psychologically sound, compared with both the self-defeating and the challenged. The psychiatric evaluation of overwhelmed women, both young and old, and of the lucky older women, as more impaired than their male cohorts may well reflect the often reported observation that women are freer in reporting symptoms than are men. The associations between femininity and freedom to complain were further strengthened by the fact that in their self-ratings of masculine and feminine traits the overwhelmed women ranked high on femininity, whereas the differences between overwhelmed and challenged men on self-ratings of masculinity (or femininity) were not great.

The challenged men were sharply differentiated in respect to physical health. They not only were more impaired than the self-defeating and the lucky but were more so than the overwhelmed, who had similar stress exposure. This is true, however, only for the middle-aged and older challenged men. In prior publications (Lowenthal and Chiriboga, 1972b, 1973), we reported preliminary evidence that some of these challenged men may in fact be or come to be "deniers," and that their unwillingness or inability to discuss or otherwise work through stressful situations has a cumulative effect, not so much on their mental health (because not complaining is considered a sign of good "adjustment") as on their physical health. They do not, however, otherwise resemble Horowitz's "deniers," described as emotionally numbed and behaviorally constricted (Horowitz and Becker, 1972). In fact, when their tendency to develop physical illness in later life is taken into account, these men seem more closely to resemble the "repressors" reported by Weinstein and others (1968). These repressors showed greater autonomic than self-report reactions, while the "sensitizers" were more inclined to respond to stress with detailed and expressive verbal reports.

Unlike the older women, who in all stress types also ranked high in self-reports of (relatively minor) physical problems, these older challenged men were somewhat likely to suffer from serious illnesses. As with psychiatric symptoms, the women again were complaining more, but about less serious matters. Significantly, none of the physically impaired older challenged men appraised themselves as in poor health: one considered his health fair; the rest reported that, in comparison with others their age, they were in good or very good health, despite such illnesses as severe heart attacks, emphysema, and diabetes. By contrast, the overwhelmed men were more likely to report no physical problems. Those who did have some impairment were, like the older women, for the most part not so handicapped that they were forced to curtail their activities. At the same time, in self-reports of their general physical health, these overwhelmed men were far more negative than were the much sicker but challenged men.

We know that the life expectancy of older women (most of whom complain about their stresses and their health) is considerably greater than that of older men. It will be interesting to see, in the five-year follow-up study, the extent to which men of the overwhelmed (complaining) type continue to be healthier than their challenged or denying peers.

IX

Perceived Stress
Across Life Course

In Chapter Eight we reported evidence indicating that the individual's characteristic mode of perceiving and responding to stress may be as important for adaptation as his actual exposure to stressful events. In this chapter we will consider in some detail what those perceived stresses were that seemed to have an influence on adaptation. While studies of the association between stress and adaptation have suggested the crucial mediating role played by subjective perception, little attention has been devoted to variations in such perceptions. For example, some of the key studies of stress report that people can generally agree on the rank order of stressful life

The authors express thanks to staff and students of the Human Development Research and Training Program. This chapter is a follow-up of ideas discussed in a summer practicum stress seminar (1972) led by Marjorie Fiske Lowenthal and David Chiriboga. Thanks are also due to Robert Pierce and David Chiriboga and the members of their methods seminar for suggestions and criticisms in the early stages of this work and to Robert Pierce for his continued help with programming and methodological problems.

163

events (see, for example, Holmes and Rahe, 1967; Masuda and Holmes, 1967; Harmon, Masuda, and Holmes, 1970); a careful reading of the results from these same studies, however, reveals the existence of considerable intergroup variation. The existence of differences in the subjective evaluations of potential stressors was also reported by Lowenthal, Berkman, and Associates (1967).

Our discussion will be based on the Life Evaluation Charts (LEC) completed by our respondents (see Chapter Seven for further description of the LEC). For each upward or downward trend in life satisfaction in the individual's chart, he or she was asked to describe the event or events which led to that change. Inspection of the LEC and the causes for the shifts therein were limited to the ten years preceding the interview. For convenience we shall refer to those life events which required adjustment on the part of the individual involved as "stresses." According to some writers (Selye, 1956; Dohrenwend, 1973; Holmes and Rahe, 1967), any such change, regardless of whether it was welcomed or not, involves stress. Even though Selye (1974) has come to the position that "positive stress" is less destructive than "frustrative stress," we will continue to use the convenient shortcut term *stresses* in referring to events that bring about changes.

Three dimensions emerged from preliminary analyses of the charts and the explanatory material: the nature or content of the circumstances perceived as stressful; the primary person to whom the event or circumstances occurred ("person focus"); and direction of the impact—that is, whether the situation produced a positive or negative change in affect.

Twenty categories of stressful events or circumstances were clearly discernible in the subjects' explanations. Many of these focused on both normative and idiosyncratic transitions, such as marriage, divorce or separation, the draft, residential moves, and religious events, including conversions. These empirically derived categories tend to be more general than the items included in our measure of presumed stress (Appendix B). Several events on the Holmes and Rahe scale (events such as Christmas, changes in sleeping patterns, and violations of the law) were not mentioned at all by our respondents.

Analysis of the stresses pinpointed by our subjects suggested the possibility of a sex bias implicit in the Holmes and Rahe scale; clearly, women were reacting to circumstances experienced by others. We therefore added "person focus" (the person first and primarily affected) as a separate dimension. In our data, this dimension included the self and eight others: spouse, child(ren), parent(s), sibling(s), family in general, other relative(s), friend, people-at-large.

The third dimension of perceived stress consisted of whether a particular stressor served as an explanation for a rise or drop in life satisfaction. A residential move or a job change, for example, may be interpreted as positive or negative. As Langner and Michael (1963, p. 9) have pointed out, man's capacity to symbolize allows one person to view an event as a catastrophe and another person to see it as a blessing; at the same time, they also note that there are broad sociocultural uniformities in definitions of stress. This third dimension—"directionality"—was included with the intention of documenting some of these uniformities and reactions.

Sex and Stage Differences

While we shall primarily report on stresses occurring in the decade prior to the interview, a brief look at events and circumstances occurring throughout the life span provides an overview of differences between what women and men in the four stages retrospectively considered stressful. From a life-course perspective, the most salient areas for women were education (mentioned by 71 percent); the family (55 percent); health (51 percent); and dating and marital relationships (50 percent). Work, their own and their husbands' combined (41 percent), was also identified as an area of perceived stress. In contrast, there were only two broad categories in which half or more of the men reported stresses: education (69 percent) and work (50 percent). These sources of stress were not only reported by more men than were other stresses, but were reported more frequently by individual men. Additional stressful issues among our male subjects were residential changes (47 percent), marriage (44 percent), military (42 percent), and family (41 percent).

Turning now to events and circumstances identified by our subjects as sources of stress in the ten years preceding the interview, we find notable differences between the life-stage cohorts, as well as clear differences between the sexes within the four stages. Young persons reported exposure to more circumstances they considered stressful than did people in the two later stages of life. In fact, these young respondents listed nearly two and a half times as many stresses in the past ten years as did the older half of the sample, the newly-weds reporting more than half again as many stresses as the high school seniors. The middle-aged and the preretirement groups, in addition to reporting considerably fewer stresses, resembled each other more than did the two younger groups. This pattern resembles that emerging from the measure of presumed stress derived from our slight revision of the Holmes and Rahe scale (Chiriboga and Lowenthal, 1972). Older subjects reported fewer stresses; in fact, more than a quarter of them reported none at all in the ten years preceding the interview, compared with only one in the two younger groups.

The newlyweds were the only group in which both sexes reported more circumstances producing positive than negative stress (the ratio was 1.5 to 1). The ratio was reversed among the middle-aged parents (.73 to 1). While women in both of the later stages reported fewer stresses than the two cohorts of younger women, what they did report was far more likely to have had a negative influence on life satisfaction. Men reported the lowest ratio of positive to negative stresses in middle age. At the preretirement stage, however, men reported more positive than negative stresses. (As indicated in the preceding chapter, many of these oldest men are mellower and more philosophical than the middle-aged men.)

As Table 16 shows, the major cause of stress in the younger stages was education. Such stressors were reported an average of three times each by four fifths of the women and nearly three fourths of the men. While two thirds of those who mentioned such stresses reported both increases and decreases in life satisfaction associated with educational problems and achievements, there was a tendency for men to perceive more positive stresses than women.

Neither men nor women clearly distinguished between the social and the academic aspects of such stresses as changing schools, adapting to new teachers and classmates, or making progress or failing in school. Teachers had a profound impact on the lives of

Table 16.

STRESSES (INCLUDING POSITIVE AND NEGATIVE)
OVER LAST TEN YEARS[a]
(percent mentioning at least one such stress)

	Younger			*Older*		
	Men	Women	*Total*	Men	Women	*Total*
Education	71	80	76[e]	2	9	6
Residential	33[b]	40[b]	36[e]	9	4	6
Dating/Marriage	33[b]	50[b]	40[e]	2	12	8
Friends	27	44	35[e]	13	5	9
Family	24	36	30	13[b]	26[b]	20
Marriage	18	28	23[d]	9	12	11
Health	10	22	16	13[e]	38[e]	27
Work	22	14	18[d]	45[e]	21[e]	32[d]
Leisure						
Activities	35[b]	12[b]	23[e]	6	2	4
Military	27[e]	2[e]	14[e]	0	4	2
Death	14	12	13	18	19	19
Finances	6	4	5	18	11	14

[a] This is not an exhaustive list of the stresses found in the protocols;
some categories were omitted because they occurred very rarely
or because they were not substantively interesting in the present
analysis.

[b] Differences between men and women within the cohort are significant with $p < .05$.

[c] Differences between men and women within the cohort are significant with $p < .01$.

[d] Differences between young and old are significant with $p < .05$.

[e] Differences between young and old are significant with $p < .01$.

their students, as indicated by statements accompanying indications
of stress: "I couldn't stand [my teacher]. She had pets, so that year
was an absolute loser." "I had a very bad teacher. Somehow she
disliked me and I resented it. I couldn't go her way. She was always
putting me down. I was depressed and down to a point where I
didn't want to go to school at all." "Bad" teachers, who produced
negative stresses, were far more likely to be reported than "good"
ones, who might have produced an increase in life satisfaction; in a
few instances, however, these young people reported having been
"in love" with their teachers.

Residential moves were recalled as the next most salient source of stress among the younger respondents. These moves ranged from immigration—spending a year abroad in the Peace Corps, for example—to moving into another house in the same residential area. Residential moves were often accompanied by stresses in other areas (such as friends, work, and school) and were as likely to have had a positive impact as a negative one among young respondents in general—although women were significantly more negative about such moves than men were. As one young woman explained: "We moved down to —— Street, which was moving away from all my friends; just fourteen blocks from our old house and my whole life was shattered. I was leaving behind all my good friends and I figured I would never see them again."

Among the young, friends led family by a small margin as a source of stress. Just over one third of them singled out extrafamilial stresses (such as "made new friends," "couldn't make friends," "started dating"); fewer than one third reported familial ones (including conflict over parental restrictions, sibling rivalry, reunions, and resolution of conflict). The family was as likely to be a source of negative stress, reflected by a drop in life satisfaction, as it was a positive stress; friendship-related stresses tended to be positive, in a ratio of two to one. Young men, however, were more likely to report family as a source of negative stress than were young women. A common theme was the sense of pressure from parents (probably because, in this socioeconomic group, the men are expected to perpetuate family mores). In one case this pressure was to achieve in sports, which our respondent was not as good at or as interested in as his brother. Another young man explained: "Well, it just bothers me to be at home because I don't want to hear. I just can't sit there and relax. She's always asking me what I plan to do later on." The positive stressors reported by young women, relatively absent in male reports, were mainly of two types: increasing freedom and improvement in their relationships with their parents. In keeping with their emphasis on interpersonal issues within the family context, more young women than men singled out friendships as sources of stress, but the women were more likely to include negative stress in this area than were the men. In the newlywed stage, over half of the men and the women reported positive stresses in dating or marital relationships, but significantly more women also reported stresses perceived as negative.

Nearly one fourth of the young people indicated leisure activities (successes or failures in sports and involvement with music, dancing, and various other hobbies) as an area of perceived stress. Significantly more men than women reported such stresses. They also found them positive more frequently than did women, who perceived a roughly equal proportion of positive and negative stresses in this area.

High school seniors and newlyweds rather closely resembled each other in singling out most of the stressors we have just described. As might be expected, however, newlyweds had experienced additional stresses—marriage, work, and the military.

Marriage was rarely seen as negative. It was reflected by increasing life satisfaction in over half of the married women and one third of the married males. On the other hand, a surprisingly high proportion of newlyweds, particularly among the men, did not perceive marriage as either a positive or a negative source of stress.

Work did not appear as a source of stress among high school seniors, even though the majority of them had part-time jobs at the time of the baseline interview. And although nine tenths of the newlyweds worked at least part time, fewer than two fifths of them reported it as stressful. The low salience of work, surprising especially for the young men, reflects the fact that, during the greater part of the time span covered, most of them were in school and many of them were still students at the time of the interviews. Sex differences in viewing work as a source of stress were smallest at this stage, and more women reported stresses in this category than did women in the other three stages.

The threat of the draft or recent military experience impinged on the life satisfaction of over half of the newlywed men, and constituted the major difference in perceived stress between young men and women. While many changes in the life satisfaction at this stage were positive ones, war experience or the threat of it was associated with at least one negative stress. Two fifths of those with military experience reported that it provided, along with stresses perceived as negative, at least one positive stress. That change may have been a discharge or an enlistment, but occasionally was related to specific experiences within military life.

In previous chapters we have indicated that time was perceived as much less filled or "busy" for older subjects, at least insofar as changes in life satisfaction were concerned. This slower tempo also is demonstrated in the current analysis: more than one quarter of the older subjects reported no stresses whatsoever for the decade preceding the baseline interview; moreover, those who did report stresses reported less than half as many as did the younger respondents. Differences between the sexes, however, were much more dramatic among the older respondents. The main area which middle-aged men perceived as stressful was work (changing jobs; getting fired, hired, or promoted; or being without a job); nearly half reported changes in life satisfaction attributable to work. Work-related issues had less salience as a source of stress for the men in the preretirement stage than in middle age, no doubt because most of them expected to be well out of it soon; yet it was still a stress for one third of the oldest cohort. Even though nearly three fifths of the women in these two later life stages worked, fewer than one fifth reported stresses related to their own work, once more confirming the low salience of the occupational sphere for these women. They were most likely to view health issues, more likely someone else's than their own, as stressful (although women also worried more about their own health than men did). Approximately three times as many women as men reported health-related stresses; and among both men and women, unsurprisingly, they were almost invariably negative.

Aside from work, there was no single area which even a fifth of the men agreed was stressful. Among women, however, familial relationships constituted a third area of perceived stress pertaining to family members. Changes in events or circumstances in this area were as likely to be positive as negative. Those who were parents viewed their families from a position of tremendous responsibility—not only toward their children but toward their own parents, who were getting too old to care for themselves: "[These years] are lower because my mother came to live with us for about eight or eight and a half years. She was a burden, quite a burden. Had no privacy, you know. But, of course, it was my mother. I would have done anything in the world for her. She was a wonderful woman. But it's different with someone like that around. Our freedom was gone, our freedom as a family." "I guess it's terribly selfish of me, but in 1953 his mother and father moved out here, and in 1954 my mother and father moved out here. And you're never free. . . . That is the only thing that has depressed our lives at all. . . . For many years we've been building up to the future, and now we feel constrained."

The increase between the younger and older stages in those reporting death as a stressor was slight; but since other areas of stress had waned, it assumed more importance for older people. Except for a few instances where the death of others involved relief from suffering, the impact of the deaths of others on life satisfaction as measured by the life chart was, understandably, negative.

Finances constituted a stress for one seventh of our older respondents. Raises, business successes, bonuses, inheritances accounted for those perceived as positive. An equal number were negative, however, and included various kinds of economic losses, occasionally resulting from loss of job. A tendency was observed for some of the preretirement men to evaluate much of their past lives in economic terms—in part, no doubt, because many of them would suffer a reduction in income after they retired; but there was also frequent reference to the Depression of the 1930s, which many had experienced as traumatic.

Significant Others as Focus of Stress

To determine the extent to which stresses were reacted to by our respondents, we noted whether the various circumstances associated with change in life satisfaction were directly experienced by the respondent or by someone else. That is, the losses or other stressors suffered by a significant other (a loved one's illness, a child's marriage, a friend's death) can be distinguished from one's own, but may have as much or more impact on the individual's life satisfaction. To measure this dimension (which we call "person focus"), we derived an affiliation score from the proportion of stresses focused on others. Dichotomizing the respondents on the basis of high and low affiliation, we found that three quarters of the young, as opposed to only one quarter of the older respondents, were in the low-affiliation group. Sex differences among the young are insignificant but are very pronounced in the older groups. The most affiliative groups are the middle-aged and preretirement women—as is indicated by some of their statements: "That was when my daughter left her husband and three children. I should rate it '1' because it nearly killed me. I am a worry-wart and it made my life very unhappy." "Michael [son] got sick in school and dropped out, and he was very unhappy. When he is unhappy, I am unhappy."

Stresses focused on others had three main themes: children, health, and death (spouses' work and miscellaneous problems involving parents were among the remaining one fifth of other-centered stresses). Together, these themes accounted for more than four fifths of all stresses which were not self-centered. Children were the principal focus of stress; many aspects of their children's lives were experienced as stressful by parents, particularly by mothers. These included a child's conflict with other family members, educational or occupational stresses, and marital and parental changes in their children's lives. Health problems of children were more stressful than those of spouse, parents, or self, even though their ages suggest less objective basis for concern.

Twice as many middle-aged as preretirement women reported that their children were sources of stress. Children did not appear as a source of stress for the fathers, except for the fathers in the preretirement stage—and even then children were rarely mentioned.

Spouses were a source of stress only to the older men and women. However, while more than one third of the middle-aged women reported stresses centered on their spouses, only two of the men at the same stage did so. Women were also likely to mention more than one stress centering on their husbands. They were concerned primarily with health, mainly physical but also emotional problems; and a few reported stresses relating to their husbands' work or lack thereof. In the preretirement period, we find only four men and four women reporting stresses originating in spouses, mainly death and health problems.

Death was a consistent theme in other-focused stresses, accounting for more than one third of the other-centered stresses, of roughly equal significance to men and women and of only slightly less importance to the young than to the older groups. There was a tendency for deaths of friends and members of the extended family to be reported more frequently by the two younger groups than by the older, whereas deaths of parents predominated among the latter.

Differences in Stress Appraisal and Response

As the foregoing sections suggest, the usefulness of the "life events" or "life change" concept of stress utilized in various stress scales and in the stress typology discussed in Chapter Eight is to a considerable extent supported when we ask people directly about the causes of change in their satisfaction with life. In the later stages of life, however (middle age and beyond), we begin to detect more subtle factors which seem to be causing positive or negative changes in life satisfaction. Stress reaction may result from (1) the general absence of change or new life events, (2) the failure of an expectable event or change to occur, or (3) the mitigation of events or circumstances formerly considered stressful. We shall therefore conclude this chapter with a few examples of these perspectives in the hope of stimulating more systematic research into the subtleties and complexities of stress appraisal and response.

The most common form of "nonevent" as a source of stress was associated with being off-time with respect to some personally meaningful schedule. For example, middle-aged men often reported that the awareness of coming to a standstill in promotions or salary increases was a major reason for a lowering of their life satisfaction. "There was no movement, no promotion in the department. . . . It was pretty discouraging, and here I was in the prime of life. It didn't look very promising." "I was getting sort of fed up by being at the same level, and felt that I should have gotten more [promotions]." Such observations were often couched in terms suggesting a rather gradual heightening of the awareness of "nothing happening" as stressful. This slowly developing sense of being stressed is to be distinguished from sudden knowledge or awareness, at an identifiable point in time, that one has been bypassed for a specific promotion or denied a raise at a particular juncture.

The absence of an expectable event, signaling a deviation

from an anticipated career trajectory, is a source of stress not only in the occupational career but in such other "careers" as marriage, child rearing, and leisure-time pursuits. The importance of the nonevent is suggested by Neugarten's (1968b) report that the middle-aged and the old seem more likely than the young to evaluate behavior on the basis of whether or not it is "on" or "off" some idiosyncratic or normative time schedule. Young widows are more acutely stressed than older ones (Blau, 1973); a slower pacing in the development of career and marriage plans in their young—rather than any basic differences in values and aspirations—is a source of stress for the parent generation (Thurnher, Spence, and Lowenthal, 1974); and we all know about the sudden jolts to awareness of middle age some fathers and mothers receive when their offspring "prematurely" win a tennis—or chess—match against them.

Just as a gradual increase in the awareness of the absence of change or of an expected event may become stressful, so may a sudden, acute awareness of a slow change cause a rather abrupt shift in morale. For example, a preretirement woman explained a drop in life satisfaction at age fifty-five by saying: "I just sort of realized that I was getting a little older, and I realized that I was just doing the same thing."

Reappraisal may also result from the acquisition of new information about a condition or situation previously perceived as stressful. One woman, for example, who suffered from nervous tension at the time of menopause, reported it as a negative stressor on her life chart until a friend told her that what she was experiencing was normal and would not lead to mental illness. A more philosophical reappraisal of a situation may also lower the level of negative response through the process of accepting it as inevitable or beyond control. This type of reappraisal was reported by a woman who rated herself as negatively stressed when her husband refused to stop smoking and to lose weight after a heart attack. Her chart reflected a sharp increase in life satisfaction when "I finally reconciled to the fact that my husband wouldn't listen to the doctor's instructions."

In middle age and later, too, circumstances or events formerly assessed as stressful may be reappraised in the light of changing configurations, perceptions of which often suggest the possibility of an increase in cognitive complexity with the accumulation of life experience. Take, for example, the assessment of health status as stressful. A man or woman may be complaining about minor aches and pains which he or she considers sufficiently stressful to cause a change in life satisfaction. But if this state is followed by a critical illness such as a heart attack, recovery to the less than perfect health level just preceding the attack may well result in a new peak of life satisfaction.

Implicit in many of these appraisals common to those in the two older cohorts is a shift in time perspective, the assessment of events (or their absence) on the basis of prior experience and in the light of future expectations. The fact that our older subjects reported fewer stresses than the younger ones may in part reflect a broader frame of reference. There are two major sources for this increase in breadth of perspective: one is the accumulation of personal experience—the assessment of present events in the light of earlier events appraised as even more stressful; the second is the inevitable expansion of awareness, from middle age on, of the "insults of aging" striking at one's peers.

X

Continuities and Discontinuities in Value Orientations

In this chapter we address ourselves to the issue of value change across the life course. Starting on the most global and abstract level of philosophies of life, the discussion moves to the individual's present hierarchy of values and to his subjective perceptions of how his values have changed since the past and what changes he anticipates in the future. Concerned with the role of values in the adaptive process, we examine the relationship between value orientations and levels of adaptation and, as a further step, seek to determine the characteristics which distinguish individuals reporting marked discontinuity in their values from those who report little or no value change.

Philosophies of Life

Our subjects were not given to ruminating over existential problems and the meaning of life. However, when asked "What is the main purpose or task in life?" only the very rare individual expressed some uncertainty. Phrased either in terms of end states to be attained, rules of conduct, or sometimes both, their responses reflected the acceptance of traditional social and religious values. In keeping with their predominantly pragmatic bent, their statements more often conveyed the sense of "task," things to be done, than "purpose," reasons for being. To the extent that the "individualistic achievement complex" said to describe our society (Parsons and Shils, [1951] 1962) was evident, it was less in the form of status aspirations or ambitions for outstanding achievement than in the more muted sense that the individual should engage in some useful activity, show some tangible accomplishments, and exert effort in the pursuit of his goals. Although strictly religious formulations of life's purpose tended to be rare, religious teachings seem to underlie the frequent injunctions regarding conduct toward others, and the belief that the individual should contribute something toward the welfare of mankind. A content analysis of recurrent themes yielded the following major categories: personal achievement (social or occupational success, fulfilling one's unique potential); marriage and family (the proper raising of children, the assurance of a "happy home life"); humanitarian-moral concerns (love or decency toward others, making a contribution to society); coping with the givens of life (earning a living, adjusting to limitations and frustrations); happiness (the notion that life should be pleasurable and enjoyable); religious life (doing God's will, following religious commandments); and legacy (the notion of personal immortality in that one's life will have some effect on the coming generations).

The main difference noted between the early and later life stages was the more expansive orientation and higher expectations from life shown by the former, and the more self-limiting orientation of the latter (see also Bühler, Brind, and Horner, 1968). The younger groups were more likely to refer to success and self-fulfillment; the older, though not ignoring personal accomplishment or gratification, were more likely to caution against setting goals too high ("Do what you are comfortable doing") and to emphasize coping with the contingencies of life—that is, the need to cultivate a positive frame of mind and to continue to do one's best regardless of circumstances or outcome. Women in all stages tended to emphasize marriage and family and general concern for others.

High school boys and girls differed markedly from the remaining groups, except newlywed men, in the predominance given to personal achievement and in the high value placed on happiness. Among boys, personal achievement tended more often to be phrased in terms of occupational attainment and social success than in the perhaps more diffuse terms of self-actualization or self-fulfillment. Conscious of the adult world of work that awaited them, boys tended also to allude to coping with earning a living. The central issue that emerged from the boys' responses was how best to bridge the potential conflict between occupational demands and personal freedom and enjoyment. A not infrequent solution was to combine occupation with enjoyment: "I figure that I'll be working for the most of my life, so I want to get a good job that I'll be able to enjoy. So then I'll be able to enjoy my life, because that will be my life. Of course, you can't really enjoy life unless you have a lot of money. It's important, though, to get a good job that you enjoy, because I couldn't stand doing a job that I didn't like even if it paid good."

The occupational world did not serve as a frame of reference for girls. Their themes of personal achievement focused on self-actualization and self-fulfillment. The underlying concern was to develop one's potential to the full and to evolve a life style uniquely suited to one's individuality. At the same time, there was little awareness of the specific directions these endeavors might take. Like the boys, the girls expressed some apprehension that entry into the adult world might result in some loss of individuality. Themes of proving one's worth were not lacking: "I think if people want something bad enough, they should go after it and prove themselves." Perhaps their observations that adult life can be relatively joyless prompted the high school seniors to stress happiness and enjoyment as one of the main purposes of life. One girl expressed herself rather forcefully: "To find happiness somehow, even if it means killing yourself."

Conceptions of life's purpose or tasks presented by newlywed men resembled those of high school seniors. They, too, seemed bent on reconciling the demands of adult-role obligations with the pursuit of personal inclinations. Conscious that they had made their first major commitment—and that further commitments, which would further circumscribe their future life style, would soon follow—they seemed eager to ensure maximum satisfaction and self-expression. One younger man, anticipating the time when he would settle down, put it as follows: "To be satisfied with what he's doing. What I mean is that if he is satisfied with what he is and where he is—occupationally, physically, philosophically, environmentally . . . he's certainly going to be perfectly happy and not want to go anywhere else." Newlywed women's stated philosophies of life showed a relative unconcern with personal achievement. An essentially nurturant orientation underlay their responses—the notion of giving oneself to others, first to one's family and secondarily to more generalized others. The idea that happiness would follow in the wake of such pursuits tended to be implicit. While the following statement is unusually euphoric, personal, and detailed, it captures the basic theme: "To bring good into the world. I find now that my main purpose is to please my husband, my family, to find happiness in life myself. I think happiness is important. Every time I can make him smile, it crosses out a frown he's had. If more people smiled, it would make a lot happier world. . . . You do your best at your job; that makes yourself happy. And you go through a routine of going to work five days a week so that you can earn money to make your family happy."

Whereas the young seemed concerned not to miss out on any of the satisfactions that life may offer, the older groups seemed more concerned to minimize frustrations. The notion of *coping* was the dominant theme among middle-aged men and those facing retirement. In general, the responses of the middle-aged men were dry and conformist, most often touching upon the dual tasks of earning a living and raising a family: "Well, I'd say probably earning a living. I don't know, everybody has their hand out today. . . . I just think it's the responsibility that the husband should have to his family, to see that they're taken care of." After twenty or thirty years of work, stipulations that the job be satisfying were conspicuously absent; rather, the emphasis was on meeting economic requisites and achieving financial security. Those who expressed themes of personal achievement almost invariably imposed sensible limits: "I think everybody should better themselves, but they should not set their goals so high that they're difficult to achieve." Given essentially materialistic and austere perceptions of life's purpose, the relative absence of humanitarian concerns is not surprising. Unlike the other groups, these middle-aged men at times digressed and questioned the motivations of others: "People are never satisfied; they always want more." "A lot of them are doing just the opposite of what they should be doing." Pressured and struggling, questioning their own achievements, and conscious of compromises and sacrifice, many men seemed concerned with validating their life style by downgrading those with more carefree orientations. This need for justification was also noted in their often negative appraisals of the goals of the younger generation (Thurnher, Spence, and Lowenthal, 1974).

Women facing an empty nest tended to speak of "living a good life and bringing up your family well so they have a good life," of "creating a happy home," and of "giving happiness to my husband and children as well as receiving it." The raising of children tended to be viewed as the primary task and an "accomplishment," and references to occupational activities were singularly lacking. Coping took the form of doing one's job "efficiently and to the best of one's abilities," of "living as best you can," and of "not regretting the past." Ambitions toward personal achievement were often viewed as incompatible with the essential responsibility of raising a family: "Once you get married and have children, the task is just to see they are raised properly. Because unless your children develop well, you are bound to be unhappy no matter what else you do. To keep your home happy, your job is bound to be secondary." That statement was made by a competent women who enjoyed her job and had turned down an offer of promotion. Women who mentioned personal achievement or self-fulfillment as the main purpose in life (about one fifth) were usually in the higher occupational ranks, or were widowed or divorced, or had precarious marriages.

Among men and women in the preretirement stage, the most distinctive feature was an increase in humanitarian and moral purposes, with a further stress on legacy on the part of men and on religious life on the part of women. These themes have in common a certain transcendence of self and family and suggest the expansion of concerns to encompass wider segments of society—which, some authors believe, usually occurs during the later years of life (Linden and Courtney, 1953; Erikson, 1959; Dunn, 1966).

The humanitarian-moral concerns of women in the preretirement stage tended to be personal, stressing the need to "care for," "be kind to," and "help" people, or in some way to be "useful" to others. In contrast, the humanitarian-moral themes of preretirement men most frequently took the form of making a tangible contribution to society: "I think [a man] does well if he makes himself a decent and satisfactory part of society, with at least some sort of contribution that is recognized or recognizable." Themes of legacy (Butler, 1970) contained a variant of this thought, most often phrased as "leaving the place better than you found it." The theme of legacy, in this instance with evolutionary overtones, is most fully expressed in the following example: "The idea is to leave the world a little better than you found it. At least a little easier for the next ones. I think that's the way it's been all through life. You can put it this way: through the effort of each generation, which one should always be an active part of, they should come up with something that takes the drudgery out of living. The drudgery, not the work. Taking the drudgery out of life, making it a better place." A sense of duty, of "paying one's dues," seemed to be attached to these responses; and the impression conveyed was that the contributions these men had in mind were essentially material, perhaps most directly related to improvements in the standard of living. They reflect the values of technologically expanding society and also perhaps those of an earlier frontier society.

The coping themes of people in the preretirement stage took on a different cast. Rules of personal conduct were less instrumental in emphasis. Statements about "doing one's best" and the requisites of job and earning a living were replaced by references to "independence" and "not being a burden," along with "remaining alive," "functioning," and taking care of one's self. In later years of life, achievement may be redefined in terms of survival (Riley and others, 1969).

These statements about philosophies of life are different from the subjects' descriptions of what they hoped for in the way of personal attainment. In response to the question "What do you

personally want out of life?" subjects were more likely to allude to
social-role norms, the requirements of work and family, material
assets, and specific personal avocations and enjoyments. Similarly,
the values manifest in their descriptions of their concrete short-range
and long-range goals also often deviated from those reflected in their
philosophies and personal desiderata.

Life-Course Variations

Most theoretical works conceptualize at least two major fields
of value and draw distinctions variously described as "ideal" versus
"real" (Linton, 1936), "conceived" versus "operative" (Morris,
1956), "desirable" versus "desired" (Kluckhohn and others, [1951]
1962), or "superego-required" versus "self-required" (Smith, 1969).
These important distinctions have, however, never been successfully
operationalized or controlled for in empirical study, a serious problem which remains to be solved in systematic research (Smith,
1969). Faced with the difficulty of reliably assessing the degree to
which a given statement reflected the "real" as opposed to the
"ideal," we resorted to a composite measure. Questions representing
several different levels of the value/goal domain were coded in
terms of a seven-item value typology; and the frequency of occur-
rence of a given value, the value summary score (see Appendix B)
was used as a measure of its salience for the subject. The value
typology developed for this purpose was based on an extensive
literature reveiw of value classifications, supplemented by an analysis
of empirical pretest data, and contained the following categories:
instrumental-material, interpersonal-expressive, philosophical-religious, social service, ease-contentment, hedonistic, and personal
growth.

The analysis of values showed instrumental-material values
to predominate among high school subjects and newlywed men;
newlywed women and middle-aged subjects gave priority to interpersonal-expressive values; men and women in the preretirement
stage, in turn, placed highest emphasis on ease and contentment.
Sketched in broadest terms, the curve of the adult life course seems
to begin with concerns for educational, occupational, and material
requisities or achievements (the establishment of one's socioeconomic

status), flows on to responsibilities of marriage and family, and recedes toward contentment and withdrawal from strivings and struggles. While upholding this general trend, the systematic analysis of stage and sex differences served to pinpoint a series of shifts in values.

High school boys were found to differ significantly from newlywed men only in a decline in instrumental-material values among the latter; and, compared to newlywed men, middle-aged men showed a pronounced abatement of personal-growth values. The greatest differences between adjacent stages occurred between the middle-aged and preretirement stages, with the older men showing a decline in instrumental-material and interpersonal-expressive values, along with a concomitant increase in ease-contentment and in hedonistic values. In contrast to men, the most marked differences among women took place between the high school and newlywed stages: newlywed women were significantly lower on instrumental-material and hedonistic values than girls, and directed more emphasis to interpersonal-expressive values. Middle-aged women differed from the newlywed women in less emphasis on instrumental-material values and a rising concern for ease and contentment. Less change appears to occur at the preretirement stage, with the older women showing a significant decline only in interpersonal-expressive values when compared to the middle-aged. These findings indicate that value shifts across the life course differ for men and women both with respect to content and timing, and suggest that whereas the major value reorientation for men is linked to retirement, among women it occurs upon marriage.

Socialization to sex-role norms seemed largely to account for sex differences within stages. With adult sex roles not fully crystallized, no significant value differences were obtained between high school boys and girls. The most pronounced sex difference at the newlywed stage was the higher salience of interpersonal-expressive values among women. By middle age, men also become engulfed in the family world; at this stage, therefore, men's higher instrumental-material concerns, rather than differences in interpersonal-expressive values, most distinguished the sexes. At the preretirement stage, men placed greater emphasis on hedonism than did women. These hedonistic values undoubtedly reflect emerging social norms for retirement, but they may also be attributed to the surfacing of personal needs following the cessation of social expectations. As will be shown later, a strong hedonistic orientation among these older men had negative implications for adaptation.

In our study we were interested in the relationship between value orientations and the negotiation of normative life transitions and, more generally, their influence on adaptation at successive stages of life. Values may be regarded as either viable or dysfunctional, dependent on the ease with which they can be translated into goals and behavior and successfully pursued. The viability of a given value will be affected by both extrapersonal and intrapersonal factors; on the one hand, the individual's social setting may, or may not, sanction or provide opportunity for the expression of his values; on the other, his psychological and physical resources may, or may not, meet the demands necessary for their successful pursuit. Since both factors are likely to change through time, values functional at one stage of life are not always functional at another, and some reorientation across the life span tends to be the rule rather than the exception. We therefore assessed the relationship between value orientations and adaptation at different stages of life. To this end, values were examined in relation to measures of life satisfaction (Life Satisfaction Index, see Chapter Five). In addition, because of the pivotal position of the family in this sample, we also examined the association between values and positive or negative feelings toward family members (overall familial-affect scores, Appendix B).

Values most strongly linked to positive adaptation at the high school stage proved to be instrumental-material. Boys high on these values were likely to be high on life satisfaction, and a parallel though weaker trend also prevailed among girls. In contrast, personal-growth values were linked to low life satisfaction, with the association again stronger among boys than girls. These findings suggest that boys and girls who are able to channel their goals into the areas of education and job, and who are receptive to the conventional demands of adult roles, experience a higher sense of psychological well-being than boys and girls who are concerned with the discovery of their identities and potential, and with the exploration of the world around them. The different implications of these values would partly relate to our findings (Thurnher, Spence, and Lowenthal,

1974) that early espousal of instrumental-material values and goals is approved and rewarded by parents, whereas the more diffuse search for personal growth (which may lead a young person to postpone or reject occupational and educational commitments) gives rise to anxiety among parents and is likely to meet with impatience and disapprobation.

Emphasis on social values—that is, the concern to alleviate the suffering of others, to work toward the solution of social problems, and to contribute to the welfare of society—was associated significantly with low life satisfaction among both boys and girls. Various explanations may be offered to account for the unwelcome finding that happy individuals are less likely to strive to ameliorate social ills. First of all, the high school seniors who were satisfied with themselves and what they were doing may have been personally less exposed to social problems, or less prone to empathize with the plight of others. Or perhaps social-service activities were not encouraged by parents or by peers. In any event, similar to Offer's (1969) sample, our high school seniors were not an idealistic group when it came to actively working for a cause.

Though associations between value orientations and family affect did not reach levels of significance, some trends were suggested. Boys and girls who expressed warm feelings toward family members tended to give higher importance to interpersonal-expressive values than those who viewed their families less favorably. Positive experiences within one's family of origin would logically seem to lead to the desire of establishing a family of one's own, as well as to general concern for close interpersonal ties. Among girls, family affect tended also to be associated with instrumental-material values. Girls with good family relationships were more likely to show commitment to the occupational or educational goals endorsed by their parents; motivated to fulfill parental expectations, they were at the same time assured of parental support.

Value orientations among newlywed men and women were not related to overall life satisfaction, except for a tendency for women with high philosophical-religious values to express more satisfaction. Conflict with parental values, which may have influenced morale among high school seniors, was no longer an issue. Relevant also is the consideration that, compared to the other life stages, early

adulthood (as represented by the newlyweds) offers the individual
the greatest freedom and options in the values he may choose to
pursue and fewest structural obstacles in the path of their attainment.
Affect toward the family was associated with value orientations only
among men, and was linked to hedonism. Newlywed men who
cherished warm feelings toward family members in general, and
wives in particular, were likely to stress happiness and enjoyment
and seemed determined that no joyful experiences pass them by.

Among middle-aged men, values most likely to influence
well-being were those relating to family and work. Whereas interpersonal-expressive values tended to be linked with high life satisfaction, instrumental-material values showed the opposite trend.
Among some of the men with high instrumental-material values,
low life satisfaction seemed to stem from a realization that original
occupational and material goals could never be met; among others,
it seemed to reflect increased pressure and exertion to achieve certain
goals before the gates to occupational advancement were closed.
Middle-aged women showed a strong association between high
social-service values and low life satisfaction, resembling high school
seniors in this respect. In addition to the interpretations offered for
the younger stage (having to do with personal experiences and
capacity for empathy), the decline in life satisfaction among these
women may arise from the frustration of not being able to work
effectively toward the improvement of social conditions. That is,
whereas the high school seniors were handicapped by youth and lack
of independence, the middle-aged women were tied down by
parental responsibilities.

Most interesting were sex differences in relation to affective
involvement with the family. Among middle-aged men, family affect
showed an inverse relationship to personal-growth values, while
among women it tended to be inversely related to hedonistic values.
Women high on nurturance and satisfied with family life tended not
to seek hedonistic gratifications; such concerns were most likely to be
expressed by women for whom family relationships were less satisfying or meaningful. On the other hand, middle-aged men who were
less committed to their families were most likely to entertain personal-
growth values. Since a decline in personal-growth values most
significantly differentiated middle-aged men from newlywed men,

the findings suggest that rising responsibilities of parenthood strongly contribute to this decline.

A further shift in the implication of value orientations was indicated at the preretirement stage. Values of ease-contentment appeared to be adaptive among men, tending to be associated with high life satisfaction. In contrast, high emphasis on hedonistic values showed a strong relationship with low life satisfaction. Thus, while goals of contentment and the more passive pursuit of simple pleasures were adaptive for men in this stage of life, a very active concern for hedonistic gratification was not. Some of these men may have been individuals with a lifelong hedonistic orientation who find themselves at a point in life where the fulfillment of their goals becomes less feasible; others may have been individuals who wished strenuously and anxiously to compensate for the gratifications they had formerly denied themselves; yet others may have been driven and successful career men who, finding themselves bereft of challenges, felt compelled to pursue "enjoyment" with equal vigor. Riley and others (1969, pp. 971–972) point to the dearth and ambiguity of retirement norms and conclude that immediate personal gratification remains the only socially defined criterion of successful performance in the retirement role. Some men, they state, may "overconform" to the new role "by hedonistic pleasure seeking as a summum bonum." Our data suggest that such "overconformity" may have certain drawbacks and is not likely to ensure high life satisfaction.

Among women in the preretirement stage, significant associations with life satisfaction were shown for philosophical-religious values. It was the unhappier women who were more likely to stress these values. If the intensification of religious beliefs and practices arose from a search for solace, the comfort derived would seem only partial and not such as to result in full acceptance of one's self or one's life course.

Lastly, turning to the influence of family relationships, it was men with strong philosophical-religious values who expressed most positive affect toward family members. Noted among men was a tendency for low family affect to be associated with social-service values, whereas among women low family affect tended to be linked with high instrumental-material values. While the associations are not strong and the dynamics involved are not immediately apparent, it seems worth noting that these sex differences are consistent with the direction of personality change among these men and women (see Chapter Four). Older women with low family investment seem to endorse values traditionally viewed as characteristic of men; older men under similar conditions seem to grant importance to the more nurturant values of social service.

Subjective Perceptions

In the preceding sections, we attempted to assess "objective" differences in values across the adult life course. We now turn to the individuals' subjective evaluations of how their values had changed and were likely to change.

From a psychological perspective, subjective appraisals yield insight into the individual's perception of himself as changing or unchanging; from a sociological perspective, they illustrate the individual's conception of the social norms of succeeding life stages. On the one hand, he may regard value change as self-generated, a concomitant of developmental changes in himself; on the other, he may be aware of the influence of social-role expectations and of situational circumstances which sanction some values rather than others at particular stages. The effects of both perspectives are often closely intertwined, and our subjects did not always consciously make such distinctions. For the most part, they resorted to social-role models when predicting change in themselves, perhaps more so when relatively satisfied with their present selves and life circumstances, less so when not. In the latter instance, one might venture to speculate, the motivation for change may have been linked with the need to escape, and the direction of change may have been more idiosyncratic.

A structured instrument in the form of a card sort representing the seven categories of our value typology provided a useful method of measuring the magnitude and direction of perceived change. Subjects were asked to rank the value categories three times: first, in order of their importance at present; second, in order of their importance when they were eighteen years old (for high school seniors, when they were fourteen years old); third, in order of their anticipated importance ten years hence. These data were used to assess the consistency of an individual's values over time and further to determine group differences in the direction of retrospective and prospective value change. Measures developed to assess how an individual's values change, the value-discrepancy scores, were based on shifts in the subject's ranking of value categories in the different value sorts. Value-discrepancy scores were computed for shifts between past and present value sorts, shifts between present and future sorts, and overall change (past, present, and future sorts). The following questions were explored: Are there life-course differences in the extent to which people see their values as stable and enduring? To what extent is there continuity in the values espoused in youth? As the people in our four life stages project their values into the future, is there evidence that, across the adult life span, some values wax while others wane? Is value stability or instability correlated with other characteristics of the individual?

Influenced by the common-sense, if mechanistic, assumption that longer time intervals would permit and hence be followed by more change than shorter ones, we expected that the younger groups would report less change in values than the older groups. This expectation, however, was not confirmed by the value-discrepancy scores, for differences among the groups proved not to be statistically significant. Sex differences, too, were found to be negligible. Block (1971) reports extraordinary variation in personality continuity and shows the two periods, from junior high school to senior high school and from senior high school to the mid-thirties, to be roughly similar in potential for overall change. These findings accord with the similarities noted between the high school and newlywed groups, suggesting also that their subjective perceptions may not have been inaccurate. It would, however, be erroneous to conclude from the absence of differences between the older and younger groups that little further change occurs after the third decade of life. Much discussion has been given to developmental changes in time perspective and the sense of time lapse (Fraisse, 1963; Aisenberg, 1964). The same period of time, for example, which is experienced by the young as long in duration and rich in variety tends to be experienced by older persons as shorter and less eventful. That the older groups did not perceive more value change than the younger may in part have been due to developmental differences in time experience.

All groups believed that they had changed more in the past than they were likely to in the next ten years, and there were significant differences across the life course with respect to projected change. The younger groups anticipated more discontinuity in values than did the older groups, with the notable exception of newlywed and middle-aged men. The continuities noted among newlywed men equaled those of the oldest stage, whereas middle-aged men resembled the youngest stage in showing relatively high levels of discontinuity. The patterns shown by high school seniors, by newlywed women and empty-nest women, and by preretirees seem congruent with their position along the adult life span. Given the proposition that probability of change bears a direct relationship to extension of futurity, it would seem logical, if not inevitable, for persons with "their whole lives ahead of them" to anticipate much change, and for those conscious that remaining years are numbered to anticipate less. A different explanation, however, must be sought for the seemingly incongruent patterns of newlywed and middle-aged men. Marriage has been said to evoke new definitions of the self and to be characterized by general euphoria (Clausen, 1972), and the younger men were, as we have seen in previous chapters, highly satisfied with their lives and themselves. They seemed to feel that they had finally discovered their potential and were to actualize it. Under these rather optimal conditions, they probably would not want to look forward to marked change in any sphere of their lives. The opposite trend, anticipation of high value change in the future on the part of middle-aged men, clearly reflects, as will be shown later, their expectations for the retirement phase.

Having assessed the magnitude of change, we next examined the direction of value change. When comparing present values with those recalled from youth, the people in the preretirement stage showed more systematic change in more values than did any other group. They revealed important shifts in five of the seven value categories, while change in the other groups was limited to two or three. The one change which all groups reported as differentiating their later from their earlier selves was a decline in hedonism. In addition, high school girls showed an increase in the importance of social-service values; newlywed men felt that personal-growth values had become more important to them; newlywed women and middle-aged men reported an increase in interpersonal-expressive values, whereas middle-aged women reported an increase in social-service values. (Perhaps because they felt that interpersonal-expressive values had been central to them throughout all their lives, the middle-aged and older groups of women failed to report any change in this area.) Men and women facing retirement reported a decline in instrumental-material values and an increase in social-service and ease-contentment values. The men further reported an increase in interpersonal-expressive values and the women an increase in philosophical-religious values.

These differences between recollected and current values seem to relate most directly to two characteristics: the social-role statuses our subjects had assumed in the meantime, and a broader question of immediate gratification versus personal responsibilities and obligations to others. Thus, the increased importance of inter-personal-expressive values reported by newlywed women and the middle-aged and older men reflects their sense of responsibility for marital and other familial relationships. Similarly, the changes noted among those in the preretirement stage clearly coincide with the transition from the world of work to that of leisure. At the same time, however, all subjects perceived themselves as becoming less self-indulgent and more responsible as they grew older. The demands of adult roles do, indeed, interfere with the pursuit of hedonistic values; nevertheless, the increasingly insistent rejection of hedonistic values also suggests a rising sense of social ethics and concern for others, including and extending beyond the family. This notion that an individual should become more socially responsible as he grows older also seems to be the basis for the increase in social-service values, reported by all women (except the newlyweds) and also by preretired men.

At this point we digress to comment about the accuracy of perceived change. Though the material for such an evaluation was not available, it seemed meaningful to examine the changes reported by the three older groups in relationship to the present value orientations of the high school seniors. To this end, we compared the

value summary scores (see Appendix B) for each of the older groups
with the scores of high school seniors of the same sex, and we found
some significant shifts. We then examined these shifts for congruence
with the direction of self-reported change. The overlap between the
value shifts indicated by these two sets of data was only moderate;
there were, however, no reversals in the direction of change. Newlywed women showed the greatest agreement, which may in part be
attributed to more accurate recall because they had left high school
most recently. Most notably, however, our comparison of value
summary scores did not support the consistent self-reports of rising
social-service and declining hedonistic values. Explanations would
rest on questions of sociohistorical change and the accuracy of
retrospective recall. On the one hand, the present high school cohort
may indeed have been more altruistic and less hedonistic than earlier
cohorts; on the other hand, the older groups may have been given
to retrospective distortions and to the stereotype of youth as a period
of self-centered gratification.

   Compared to perceptions of past change, systematic shifts
between values held in the present and those projected for the future
were very rare. In general, predictions were governed more by
individualistic and circumstantial considerations than by stage-
linked or socially circumscribed stereotypes, and subjects appeared to
be describing the directions they personally wished to follow, as
opposed to the directions that social forces might mold them into.
Among the younger groups, systematic shifts were found only among
high school girls, who showed a significant decline in personal-growth
values. The anticipated decline in values, centered on personal development, comes as something of a surprise from so young a group.
For many of these young people, perceptions of responsibilities and rewards of marriage and family apparently precluded further opportu-
ntiy for educational or avocational pursuits, or interest in the
acquisition of new knowledge and skills. Among the older groups, only
middle-aged men showed systematic value shifts—namely, a decline
in instrumental values and a rise in hedonistic ones. These projected
changes, which would bring their values closer to those held by men
in the preretirement stage, reflect effective anticipatory socialization:
these middle-aged men were aware of the influences of their changing role statuses and social environment; and the direction of change

for many of them, as evidenced by case-history material, also seemed to accord with their personal inclinations.

Definitive studies of value change, whether concerned with objective or subjective perspectives, would require a longitudinal research design. Thus far, investigations of developmental change in values have been based on cross-sectional data (Bühler, 1959; Kuhlen and Johnson, 1952; Cyrus-Lutz and Gaitz, 1971; Chinoy, 1955); and though there has been a steady increase in longitudinal research, these longitudinal studies (for example, Block, 1971; Brooks and Elliott, 1971; Lowenthal, Berkman, and Associates, 1967) have for the most part dealt with psychological, social, and behavioral variables and have not included goals and values. The longitudinal phase of our study will allow us to assess actual value changes, to explore agreements and discrepancies between subjective perceptions and objective change, and to determine the implications of subjective anticipations for personal development.

Correlates of Value Change

Transitions to successive stages of the adult life course differ in the nature and magnitude of change they normatively require of the individual (Burr, 1972; Brim, 1968). In turn, individuals vary markedly in their inclination or capacity to change their values. Thus, the mode of adaptation to and outcome of any given life-course transition will be determined by features inherent in the transition and by the characteristics of the individual (Lowenthal, 1971). The analysis below may be viewed as a preliminary exploration of these propositions. It seeks to examine the adaptive implications of value change at different life stages, and to assess the characteristics of individuals who perceive themselves as changing, as compared to those who do not.

In order to understand how an individual's perception of values interrelates with his sense of self-worth and of psychological well-being, we correlated retrospective and prospective value change with self-concept and with life satisfaction (Table 17). In addition, we assessed value continuity and discontinuity in relation to judges' ratings of perceived and presumed stress (see Chapter Eight). Since we hypothesized that intelligence may well play a role in the assessment of retrospective change and the prediction of future change, we also established correlations with the WAIS scores (Vocabulary and Block Design subtests, combined). Finally, we correlated these value changes with various adaptive characteristics (see Appendix B, Adaptive Ratings).

No relationship was noted between degree of retrospective change and degree of prospective change. In other words, people who felt that they had changed much since the past were not necessarily those who anticipated much change in the future. Consistent with this finding, the two directions of value change were shown to be related to different sets of factors. Thus, for the sample as a whole, presumed stress, the exposure to a variety of life events requiring readjustment, was strongly linked to perceptions of retrospective change but did not seem to influence anticipation of prospective change. Perceptions of retrospective change tended to be correlated predominantly with cognitive characteristics (foremost among them, WAIS scores and judges' ratings of insight) and to a lesser extent also with life-cycle and contextual perspectives and with competence. In contrast, cognition appeared to have little relevance for the anticipation of prospective change, which, for the sample as a whole, tended to be associated with positive self-concept and resolution of losses, that is, the acceptance of losses with fortitude, the willingness to try again, and the attempt to effect restitutions. Individuals who have a tendency to dwell on the past and are unable to surmount its shortcomings tend not to envisage future change as likely. Openness to future change—whether reflecting merely an individual's receptivity to the idea that external life experiences will bring about changes in his values, or whether linked to the personal desire to improve and grow—seems to require at least a modicum of self-assurance and acceptance of one's self and one's life history.

High school boys stood out from other groups in that perception of high retrospective change was associated with negative characteristics. Boys who felt that they had changed greatly showed a tendency to score high in negative self-concept, ascribing to themselves such traits as defensive, rebellious, resentful, restless, or worried; and they were given low ratings in competence. In contrast, boys who were high in prospective change scored high in positive self-concept—that is, self-ascription of such traits as coopera-

Table 17.

PSYCHOLOGICAL CORRELATES OF VALUE CHANGE (Pearson product-moment correlation coefficients)[a]

	High School		Newlywed		Middle-Aged		Preretirement		Total
	Men	Women	Men	Women	Men	Women	Men	Women	
Retrospective Change									
Life satisfaction									
Self-criticism	.57**			(.40)			.47*		
Negative self-concept		.43*							
Positive self-concept								(.44)	.17*
WAIS (Vocabulary and Block Design)									(.12)
Life-cycle perspective		.45*							(.12)
Contextual perspective									
Growth		.53**							
Insight		(.36)				.39*			.17*
Familial mutuality		(.36)							
Accommodation (judged)	— .48*			.50*					
Competence		.43*						(.36)	(.13)
Satisfaction with competence		(.39)							
Resolution of losses						.38*			
Low psychological impairment		(.37)				.41*			
Perceived stress			.48*						
Presumed stress			(.36)						.20**
Prospective Change									
Life satisfaction					.46*				
Negative self-concept	.53**	(.36)							
Positive self-concept						.48*			.18*
Insight					(.36)		(.34)		
Familial mutuality					.40*		.39*		
Competence					.43*		(.38)		
Satisfaction with competence	(— .40)								
Hope			(— .36)				.53**		
Resolution of losses		.50**							(.13)
Low psychological impairment		.40*							
Perceived stress		— .51**							
Presumed stress						.43*			

[a] Positive correlation indicates a direct relationship between value change and positive status on the other variable. Parenthesized correlations attain a probability between .10 and .05; correlations with one asterisk have a probability between .05 and .01; correlations with two asterisks have a probability of less than .01.

tive, energetic, intelligent, and reasonable—but low in satisfaction with competence. The reason for these differences rests primarily in the fact that very high past change in values could generally be linked to the desire to stress one's membership—sometimes real, more often spurious—in the counterculture. These boys wished to convey that they had undergone a conversion and gained insight into things that really mattered. Not surprisingly, they were not willing to envisage any future change. On the other hand, boys who felt that their values would change in the future were, as shown in a comparison of present values, more likely to be concerned with social issues and were also less likely to opt for security and contentment.

Among newlywed men, value change was not associated with personality attributes or competence, but seemed most closely related to the peculiarities of individual life histories. Newlywed men who felt that their values had changed considerably in the past tended to be characterized by exposure to stress as well as some preoccupation with stress.

The peculiarities of individual life histories did not affect perceptions of value change among the middle-aged men and those in the preretirement stage—perhaps because they had had more experience with the inevitable fluctuations in life's satisfactions and dissatisfactions. A single association was noted with respect to retrospective change; namely, the tendency of the oldest men to score high in negative self-concept. Why older men who were given to ascribing to themselves such traits as stubborn, lazy, suspicious, and jealous tended to perceive more retrospective value change in themselves is difficult to interpret. Negative appraisals of successes in past life were shown to affect the morale of these men (Thurnher, 1974), and one can offer the tentative explanation that they may have been frustrated about their life goals and achievements, that they had accordingly lowered their aspirations and modified their values and hated themselves for doing so.

On the other hand, differences between prospective changers and nonchangers were more marked and clearcut. Prospective change among middle-aged men was associated with insight and competence, and a similar tendency was also shown by men in the preretirement stage. Middle-aged men who projected much value change were further characterized by low life satisfaction, suggesting that their motivation for change was highly influenced by distress over present circumstances. Changers among the older group of men tended to be high on familial mutuality and on hope, which suggests that one is more likely to envisage or venture change in late life if a close interpersonal relationship provides support.

Turning next to women, we find that high school girls' perceptions of past value change reflected psychological and social maturation. Retrospective change was associated not only with high rating of growth but also with life-cycle perspective and competence. Furthermore, girls reporting change tended to have a more positive self-concept, to be higher on insight and familial mutuality, and also to have little psychological impairment. While one might expect girls with these attributes also to be the ones most likely to anticipate further change and growth, this was not the case. Prospective change seemed to be linked to the nature and density of life experiences; girls low on perceived stress, whose lives had been uneventful, were most likely to foresee value change in the future. Though prospective changers showed a tendency toward negative self-concept, they were not without psychological resources, for they were rated high on loss resolution and low on psychological, impairment. These findings suggest that girls, by and large, appraise their maturation with relative accuracy. Retrospective changers may feel that they have reached a state of maturity (raters' judgments would, on the whole, support this conclusion); having reached this state, they seem, at least temporarily, not to feel compelled or motivated to envisage further change. Girls who are late maturers and off pace in their developmental cycle are the ones who anticipate and hope for further change.

Among women in the remaining three life stages, marked differences between changers and nonchangers were found only among those confronting the empty nest, where value change was shown to have positive implications. Empty-nest women who felt that their values had changed considerably since high school tended to be more insightful and were less likely to be rated psychologically impaired; they were also rated high on loss resolution. On the whole, they gave the impression of mature women who were aware and accepting of the developmental changes that had taken place. It is interesting to note (since it seems to underline sex differences in overall orientation and also in the timing of life events) that the psychologically more resourceful middle-aged women focused on retrospective change, while resourceful men at the same stage focused on prospective change. One is also struck by certain parallels in the characteristics of middle-aged women and high school girls who report high retrospective change, these findings suggesting that similar psychodynamic processes may be involved. The two groups seem to share an intensified consciousness of proximity to critical life transitions: in the case of girls, entry into the world of women and the reproductive cycle; in the case of women, the completion of maternal tasks. Again, as in the case of girls, these positive psychological attributes do not encompass notions of future change and development. One is reminded of Freud's ([1933] 1965) observation that women, unlike men, appear to have completed the whole course of their psychosexual development by midlife, the difficulty of this process seemingly exhausting the potential for further development. At the same time, Freud does not rule out the possible influences of "social breeding"; and perhaps in some measure the dearth of further change anticipated is due to the constraints and lack of alternatives provided by the social structure. Those women who anticipated a change in values tended to have a positive self-concept, reporting themselves as confident, energetic, intelligent, likeable, and cooperative. They also tended to be women who had been exposed to considerable stress in the course of their lives. In short, there is a suggestion that women in this stage are unlikely to envision the possibility or feel the need for future change unless they have some confidence in their ability to structure or control their environments, or unless they have a keen, perhaps desperate, desire to somehow make up for the frustrations of the past. Some of them may hope that the coming years will allow for greater expression of ease and contentment values; others may hope that the future will provide new opportunity to pursue goals of personal growth.

Newlywed women who reported considerable value change tended to be somewhat self-critical and more accommodating to others. Since both these variables are linked to the marital role (self-criticality among newlywed women involved predominantly the rejection or removal of traits which deviated from the wifely ideal), the magnitude of perceived change may reflect the readjustment evoked or necessitated by marriage. At the other extreme, women in the preretirement stage give the impression of being less influenced by situational factors in their appraisals of change than were those in earlier stages of the life course. Perceptions of high retrospective change tended to be associated with relatively high intelligence scores and with ratings of overall competence. No correlations were noted for prospective change.

Lastly, since measures of perceived and presumed stress had proved relevant to the study of value change, we were interested in assessing to what extent individuals falling within the four categories of the stress typology (see Table 13) also differed in their perceptions of personal value change. For this purpose, the measures of value discontinuity (value-discrepancy scores) were dichotomized into high and low within each group and cross-tabulated with the four stress types; the two younger and the two older life stages were combined. While no statistically significant differences were obtained, a number of interesting trends were noted. First of all, challenged older men, challenged older women, and lucky older women were most likely to perceive high retrospective change. Groups most likely to anticipate prospective change were overwhelmed women (both younger and older) and lucky younger men. The groups least likely to anticipate prospective change were lucky older women.

That external life events and stresses may have different implications for the sexes is suggested by the finding that challenged older men and lucky older women reported most retrospective change. Perhaps, to venture a bold and admittedly oversimplified interpretation, among women an environment that is free of undue change and stress may promote a sense of personal change and development, whereas men require an environment that is rich in external life events and stresses (provided, of course, that preoccupation with stress does not set in). Such differences point again to the overriding influence of social sex roles. In women, a sense of personal change may be linked to the domestic group (relevant here is Brim's [1968] observation that too little attention has been given to the influence of growing children in evoking personality change in parents). Change occurs within the confines of the family, in some measure vicariously, and no external events are necessary to introduce a sense of progression. Indeed, it can be argued that external events may deflect from this orderly progression. (For example, a woman harassed by a series of stressful events may fail to make the necessary reorientation which her growing family would ideally foster and may continue to treat near-adult children the same way she treated them when they were youngsters.) Because her traditional role does not call for the mastery of external circumstances and events, such mastery may not contribute to her sense of personal development (except insofar as she tends to support her husband, who does face them). In men, feelings of personal change or of value change are not attuned to the family life cycle; that is, to the changing modes of interaction with and responsibilities toward the maturing family members. Rather, their sense of change arises from exposure to external events and to interaction with individuals outside the family. As reported in Garai's (1970) review, men's sense of identity, "happiness," and anxieties center on occupational attainments, women's on intimacy and interpersonal relationships.

The above proposition relating to men would seem to be substantiated by the finding that it is lucky young men who are most likely to anticipate prospective value change. On the one hand, a stressless past devoid of setbacks may well be conducive to optimism, venturesomeness, and perhaps also to pleasing fantasies regarding potentials of future change. On the other hand, it can also be argued that precisely because of the uneventful nature of their past experiences the lucky young men welcome change. The above interpretation given for women is supported by findings on retrospective change. Lucky older women with relatively smooth lives—who, it would logically follow, have by and large successfully met their family responsibilities—have little desire for further change. In contrast, the overwhelmed—that is, women whose life course has been more turbulent and less successful than they would have wished—look forward to further change.

XI

The Pretransitional Stance

In this chapter, we turn first to an evaluation of attitudes toward what our informants themselves considered to be their principal future transition. We next examine their evaluation of the present, the pretransitional stage, as compared with immediate past and future five-year periods, an indirect method of evaluating the salience of the pretransitional periods for which we sampled. The summary profiles of the four pretransitional groups which follow this appraisal place the cognitive evaluations of the pending transition within the context of other domains of our respondents' lives. This broader perspective suggests, at least for some subgroups, that the conscious orientation toward the future transition does not necessarily reflect an underlying or unconscious anxiety.

Attitudes Toward Transition

In assessing our respondents' attitudes toward the future changes in their lives, we drew on many open-ended questions, where

Robert Pierce collaborated in the first section of this chapter.

a potential transition could be spontaneously introduced if it seemed important to the respondent. In this way, we tried to focus on what they themselves foresaw as major future changes in their lives, and circumvented the possibility of overemphasis on the transitions that we had selected for sampling purposes. To this end, all promising sections of the protocols were analyzed, and the salient future transitions were identified. Four dimensions of the cognitive stance toward what each informant considered to be his or her main transition were delineated: evaluation (in positive or negative terms), amount of planning, problems envisaged, and the individual's own feeling of control over the circumstance.

Many subjects anticipated more than one transition. The younger groups, facing role increments, cited an average of nearly three apiece, of which parenthood was most frequently mentioned (over four fifths). The two older groups envisaged only "decremental" or role-loss transitions: first, their own retirement; second, the empty nest; and third, retirement of spouse (which was a salient transition only to women in our sample). In the ensuing discussion, we shall focus primarily on the transition which our subjects cited as their principal one (Table 18).

The men in the preretirement group, not surprisingly, were unanimous in considering retirement the principal change that they confronted. Although about one fourth had children still living at home, none of them singled out the empty-nest or "postparental" stage as most important. The next-greatest consensus was among newlywed women, four fifths of whom considered parenthood as their primary pending transition. This is about twice as many as was true for newlywed men, who were just as likely to view the completion of their education as the main change confronting them. None of the high school girls cited parenthood as their most important change; when *all* mentions are considered, however, these girls envisaged education, a job, marriage, and parenthood with roughly the same frequency.

Although their youngest child would be leaving home within a year, and retirement was still ten or more years in the future, three fifths of the middle-aged men singled out the remoter event; fewer than a third mentioned the more imminent empty nest, a change which twice as many middle-aged women considered to be the

Table 18.

Principal Transition[a] (percentages)

	High School		Newlywed		Middle-Aged		Preretirement	
	Men	Women	Men	Women	Men	Women	Men	Women
Work	16	30	16	8				
Education	72	36	40	8				
Marriage	4	30						
Parenthood	0	0	40	84				
Military	4		4					
Empty Nest					30	59	0	10
Retirement of Self					59	0	100	50
Retirement of Spouse					0	30	0	40
No "Main" Transition	4	4	0	0	11	11	0	0

[a] Empty cells indicate that the event was not coded for that group.

most important. About one third of these women cited their husbands' eventual retirement; although about half of them were
working, none mentioned her own retirement. The oldest women,
on the other hand, were more likely to give primary emphasis to
their own retirement; although three fifths of them were married
and living with their husbands, only two fifths considered spouses'
retirement to be the most crucial future change.

Whether they foresaw an incremental or a decremental
transition, men and women at all stages maintained a generally
positive evaluation of it. While the older groups, on the whole, were
somewhat less sanguine than the young, nearly three fourths of the
oldest men envisaging retirement looked forward to it in positive
terms, a stance nearly as optimistic as that of men in the two
youngest groups, who confronted incremental transitions. The middle-aged were the least cheerful about whatever they construed to
be their main transition; only a few more than half of the men and
the women had adopted a positive attitude toward it. Reflecting
some dismay about the trajectory of their lives, many middle-aged
men worried about the economic aspect of their present life stage,
its implications for the retirement period, and the financial consequences of growing older. As one of them elaborated: "Now I can't
buy a house on a twenty-five-year basis. You have statistics proving
that you have little chance of living up to seventy-five." The more
pessimistic women were those who considered their husbands' rather
remote retirement rather than the imminent departure of the
youngest child as their main transition. These tended to be women
who were dissatisfied with their marriages and concerned about the
quality of life at a time when the diversion of children in the home
would be lacking and their husbands, as they sometimes put it,
would be underfoot all day.

Across all stages, very few people (6 percent) had a completely negative attitude toward their principal transition. Except
for about a tenth of the high school boys, these negative appraisals
were found only among the two older groups, especially the oldest
women (14 percent), where it was primarily the widowed, divorced,
and single women (who pinpointed their own retirement as their
main transition) who adopted an outright negative stance. As a
sixty-two-year-old secretary expressed it: "When I think about

retirement, it gives me some thought sometimes. I could really and truly retire if I wanted to right now. But I don't want to because I don't know what I'm going to do with myself. It's because I don't really have any real interests, any real concrete outside interests that would keep me going. . . . What can you do? Your life is practically over at my age." The potential vacuum in their lives, the lack of interpersonal and other kinds of resources of some of these women, supports our earlier thesis that retirement may often be more traumatic for women than it is for men, or at least for those men whose wives have had time to keep the familial and extrafamilial social networks intact (Lowenthal, Berkman, and Associates, 1967).

Although the possible range of planning was from "none" to "many plans," the actual planning was minimal at all stages. Among women, it was almost nonexistent except at the preretirement stage, and even there the few who did have plans were more likely to be focusing on a (usually brief) postretirement trip than preparing for a new way of life. Several of these women almost superstitiously avoided planning, as the following explanation by a sixty-five-year-old housewife illustrates: "I'm not sure about anything. I'm not a great planner. Plans have a way of exploding in your face. I hope that things work out, let's put it that way. . . . I hope to take a trip with my husband." High school senior girls were even less likely to plan, suggesting that they were engrossed in what they (and, in many instances, their mothers) viewed as the last relatively carefree year of their lives. Only one girl had any plans for a particular career, and she was already dubious about it, because, although she would "like" to become a doctor, "I'll probably want kids and to raise a family and that'll be a conflicting thing." Although the vast majority of newlywed women singled out parenthood as their main future transition, their planning, too, was minimal; and most deferred to their husbands, whom (as noted in Chapter Two) they generally identified as the "boss" of the family: "Well, now Don says we're going to wait until we can afford them [children]. That means a couple of years until we have our house bought and he gets a raise or two. . . . We're not the type to be in debt, you know; we don't want to live beyond our means. . . . And as long as I work, it helps us to get the things we need. And we also have to get better acquainted, which he thinks will take two years." Newly-

wed women whose husbands were not doing any planning tended to
be ambivalent about whether they wanted children and to resent
their spouses' lack of assertion: "Someone once mentioned to me
that if I didn't have children there would be a couple of children
who could possibly have been in the world with just a fantastic
mother. . . . [My husband] is a little boy in a way. I suppose with
his dependency and insecurity and nonaggressiveness that you might
say I already had my child. I really don't need another little boy in
addition to the one that I have now." The few women earmarking
the empty nest as critical, and who did have plans, did not center
them on themselves as much as on their children—getting them
through college or seeing them happily married. The handful who
were thinking about how to use the additional time that would
presumably be available when the youngest child had departed were
diffuse and vague, mentioning many possibilities but without much
enthusiasm, and sometimes beset with strong doubts: "[I'd like to
do] volunteer work. Or travel. If I ever have the time, I hope to be
able to write. I did quite well when I was in school, both high school
and college. This probably belongs more to daydreaming, because I
think I never will have the time."

The plans of men—except for the high school boys—were
more specific, realistic, and motivated. High school boys, who were
most likely to talk at length about plans, were as vague and un-
focused as the middle-aged women. One student, for instance,
wanted to become a rich businessman *or* a commercial pilot *or* a
ticket agent, and had made no realistic plans for preparing for any
of these career lines. Another thought that he might become a
dentist because of the "bread," but his immediate (and recurrently
expressed) goal was to go to India or the Middle East.

Perhaps responding to the notable lack of initiative among
some newlywed women, and feeling the economic press of marriage
and eventual parenthood, there were by contrast a few newlywed
men who were realistic, highly motivated, and planning step by
step: "Well, we're saving money. The savings are going for the
house right now, but that would ultimately be for the baby anyhow.
Getting the house was technically one of the steps for having a
family. Going to college is really one of the steps toward it too. I
have to finish college; that's the limitation I put on myself. I don't

want my wife working when we have a baby, so that means we'll have to be in some economic situation to have one. The child should have some time with me, too, so I shouldn't be going to school all day and working all night."

The middle-aged men, who generally envisaged retirement as their main (but by no means imminent) transition, were, as we have noted, concerned primarily with the economic aspects of that life stage. The oldest men, on the other hand, if they mentioned the economic aspects of retirement at all, simply summarized what they had already accomplished in that sphere. About a fifth of them were planning second careers, usually with considerable realism about their talents, the need for additional training, and the obstacles they expected to confront: "I want to retire. I want to get myself the kind of job where I can work two or three days a week for five to six hours. That's to make up the difference between retirement [income] and what I'm living at now. The best thing I could do is work in my own game, except that maybe I wouldn't want to do that. I might consider myself getting involved in real estate. I would probably start off in sales, get myself a broker's license and learn about the sales aspects of it. I would like to have a combination of the electrical [background] and real estate. I think this is a natural trend I've been working at. Maybe even since 1932. . . . I'm going to take up a number of courses before I retire, such as accounting, speed reading, and so on." This is in sharp contrast to the offhand, rather uninterested, tone of the women in this stage, regardless of whether they singled out their own or their husbands' retirement: "I don't really think too much of the future. You just kind of live from day to day. You just sort of know that you're going to retire and that you'll be able to come up with something after you do."

The sense of being in control of the pending transition ranged from active to almost completely passive, with other people or external circumstances viewed as decisive. Nearly two thirds of the sample as a whole believed that they had some control over the timing or sequelae of their main transition. Women were less likely to feel in control than men, though the differences between the sexes were not as marked as they were for planning. Younger people, who presumably had more viable alternatives about which to exercise choice, were only slightly more likely to sense themselves in control

than the older. The middle-aged men and women (despite belonging
to what has been called the "command" generation) felt least in
control, even less (though again not significantly) than the oldest
group, most of whom confronted imminent and often mandatory retirement. This trend does not support Gutmann (1969), who,
utilizing projective data with older samples than ours, found a
decrease in active mastery across successive groups.

Among middle-aged women, there was a very strong relationship between little sense of control and little planning; conversely, there was a trend toward a relationship between internal
control and having some plans. As with the sources of stress, the
focus for the sense of control and planning among these women
facing the empty nest was not themselves but their children, and the
relationship between planning and control among them is largely
accounted for by those whose children were doing what they (the
mothers) wished them to do—mainly preparing to go on to college.
Women who were uncertain about whether their children would
continue their education had less sense of control. Among preretirement women, on the other hand, the relationship between control and planning was in large part accounted for by the unattached
working women, who earmarked their own retiremment as crucial.
Older women who envisaged their spouses' retirement as the main
transition, while they may have encouraged or pled for one option
or another, were by no means convinced that they would be successful: "[My husband] has been thinking of retiring because he
has a bad back. I keep on encouraging him to stay working, we
just plead with him not to retire. . . . He is miserable if I'm not
here with him. . . . If I'm home, then everything is fine. If he's
alone at home, everything is bad." Among older people, too, there
was a strong relationship between the sense of control and a positive
evaluation of the transition. Middle-aged women, however, were an
exception: among them, feeling in control of their next critical
transition was associated with a negative evaluation of it.

Young men expected to encounter more problems with the
pending transition than young women, while among the middle-
aged, it was the women who were most likely to anticipate difficulties. In the oldest group, there was a tendency toward convergence: the oldest were the most likely of all the women to anticipate

more than a few problems, and the oldest men were the most likely of their sex to anticipate more than a few. Across the four life stages, women showed a steady increase in the anticipation of problems. The negation of problems by the middle-aged men is impressive in comparison not only with the older but with the younger people of the same sex. Oddly enough, anticipation of problems bears no relationship to planning, nor is it significantly associated with a positive or negative evaluation or the sense of control. There is an interesting trend among middle-aged women, however: those who feel they are in control tend to report more problems associated with the transition, just as they also tend to have a negative evaluation of it. This suggests that women envisaging an imminent empty nest may be disconcerted at finding themselves, perhaps for the first time in their lives, facing a life stage in which their destinies are to some extent in their own hands.

Attitudes toward the transition appear to be more highly correlated for transitions of later life than for the earlier transitions, perhaps indicating that the decremental transitions of later life are more central to the lives of people about to undergo them than the incremental transitions of early life. The sense of inner control was clearly the most important of the pretransitional cognitions, being strongly associated with a positive attitude toward the transition, as well as with planning for it (except among middle-aged women, where the converse is true). Whether or not the individual foresaw problems in connection with his main transition had little bearing on whether his attitude toward it was positive or negative, the amount of planning undertaken, or the sense of being in control.

To explore the relationship between stance toward the future transition and other spheres of the individual's life, we examined the relationships between (a) evaluation, planning, problems, and control measures and (b) thirty-eight circumstantial, interpersonal, intrapersonal, and affective characteristics, as well as five indicators of adaptation (see Appendix C for list). This procedure, undertaken separately for the eight subgroups, yielded seventy-three relationships significant at the .05 level or better. Since, with such a great number of tests, a sizable number of .05 relationships could be attributed to chance, we shall report primarily on those significant at the .01 level or better.

Scanning all eight stage and sex groups, we find that the highly significant associations cluster at the extremes of the attitudinal types: the high school boys, who were the most positive on all dimensions of the stance toward the transition, and the middle-aged women, who were the most negative. If we add to these two subgroups men at the preretirement stage, who had the most optimistic stance of the four older groups, three fourths of the highly significant correlations are accounted for. If we take into account relationships of a lesser significance, these findings are further strengthened for preretirement men and middle-aged women, who between them account for over half of the additional associations which reach the .05 level. In addition, when the two degrees of significance are taken into account, three fourths of the associations are with the sense of control or with a positive or negative evaluation —suggesting, as did the associations among the same dimensions, that these two perspectives are more crucial in the anticipation of transitions than are amount of planning or whether or not problems are expected.

The characteristics strongly associated with the four dimensions of stance toward the transition were primarily interpersonal and intrapersonal. There was no relationship between any dimension of stance and indicators of adaptation, such as psychological symptoms, psychiatric evaluation, physical symptoms, morale, or preoccupation with stress. The only characteristics associated with stance toward the transition in more than two of the eight stage and sex groups were role scope (three), subscores of the Wechsler Adult Intelligence Scale (three), and self-concept (three). Again, these findings were also reinforced in correlations significant at the .05 level. These rather unexpected findings underscore the essentially cognitive nature of appraisals of the anticipated transition, and suggest that projective measures need to be included in order to assess fully the impact of the transition.

Present in Context of Past and Future

An indirect and perhaps more profound indication of the importance of the pending transition within the broad configuration of our subjects' lives is found in their Life Evaluation Charts. On the whole, our respondents were about evenly divided between optimism and pessimism as inferred from comparing their anticipations for the future with their evaluation of the present. For those who believe that the future will be better, the pretransitional period —that is, the present—is perhaps more stressful than the transition itself is expected to be. (A parallel to this finding appears in laboratory studies of stress, where the period of anticipation is sometimes accompanied by more symptoms of anxiety than is the period during which the subject is actually being subjected to painful stimuli [Lazarus, 1970].)

Among men, high school boys were most likely to anticipate change for the better; over three fifths of them plotted the next five years at a higher level than the present—compared, for example, with only one tenth of the middle-aged men (Table 19). This resembles the cognitive stance of these two male groups toward the particular transition they envisaged as their main one: the senior boys had a very favorable attitude toward the next major change in their lives, whereas only half of the middle-aged men viewed their next transition (retirement) favorably. On the other hand, that as many as half of these middle-aged men viewed retirement with favor, while only a tenth saw the next five years as better than the present, supports our thesis that these men are apprehensive about the vicissitudes of their work lives and their economic status now that most of them have reached a plateau in their careers. Men at the preretirement stage showed apprehension about the next five years. Although these men, from a purely cognitive viewpoint, professed to have a very positive stance toward retirement, one third of them rated the future lower, and only one fourth rated it higher, than the present.

Among women, differences across the four stages were less dramatic: about a third of them were optimistic, except for the middle-aged, who projected a marked decline in the next five years; in their verbal appraisals of their next transition, however, these women professed to be pleased at the prospects of their youngest child's leaving home.

Within each life stage there were some dramatic differences between men and women. While the majority of high school boys rated the next five years higher than the present, the girls projected

Table 19.

EVALUATION OF PRESENT IN COMPARISON WITH PAST AND FUTURE FIVE YEARS (percentages)

The mean of the future five years compared to the rating for the present year:

	High School		Newlywed		Middle-Aged		Preretirement	
	Men	Women	Men	Women	Men	Women	Men	Women
Future Lower	24	62	37	52	33	27	35	20
Future = Present	14	8	16	17	57	54	40	45
Future Higher	62	29	47	30	10	18	25	35

The mean of the past five years compared to the rating for the present year:

	High School		Newlywed		Middle-Aged		Preretirement	
	Men	Women	Men	Women	Men	Women	Men	Women
Past Lower	60	92	76	80	44	60	62	36
Past = Present	12	0	4	4	44	12	24	43
Past Higher	28	8	20	16	12	28	14	21

a downward curve, over three fifths of them rating the future period lower than the present. There was a similar, though less dramatic, sex difference among the newlyweds. And yet the great majority of both of these groups of young women had reported a positive attitude toward the principal transition they were confronting. That in general they rate the future lower than the present may well reflect the extent to which the present year indeed appears to them as a high point in their lives. If we also examine their appraisals of the present in comparison with the *preceding* five years, we find that these high school girls and newlywed women were far more likely than any of the other groups to evaluate the present higher than the past. High school senior girls may feel that their attractiveness is now at its peak. Many are dating, and few have serious worries, because they assume that their personal destinies and life styles will be determined by their future husbands. For their part, most newlywed women are very much in love and engrossed in the marital relationship. In their orientation to their next transition, parenthood, we have seen that, indeed, they are as dependent on their husbands as the high school girls apparently expect to be.

In their past and future evaluations, as in many other areas of their lives, the middle-aged women provide evidence that their adaptive level is considerably lower than that of women who are confronting the retirement stage. Fewer than a fifth of them expect the future to be any brighter than the present, compared with over a third of the women who are on the average ten years older. Like the younger women, the majority rate the past five years lower than the present, whereas only about one third of the older women do so. And conversely, whereas over one third of the older women reveal a continuity of evaluation of the past five years with the present, only a little over one tenth of the middle-aged women do so. In light of the greater vagueness of middle-aged women in planning for the next stage, we might conclude that they are preoccupied with relishing the last year of the parenting period.

Pretransitional Profiles

On all dimensions of the cognitive stance toward the particular pending transition which they viewed as their main one, the younger groups ranked higher than the older, though not very much more so than the men facing imminent retirement. High school boys closely resembled newlywed men in having a very favorable attitude toward the transition, envisaging few problems, and feeling very much in control. High school girls, on the other hand, were somewhat less positive; like the women at all other stages, they were less likely to feel in control than the men. In fact, at the high school stage, twice as many boys as girls felt in control of their next transition. On the other hand, the girls anticipated far fewer problems and were doing little planning. Among these girls few personal characteristics were associated with their attitude toward the transition— perhaps reflecting, as we hypothesized earlier, a lack of salience of the anticipated transition. Those whose Life Evaluation Charts were most "dense" in the past, reflecting a certain amount of complexity of life style, viewed their pending transitions in the most favorable light, as did those with the broader role scopes. Inspection of their protocols indicates that these relationships are largely accounted for by the relatively few who have even a modest interest in higher education or a job.

As noted in preceding chapters, the immediate goals of these girls were diffuse—like those of the middle-aged mothers. Their most serious commitments were to the idea of eventual marriage and family. They were the least concerned with social problems of any subgroup. Like the middle-aged women, the high school girls were uneasy when they acknowledged having such characteristics as competence and self-directedness. In connection with inquiries about future values and goals, they anticipated a decline in personal growth in the next ten years; in addition, they regarded the present as better than either the past or the future five-year periods. They seemed to be saying, then, that they had reached a peak or a plateau. To the extent that their present year will continue to be perceived as a peak (which we will be able to ascertain only in the longitudinal phase), this group of middle- and lower-middle-class eighteen-year-old girls would seem to provide some support for Freud's thesis that development in women comes to a standstill very early: "A man of about thirty strikes us as a youthful, somewhat unformed individual, whom we expect to make powerful use of the possibilities for development opened up to him by analysis. A woman of the same age, however, often frightens us by her psychical rigidity and unchangeability. Her libido has taken up final positions and seems incapable of exchanging them for others. There are no paths open to further development; it is as though the whole process had already run its course and remains thenceforward insusceptible to influence—as though, indeed, the difficult development to femininity had exhausted the possibilities of the person concerned" (Freud, [1933] 1965, pp. 134–135).

Among high school boys, who had the most positive stance toward the next transition, a strong masculine self-concept was associated with the sense of being in control of the transition. Breadth of role scope was strongly associated with evaluation: boys with many roles were either positive or negative, whereas those with few roles were ambivalent—suggesting that breadth of reference groups may serve an ego-strengthening function for these young men. It is reasonable that the brighter high school boys—as assessed by the Vocabulary and Block Design tests of the Wechsler Adult Intelligence Scale—should do more thinking about their next transition than the less gifted, but rather paradoxical that their plans were unrealistic. As Erikson (1968, p. 163) points out in discussing the later stages of identity formation, "Normative crises . . . are characterized by an abundance of available energy which . . . supports new and expanded ego functions in the searching and *playful* [italics supplied] engagement of new opportunities and associations." (As we saw in Chapter Four, this kind of scattered energy also characterizes the newlywed men.) These boys seem to be searching—living a relatively complex life style and possessing a comparative breadth of social horizons. While their goals are limited, resembling those of the fathers in the parent generation, they, unlike the girls, anticipate change and growth. Their problems in regard to intimacy, and the uncertainties reflected in their self-concepts, suggest the kinds of identity crises that Erikson (1968) postulates as the precursor to the future stages, which he labels, successively, as intimacy and generativity. As the reports from the newlywed men indicate, this "crisis" seems destined to continue for at least another seven or eight years for males, while the newlywed women appear to be as happily settled (and constricted) as the high school girls clearly expect to be when they reach that stage.

Erikson, of course, postulates his life stages in large part from studies and clinical work with young men. As he says in his essay on womanhood in the same volume, and as Freud concludes in the essay quoted above, psychoanalytic theory has little to contribute in regard to developmental stages in women (see also Lindzey, 1968). We suspect that, for the girls in our sample, at least a "semifinal" stage of identity formation may come with the selection of a mate. Work and education, which most of the high school girls envisaged as their principal next transitions, are for most of them tangential in relation to their longer-range hopes. Since they view finding a mate as a matter more of fate than of conscious selection, they would not be expected to make many plans in that direction; and, in fact, whereas the boys ranked highest on considerable planning, the girls were lowest of all the eight subgroups. As we shall suggest later, women in this socioeconomic and cultural group may go through another potentially developmental stage when their child-rearing functions are completed.

Newlywed women resembled high school girls in reflecting considerable satisfaction with the present vis-à-vis the previous five years and the next. Though the great majority considered parenthood to be their principal future transition, it was clear that, by and large, they were not yet ready for it. They deferred to their husbands in regard to timing, and were engrossed in enjoying and strengthening the new marital relationship. Prospective motherhood was envisaged in a rather symbolic way; and no personal characteristics, except religion, were correlated with their stance toward it. Catholic and Jewish women had the most favorable general attitude, reflecting, no doubt, some of the tenets and mores of their respective faiths.

While over two fifths of the newlywed men viewed parenthood as a main transition, most of them envisaged this event for a rather indeterminate future, when they had established themselves in a more or less permanent occupation and perhaps acquired a home. For as many as two fifths, completion of education was the main future event; this achievement, however, was seen not as an end in itself but as a means to job and eventual parenthood.

While the boys and girls of eighteen or so shared few personal characteristics, the newlywed men and women resembled each other in being the happiest people in the sample, and they ranked highest in mutuality. They also held the most negative views of their parents and their parents' marriages (except for middle-aged women, who were also very critical, though primarily of their mothers). The newlyweds appeared to be hard at work establishing compatible life styles, and while their goals resembled those of the parent generations, the timing was slower. The young women were far more centered in their husbands than vice versa, but they both agreed that they needed time to get acquainted—and the husbands established in a job or a career—before having children. The parent generations, for the most part being children of the Depression, did not marry until the potential husband was settled in his occupation, and were likely to have had their first child soon after marriage.

Though many of the newlywed women were working (over four fifths), almost none had serious work commitments (one who did was divorced a year or two later). These young women worked so that their husbands could continue their education or experiment a bit with the job market. Like the high school girls, their range of activities was more constricted than the men in their life stage, and was limited primarily to those carried out jointly with their husbands. Their social horizons, too, were much more constricted, and they resented their husbands' outside activities and interests. They were in love, and nothing else seemed to matter.

For the newlywed men, on the other hand, the first year of marriage, rather than constricting and draining them, seemed to release energy, which spread in all directions. They were buoyant and impulsive, and they had the most complex life styles—along with senior boys—of any group. Psychically they were the most complex of all the men, and personal growth ranked high among their aims. Whatever they viewed as their main transition, they, again along with the high school boys, had the most positive stance toward it of any of the groups we are studying. Agreeing with the newlywed women that the man is boss in the family, they seemed content with the passivity of their wives. They viewed the next five years optimistically and felt very much in control.

Among the middle-aged, the women, whose view of their main pending transition (the empty nest) was the most negative, seemed to be in a critical period—more so than any other subgroup. Their conscious stance toward the imminent departure of their youngest child was strongly associated with several other personal characteristics. Furthermore, these associations were found in four domains of their lives: circumstantial (or "givens"), interpersonal, intrapersonal, and affective. In general, brighter respondents viewed their transition either positively or negatively; the less bright viewed it with ambivalence. The relatively few who were doing any planning revealed—perhaps not surprisingly—considerable "density" in the projections of their Life Evaluation Charts, reflecting a certain degree of cognitive complexity. The planners were also more flexible in goal orientation, projecting future goals different from their current ones. Those richest in family resources, as reflected by number of familial roles, expected the fewest problems. As we have seen, the locus of the stresses and hopes of these women is in others, usually children or spouse; apparently, then, the more relatives available as objects of their attention, the less threatening the future (postparental) stage will be. Among these women, too, the sense of control over the eventualities of the postparental and retirement phases of life was closely related to feminine characteristics: those with the strongest sense of control were those who had markedly feminine concepts of themselves and who ranked high on expressivity and affect in their responses to projective material. Their concerns were primarily with interpersonal relationships; judging from their anticipated changes in goals, the objects of this concern might change, but they did not expect to shift to issues bearing on their own growth or self-realization. Thus, with the imminent departure of their youngest child, their future aims were viewed as coming to be more centered in their husbands. This conclusion is in part supported by the fact that among all the other women, who were also facing a transition, a *low* self-rating on femininity was associated with a sense of control.

These middle-aged women were also the least sure of themselves of all groups, and their uneasy and often conflicting characterizations of themselves suggest identity diffusion if not outright "crisis." The future in general looked bleak and empty to them, and the majority did not feel in control. They reported themselves to be unhappy; they reported more psychological symptoms than anyone else; and they were the most likely to say that they had at some time considered suicide. Their life styles, in the terms discussed in Chapter One, were primarily simplistic. While they had more complex social horizons than the younger women, and more altruistic goals, at the same time they felt uneasy about their ability and their motivation to realize them. Regardless of the amount of stress they had experienced, they were very preoccupied with it. Many seemed in despair about their marriages and what they sensed to be an increasing dependency in their husbands. Their hopes were largely centered in their children. The relatively few who thought they had some control over the circumstances of the next anticipated life stage took a dimmer view of it than did those women who vested control in their husbands or other external agents or circumstances.

The majority of middle-aged men, as has often been noted, viewed retirement as their next transition and viewed it more negatively than did the men who were about to retire. Since for the middle-aged the anticipated event was in the relatively distant future, it is perhaps not surprising that fewer characteristics were associated with their stance toward it than was true for those expecting to enter that stage of life very soon. Among middle-aged men, positive self-concept was the most important correlate of a favorable attitude toward retirement. In contrast, for preretirement men interpersonal relationships were most important. The importance of self-assurance for middle-aged men is perhaps attributable to the fact that their main concerns were economic, whereas the older men tended to focus on substantive changes in their life styles, involving accommodation to their wives' needs and interests.

While the pretransitional profile of the women facing the empty nest is one of not very "quiet" desperation, that of their male counterparts can best be described as stoical resignation. These conscientious heads of households scheduled themselves rigidly, had very focused, work-and-family-centered life styles, and were doing a great deal of careful financial planning. Self-righteous and defensive, they tended to feel threatened by the more relaxed styles pursued by the young—mainly, at the time of the interview, by the university activists and the dropouts, but also by their own children as well. These men often digressed in the interviews to discuss and question the motives of others—those in their own generation, as well as the young—as though to justify their own. Unlike the women at this stage, who seem to have had their social horizons somewhat broadened by their children, the middle-aged men were the most likely of all subgroups to express dismay about what seemed to them a lack of "law and order" in contemporary American life, and to bemoan social indulgence of the poor. Some freely announced that they had weapons and ammunition stored away "just in case." Their self-reports enumerated their strengths: self-reliance, industry, and conservatism. On the other hand, on measures perhaps tapping deeper levels of consciousness, they seemed apprehensive. They took by far the grimmest view of the next five years; and their need for nurturance, as gauged by their reactions on projective tests, was strong. Many who had lived stressful lives fell in the challenged category, presenting a stereotypically masculine image. These challenged men (as reported in Chapter Eight) were the most likely to have serious physical illnesses, but at the same time to protest that they were in good health. It comes as no surprise that they did not rank very high on insight.

Among women in the preretirement stage, none of the variables we examined were significantly correlated with stance toward the main transition. Half stipulated their own retirement from paid jobs as their main transition, and half emphasized their husbands' retirement. These women were the most likely to anticipate problems in the next life stage, having little sense of control and a tendency to be fatalistic about the feasibility of planning, except possibly for a trip (usually short). The main goals of these women had to do with the perpetuation of a comfortable and familiar life style. Most had gone through the critical period of the "empty nest," and they were settling for goals of good health, avoidance of stress, and meeting the needs of their increasingly dependent husbands. What they seemed to be saying was "May the next stage be no worse," and leaving it to fate or to their husbands to determine whether it would be or not.

These women, who averaged about ten years older than those facing the empty nest (fifty-eight as compared with forty-eight years old), were not as distraught as the middle-aged women. They had a more optimistic stance toward the next five years, though not necessarily toward the retirement stage per se. Those of them still having children at home (about a third) had some of the intrapersonal conflicts we found in the women facing the empty nest, but for the most part they viewed themselves with more equanimity. They could readily acknowledge that competence and independence were included in their self-concepts; and, while often discerning the increasing dependency of their husbands, as did the empty-nest women, they seemed more willing to assume the role of boss in the family. Resigned to, or rising to, their husbands' needs, they revealed more themes of consolation than of affiliation in their projections about heterosexual relationships, and fewer self-ascribed "feminine" virtues. At the same time, they had a stronger interest in personal growth and socially oriented goals and more concern with moral and philosophical values than the middle-aged women—and, for that matter, than many of the men in their own life stage. A few more of them were working than was true of the women facing the empty nest. Although most retained the lifelong family-centeredness of this middle-class sample, and few had any real satisfaction in their jobs, they did convey a sense of self-acceptance, in sharp contrast to the identity diffusion found among those ten years younger.

For the oldest men, who had a quite positive cognitive stance toward the pending transition of retirement, the imminent change was perhaps more salient. They resembled the young men in that the more intelligent were doing the most planning. Unlike both the boys and the middle-aged women, however, fewer intrapersonal and more interpersonal characteristics were related to their sense of control over the situation. Those ranking high on role scope felt most in control, and those having the highest scores on recent affective experiences in a variety of contexts expected the fewest problems. These findings tend to support the hypothesis (stated in Chapter Eight) that the adaptive potential of older men, unlike that of older women, may be strongly influenced by socializing experiences and role networks beyond the familial sphere. A strong sense of reality, of knowing one's potential as well as one's limitations, permeates the protocols of these men: "I hope to remain as active as possible. I'm looking forward to that. I know a number of things that I can do and a number of things that I can't do, so I'm going to try to do the things that I can do. . . . I'm looking forward to retirement. I think it might be a very interesting time." More mellow and relaxed than their middle-aged counterparts, men facing imminent retirement also manifested less of the self-assertiveness so notable among women in this life stage. The great majority anticipated few problems and felt very much in control of their futures, although the limited projections of their Life Evaluation Charts suggest that they might have some underlying anxiety. The scope of their activities tended to be narrow, as was true for middle-aged men, but they had fewer instrumental or material values and more investment in interpersonal relationships, enjoying their adult children and often regretting that they had not had more time with them when they were younger. Unlike their female age peers, they projected a decline in goals of personal growth and a sharp increase in goals of ease and contentment, in comparison with the middle-aged.

XII

Summary and Implications

What we hope we have accomplished in this book is to direct an adult life-course perspective to issues relating to psychosocial adaptation in adulthood. Studies across the adult life course, except in literary or case-history form, have been rare. Those that have been undertaken primarily focused on changes in personality characteristics, though the longitudinal studies conducted at the Institute of Human Development, University of California, Berkeley, have recently been broadened to include sociological dimensions (Clausen, 1972; Elder, 1974).

As we noted in the Introduction, there are a few rather global theories which might or might not be applicable to the issues we have addressed. Our position is that, at this stage of our knowledge, it would be highly premature to adopt the framework of any one of them. We are content with signs of increasing interest in a life-course perspective (Clausen, 1972; Gould, 1972; Henry, 1971; Mitscherlich and others, 1970; Neugarten, 1964; Parkes, 1971; Social Science Research Council, 1973). We see our work as one more step in providing building blocks for the study of a much longer segment of the average individual's life course than that covered by child development, a field which has had a head start of about forty years.

The four life-stage cohorts we have reported on were all drawn from a closely contained urban subcommunity, and we believe that in many ways the people in our sample epitomize mainstream Americans living in similar contexts. We chose to study them at normative pretransitional life stages because we believe such circumstances maximize the individual's awareness of his life circumstances, his cognitive and emotional processes, insight into his adaptive mechanisms—and his predisposition to discuss such matters. The findings we have reported on here thus emphasize mediating factors which influence response to environmental and situational stress.

The people in our sample were anticipating rather drastic, albeit normative, changes in their life patterns; but we believe that our findings will also be useful in the study of adaptation to more idiosyncratic changes such as divorce, widowhood or other bereavements, and major occupational and geographic dislocations or relocations. Further, our findings should be helpful in formulating, if not yet answering, the still largely neglected questions of adaptation to more gradual types of change: ecological and sociopolitical developments in the outer world and intrapsychic changes such as the individual's evolving awareness that he has become an adult, or that his children are becoming so, or that he has changed in physical appearance and stamina—in short, the more gradual and subtle processes of growing up, growing older, and, for some, becoming very old in a world which is in itself rapidly changing. We have seen in this volume that there are certain underlying commonalities— such as psychic complexity or "time focus" (whether the individual mainly locates himself in the past, present, or future in the stream of his own life). Most important, we have learned that a person's time orientation (whether he is primarily past-, present-, or future-oriented in regard to such issues as stress or values) has a dramatic effect on his sense of well-being and on physical and mental health status.

Summary

In Chapter One we found the concept of complexity especially useful in evaluating the perceptions of and involvement with the outside world among these four very family-centered life-stage cohorts. Among the youngest, the high school seniors, there was a direct relationship between complex perceptions of, and involvement in, sociopolitical issues on the one hand and participation in activities outside of the home on the other. Middle-aged women and older men with the most complex involvement in sociopolitical affairs also had more complex relationships both within and outside of the family circle, while the middle-aged men who were the most sophisticated about such issues were those least involved in their families. In the two earlier life stages, men were considerably more involved than women. Among the older cohorts, however, women were more involved than men—suggesting the possibility of greater expansiveness or complexity among women released, or about to be, from the parenting stage. The oldest cohort of men, the preretirees, were not only considerably less involved than women in the same stage but than men of all other stages—emphasizing, as some of them pointed out, a desire to avoid "hassles," which they were beginning to think they had had enough of in many areas of their lives.

The life-style typology developed in this first chapter also reflected a simplicity-complexity dimension: many of the young men were pursuing a complex style with many roles and diverse activities; the life style of the middle-aged was more narrowed and focused, centering primarily on occupational roles and activities; and a significant group of the oldest men were in the process of shedding both roles and activities. The high school girls had far more diffuse styles than the boys; more girls than boys were simplistic, and fewer were complex. This situation was reversed at the newly-wed stage, where the women were, if anything, pursuing more complex life styles than the men were. Middle-aged women were most often simplistic in style—perhaps unconsciously retooling for the postparental stage. In any event, at the preretirement stage considerably fewer women were simplistic in life style, whereas the men in general were more simplistic than the middle-aged men. In short, in terms of our admittedly "simplistic" life-style typology, at some stages men and women are highly divergent, while at others their styles tend to converge.

In Chapter Two, devoted to family issues, an underlying dimension of instrumentality versus expressiveness was helpful in tracing stage and sex variations. In describing the marital relationship, for example, the newlyweds of both sexes were prone to be concerned with personality characteristics, and especially with the emotional responsiveness of their mates. Middle-aged men and women, on the other hand, used primarily instrumental or role terms in describing each other. Preretirees of both sexes fell between these two extremes of instrumentality and expressivity. In this conservative and family-centered sample we were not surprised to find both men and women identifying the husbands as boss in the family—except for the oldest women, many of whom seemed more than ready to ascribe family dominance to themselves.

Marital dissatisfaction was greatest among the middle-aged women. Interestingly, in the stories they told about a picture depicting a heterosexual relationship, these women tended to use less expressive language than the middle-aged men; and if they saw any evidence of a happy marriage in the picture, they described the couple as older than themselves. Women in the preretirement group were prone to detect dependency needs in the pictured couple; and they, unlike the men in this group, tended to express little emotion in telling the stories they associated with the picture. The possibility of intrapsychic problems among the middle-aged women was further suggested in their reports on intergenerational relationships; compared with other groups, they described their mothers in largely negative terms, but their fathers in overwhelmingly positive ones (which stands in marked contrast to their descriptions of their husbands).

While most of the men and women in the two older groups reported conflicts with their children, the conflicts were rarely serious, usually connected with minor irritations and rarely with dissonance in goals or values. Their feelings were predominantly benign. While the men who expressed the most warmth toward their children also expressed warmth toward their wives, this was not true for the middle-aged women. (Chapter Four, on self-concept, offers some possible explanations for this difference, which we shall summarize shortly.)

That the sex of the individual rather than his or her stage in life accounts for most of the variation within our sample is well documented in the chapter on friendship (Three). Within each gender, the qualities attributed to close and to ideal friends is surprisingly constant across the four life stages, men tending to emphasize shared interests and activities, women commonly more concerned with affect and reciprocity. The men apparently wished that their friends were different, or that their own capacity for friendship were different, since they did often emphasize affect and reciprocity in discussing ideal friends. Women at all stages also tended to provide more complex descriptions of friends than men did. At the preretirement stage, however, both sexes were more likely than the younger cohorts to provide elaborate and subtle descriptions of their friends—suggesting that, with pressures of job and family easing off, these men and women had more time to develop awareness and appreciation of the unique individuality of others. The relatively simplistic descriptions of friends offered by the middle-aged women (in marked contrast to the oldest women) was yet another indication that these women facing the postparental phase of life may have been preoccupied with intrapsychic problems.

Chapter Four, on self-concept, lends further support to this thesis. A perspective across the four life stages revealed a stronger and more positive self-image among men than women; it also suggested a trend among men toward mellowness, social ease, and comfort with the self. Middle-aged women were seemingly conflicted and nearly as negative, in their images of themselves, as the high school seniors. The preretired women also showed some, though milder, evidence of conflict but were far more likely to attribute assertive and other stereotypically masculine qualities to themselves; overall, preretired women had a more positive self-image than the women confronting the empty nest.

Chapter Five, on subjective sense of well-being, identified the youngest group, especially the boys, as the least happy people in our sample; the middle-aged women ranked a close second. On a more complex measure, assessing life satisfaction, the older men ranked the highest of all eight groups. On this measure, too, the middle-aged continued to be the least satisfied of all four groups of women. In neither of the two older groups was there an association between level of social involvement and life satisfaction. On yet another subjective measure, recent affective experiences, the older groups were somewhat less complex than the young; that is, the older groups had fewer positive and negative experiences. At all stages, however, women reported a greater variety of such experiences than men. Indeed, several of the measures of adaptive level, including the affect typology developed in this chapter, provided evidence of a greater affective complexity and perhaps tolerance for the emotional ambiguities of life among women than among men.

In Chapter Six we turned to a more objective appraisal of psychological adaptation and introduced a dual model which balanced off resources against deficits and vice versa. This too may be viewed as a measure of psychic complexity, and indeed the typology essentially ranged from the psychically highly complex to the simple. In general, psychic complexity was associated with behavioral complexity. One of the most disconcerting of our findings was that while psychic complexity was strongly and positively associated with the sense of well-being among the young, the happiest people at the preretirement stage were the simple, and the unhappiest were the complex.

In the exploration of perspectives on past and future, and of attitudes toward death (Chapter Seven), we found that they did not vary by life stage as much as one might expect; for example, about as many young as older subjects were primarily oriented toward the past. The quality of these orientations differed between the generations, however—the younger focusing on particular events or circumstances, the older ranging broadly over their past lives. Time in the recent past was perceived as less "dense" by the older subjects than by the younger, though it is not clear whether this perception can be accounted for by the fact that fewer changes or events actually did take place, or whether the conception of what constitutes a change differed in the older groups.

The age to which the lifeline is extended on the Life Evaluation Chart was less among the older groups than among the young, which does not reflect actuarial projections nor does it seem to be associated with the physical condition of these—essentially healthy— older groups. Time perspective was also more salient for them. Those with the most foreshortened projections of their futures were less happy, more impaired psychiatrically, and more preoccupied with stress. Those who were primarily past-oriented reported more negative emotional experiences in the recent past, and ranked low on our measure of hope. Throughout this analysis of time ran the strong suggestion that a future orientation is a critical factor in maintaining both physical and mental health in the middle and later stages of life, whereas among the young it may be an escape from problems of the present.

In the responses to our questions about death, there were surprisingly few differences between the life stages or between the sexes. The circumstances under which thoughts of death were said to occur, however, did vary by stage of life. Older people thought of death mainly in connection with specific and personal circumstances, such as the death of a friend; younger people were likely to have death thoughts in response to general events such as accidents, earthquakes, or wars. Marriage, and especially parenthood, was reported to evoke thoughts about death which transcend the self, the concern being for the survivors. The frequency of thoughts of death was associated with psychiatric impairment. The complexity or depth of the death thoughts, however, was associated with a much larger array of characteristics, including introspection, low social involvement, and more cerebral types of behavior generally. Those with more complex thoughts were also less healthy physically, and projections of their life spans tended to be restricted.

The extent to which the past intrudes on the present is the essential theme of Chapter Eight. The number of life-course events, or stressors, reported over the prior year *declined* across successive stages in the adult life course, with a sharp drop between newlyweds and the middle-aged but only slight differences between the middle-aged and the preretirement groups. Women in all stages reported more stressful experiences than men. Work-related problems were critical for the middle-aged men, mainly having to do with lack of advancement and the pressures of assuring sufficient income to maintain a comfortable life style throughout the retirement period. Since most of these men were firmly entrenched in the probable security of civil service and related bureaucracies (indeed, most of them had selected such work primarily because of its security), and since they would not be retiring for ten to fifteen years, much of this preoccupation and anxiety undoubtedly resulted from job frustration or boredom and from economic and political factors which they perceived as beyond their control. Traumatized early by the Great Depression, these men feared another one. The mixture of strain and boredom in the middle-aged men struck us as a threat to their mental and possibly their physical health in succeeding years. To the extent that their fears prove realistic, they also seem to constitute a potentially susceptible and numerically large target group for charismatic extremist leaders.

The older men, those who confronted imminent retirement, were not as anxious about financial security or the economic system, although it should be noted that the baseline fieldwork was conducted well before the recent dramatic increase in an inflationary trend. At that time, they felt that they had accomplished whatever they could in the way of a financial base for the retirement stage and were relatively comfortable about their prospects. Their concerns focused on the development of a satisfying life style for themselves and their wives, and on ways of making the time left to them as comfortable and easy-going as possible.

But not all men in the middle-aged and preretirement stages were, respectively, anomic or philosophical in their conscious stance toward the future. Roughly one third were in the category which we called, in a stress typology developed for this study, the challenged. These men had had and continued to have considerable presumptive stress but did not dwell on it. In some ways they resembled the Type A reported by Friedman and Rosenman (1974), hard-driving, competitively ambitious men whom those authors found to be at risk of heart attack or stroke. They were intelligent and the least likely to have developed self-protective life styles. Some of them, while judged psychologically "well adapted" by the reviewing psychiatrist, were suffering from physical impairments. Paradoxically, however, their appraisals of their health status were far more optimistic than was true for those (physically healthier) men who, while also exposed to much stress, felt much freer to complain about it. The challenged men, in fact, seemed to be denying to themselves and others that they had any problems at all. One might conclude that their stress reactions were in the physical sphere, whereas those more likely to dwell on or perhaps "live through" their stresses may be of the verbal response type—distinctions also noted by Richard Lazarus in his laboratory studies of response to stress (Lazarus and Alfert, 1964).

Despite the manifest boredom with jobs and uneasiness about finances among the middle-aged men, the middle-aged women appeared considerably more stressed, although they could not clearly account for their extreme malaise and unhappiness. These women were also far more likely to report an increase in marital problems, a state of affairs not reflected in the reports of their male counterparts, nor in those of the older women. Regardless of the amount of stress to which they had been exposed, they were the most preoccupied with it of all the eight groups we studied, while the highly stressed middle-aged men were the least so.

Among men across the four adult life stages, interpersonal resources increasingly served as buffers against excessive preoccupation with the past, or with stress, and were associated with a relatively positive stance toward the future in general. The stage differences among women were less clear. For about half of the two older cohorts, the traditional resources of familial roles, familial affect, and a highly feminine self-concept were as important buffers against stress as they were for younger women; for another group, especially the better educated and more intelligent, *intra*personal factors such as a sense of competence and a positive and more masculine self-image were important psychological resources, or mediators between stress and adaptation.

These observations reinforce those based on the detailed analysis of our adaptive indicators, reported in Chapters Five and Six, namely, that the psychologically less complex, who had sought and developed self-protective, stress-avoidant life styles, were aging most contentedly. Trajectories of the more complex women went in the opposite direction from those of the majority of men, who seemed content with what they had accomplished thus far and wanted only to relax into a life style best described as dependent and comfortable, spiked now and then with a bit of hedonism (the men in the challenged category were notable exceptions).

In our study of preoccupation with stress, reported in Chapter Eight, we relied on a record of *presumably* stressful circumstances. The instrument used in Chapter Eight is based on the assumption of its developers that all life changes are stressful and, by implication, that a change that produces a positive emotional effect may be as stressful as one producing a negative one. These presumed stresses are not necessarily those that any given individual might perceive as stressful. Therefore, to assess *perceived* stress (reported in Chapter Nine), we drew on the respondents' Life Evaluation Charts rather than on a checklist of presumed stressors. In analyzing these charts and our respondents' explanations of the ups and downs in life satisfaction, we isolated three dimensions. Two of these dimensions are often ignored in the stress literature: the person who experienced the stress (self or other), which we called "person focus," and whether the stressor produced a positive or a negative change in affect. The third dimension we explored, of course, was the nature of the circumstance perceived as stressful.

The younger groups (particularly the newlyweds) reported considerably more stress in the prior ten years than the older groups did. This finding was consistent with the findings yielded by the presumptive-stress scale. The young tended to report more positive stresses, and the old reported more negative stresses; but the oldest men reversed the picture and reported more positive than negative events and circumstances. For the most part, the young dwelt on stresses, positive and negative, outside of the work and family spheres (a surprisingly high proportion of newlyweds did not mention marriage as a positive or a negative change). Work (or financial problems related thereto) was the main source of stress for middle-aged men, but much less so for preretirees. For the older women, although more than half of them were working, health issues and not work problems were most significant. Work-related problems of their husbands ranked second, and familial relationships third. In general, the stresses experienced by others were a source of stress for women and not for men, but only the two older groups; among the young, other-person focus was altogether less, and there were no significant differences between men and women. The object

of the person focus of the older women was almost invariably a
family member, children for the middle-aged, husbands for the
oldest. Deaths, interestingly enough, were a source of stress for the
young almost as frequently as for the old.

Additional sources of stress (for example, lack of change or
an increasing awareness of gradual change) which clearly require
attention in future research were also unearthed. The relativity of
the appraisal of a circumstance as stressful was also of importance;
for instance, individuals who have had life-threatening illnesses in
the past seemed to regard chronic ailments in late life as less stressful
than those who had no such yardsticks in their experience. The
timing or scheduling of a stressful circumstance also warrants more
attention than it has thus far received in the assessment of impact.

In the discussion of perceptions of continuity and discontinuity in value structure (Chapter Ten), we once again saw evidence of different timing in the trajectories of men and women. For
instance, among women it was the newlyweds who were most likely
to report value change, while among men it was the oldest group
who perceived the least continuity between their past and current
values. At all life stages people of both sexes perceived more change
between past and current values than they anticipated for the future,
but the preretirees were far more likely to anticipate future change
than those in any other life stage. Sex differences in the nature of
expected change among the two older groups again suggest opposing
trajectories, women anticipating higher evaluation of doing some
good in the outside world, men expecting to place higher valuation
on what we have called interpersonal-expressive goals.

In our examination of the relationship between current
values and life satisfaction, we were surprised to find that the very
young who valued growth goals and altruistic goals were far less
satisfied than those whose most valued goals were instrumental and
material. We conjectured that the poor morale of the former might
result from a sense of conflict with what their parents expected of
them, and perhaps with the prevailing norms of their culture as well.
We were not surprised to find that the middle-aged women who
espoused expansive goals ranked low in life satisfaction, because their
realistic prospects for achieving such goals were considerably less
than those of the high school seniors. Nor were we surprised to find

middle-aged men who espoused instrumental-material values ranking low in life satisfaction, because we had already learned how
bored and frustrated they were with their jobs and how anxious they
were about financial security. That the happiest men at preretirement are those who value ease and contentment rather than any
more expansive goals is as sad a commentary on prevailing norms as
that the growth-oriented among the very young are the most miserable.

　　While, in a sense, the entire book might be described as the
pretransitional configuration at four life stages, Chapter Eleven is
based on a culling of the complete protocols in order to assess the
salience of the pending transition in the current lives of our respondents. Because we did not wish to risk exaggeration of such salience,
we addressed no direct questions to this issue, relying instead on the
many open questions where it presumably would be brought up if
the individual considered it important. The younger groups often
mentioned several anticipated transitions, the older only one or two.
Interestingly, retirement was mentioned not only by all preretirement men but by all middle-aged men as well. In fact, for three
fifths of the later it was seen as the main transition (fewer
than a third, compared with two thirds of the middle-aged women,
mentioned the empty nest).

　　Spontaneous discussions about the main transition envisaged
had four principal dimensions: evaluation (positive or negative),
degree of planning, locus of control, and problems expected. Within
these categories we found significant differences between the sexes
only in the youngest group; there the boys were much more likely to
feel in control of, and to plan for, their next transition than were the
girls. Among men there were stage differences in the sense of internal control, with the middle-aged men least likely to feel that they
could influence the conditions and circumstances of the expected
change. Stage differences among women were found in regard to the
expectation of problems surrounding the transition—nearly half of
the high school girls expecting few, as compared with only a quarter
of the women facing the postparental period and less than a tenth
of those confronting retirement. On the other hand, at all stages,
planning was minimal and almost nonexistent among women. Since

few of them felt in control, it was clear that they were leaving
eventualities to fate or to a muddling-through process.

In overall stance, men and women in all stages professed to
view whatever transition they confronted in a favorable light; in
fact, preretirement men were nearly as positive as men in the two
youngest stages. The middle-aged of both sexes were the least
optimistic.

Intercorrelations of the four dimensions suggested that the
sense of control is the most important of the pretransitional cognitions. Correlations between the dimensions of stance toward the
transition and many other circumstances and characteristics of our
subjects revealed most associations clustering in the extremes of the
attitudinal types; the high school boys and preretirement men (in
that order) were most optimistic on all counts, and the middle-aged
women were the most pessimistic or negative. The nature of the
stance was related primarily to *intra*personal rather than interpersonal or sociostructural characteristics, and noteworthy were the
significance of intelligence and self-concept.

Changing Themes Across the Adult Life Course

An almost single-minded family-centeredness was a dominant
theme through much of this book. Parenthood was the main transition envisaged by the young; work, education, and marriage were
viewed largely as a means to that end. We did see signs of expansiveness, experimentation, and interest in personal growth among the
young men; however, judging from the life styles of the parent generation which they hoped to emulate, they will accede eventually to
the nesting inclinations (and to the possessiveness) of the young
women. The middle-aged men, for whom the joys and tribulations
of active parenting were about to be over, seemed to be mustering
all their strength to get themselves through another ten or fifteen
years on the job, so that their style of life would not have to be too
drastically altered at retirement. The women approaching the postparental stage showed signs of desperation—the more so if their
children gave any indication that they were not choosing to adopt
the parental mores and way of life. Many of these women expressed

a desire for personal growth, a wish to break out of the family confines. In a youth-obsessed society, however, they could envisage few realistic possibilities for doing so.

Under these circumstances, judging from the women who were confronting the preretirement stage, the solution seemed to be to accept the need for self-assertion and to pursue the only possibility open to them for realizing it: becoming more dominant in the family, especially in relation to their husbands but sometimes with their grown children as well. The oldest women adopted a more maternal role in the marital relationship than did the middle-aged women; thus, albeit often grudgingly, they met the increasing needs of their husbands for a domestically comfortable if not pampered existence. Both spouses hoped to punctuate an increasingly relaxed mode of living with an occasional short trip. While they attached considerable value to their anticipated freedom from responsibility, only a small portion of them expected to use such freedom to develop or pursue other commitments.

Underlying the general theme of family-centeredness at four life stages was a marked lack of role diversity among women and, among both sexes, essential boredom with occupational roles. In the face of the discontinuities in the usual course of family life, and in light of increasing societal constraints at the later stages, the need for intimacy and mutuality in dyadic relationships was especially poignant but, except among the newlyweds, rarely met.

On a number of measures—style of life, self-concept, social horizons, life-course perspectives, values and goals, affective experience, and psychological resources and deficits—we noted that our informants ranged over a rather broad continuum from the very complex to the very simplistic. The more complex were often, but not always, the more intelligent, as measured by rather simple indicators. The more intelligent, too, seemed to have adopted a way of living which exposed them to more stress, in keeping with their more complex behavioral, cognitive, and emotional predilections. Among men in particular, complexity on most measures proved adaptive at the earlier stages, at least to the extent that adaptation is assessed by measures of life satisfaction. For young women psychic complexity— on which they ranked higher than men—was, by the same measures, more adaptive than behavioral or cognitive complexity. As we moved our sights across the life course, however, we found that, in terms of life satisfaction and self-appraisals of happiness, complexity in any of these spheres was less adaptive. Among the older groups it was the simple who saw themselves as fulfilled. While on the surface these findings could be construed as support for disengagement theory (Cumming and Henry, 1961), it was clear that "intrinsic disengagement" was natural and adaptive only for the self-protective and emotionally bland. Even among them, "intrinsic disengagement" did not seem to be as apt a description as would be, for example, "a deliberate sorting out and sloughing off of unwanted responsibilities."

It was the more complex among the middle-aged women who exhibited the most acute signs of desperation—with themselves, their husbands, and their marriages. In terms of the typology introduced in Chapter Eight, the complex, highly stressed women were overwhelmed, that is, very preoccupied with stress. Among the oldest women, those in the preretirement stage, the situation was less acute. In both groups of older women, the overwhelmed reflected a continuation of the influence of parental deprivation in infancy or childhood. The life styles of these exclusively family-centered women may have perpetuated, in themselves and perhaps in their children as well, the kinds of identity problems commonly assumed to develop from such early losses. Similarly deprived men, on the other hand, having forged their identities through work and other roles extending beyond the family, tended to be in the challenged group (which in any event included few women). Among them, the depth and mutuality of interpersonal relationships proved a major resource. In their talents, their activities, their stance toward stress (including their pending transitions), and their capacity for close relationships, these men resembled the creative people studied by Barron (1963) and the self-actualizers reported by Maslow ([1954] 1970). Men of other stress types, and nearly all women except the newlyweds, in their discussions of ideal friends and in their projections about dyadic relationships in their TAT stories, revealed a pronounced longing for intimacy. At the preretirement stage, many women seemed to be sublimating any needs they may have had for reciprocity and mutuality—being, perhaps defiantly, assertive and bossy, while at the same time catering to the needs of their husbands for physical comfort. They thus sustained a kind of reversal in role reciprocity within the marriage—at the expense, perhaps, of their own development.

Implications for Research

The data and insights gained from the first phase of this study have helped to refine our initial hypotheses and research concepts, now being more fully tested in the longitudinal phase of the study, and may also prove useful to other investigators. Specifically, our method of sampling for stage of life rather than by age groups appears to have merit as a means of gaining perspective on psychosocial change in adulthood. As we had anticipated, the approach of a transition often triggers reconsideration of the past, assessment of one's assets and liabilities, and projections for the future. In the process of studying the pretransitional configuration, we have learned that idiosyncratic transitions—such as sojourns in another culture, geographic moves, serious illnesses or impairments (including mental) of self or close others, divorce, and bereavement—may also have a profound bearing on growth or regression and on adaptation or maladaptation. Retrospectively, many of our subjects reported considerable change in themselves, their values, and their behavorial patterns accompanying or following such events. Prospectively, many will have undergone additional idiosyncratic transitions in the intervals between the baseline and the later follow-up studies, and we will gain further knowledge of the import of what seem to be a variety of individualized "critical periods." Since idiosyncratic transitions are so varied and our samples relatively small, we shall be unable to quantify these data to any considerable extent. Future studies, we hope, will draw samples around such events at various stages of the adult life course, paying particular attention to sex differences and to timing. For example, widowerhood, at some life stages, appears to be considerably more traumatic than does widowhood. Serious illness in adolescence often appears conducive to growth, while in middle age or later it is more likely to be accompanied by psychological regression.

While we have found life-stage sampling useful and meaningful, our data make it abundantly clear that a cross-sequential design (Schaie and Strother, 1968) is essential if we are to determine whether, for example, the interpersonal and expressive values of the newlywed men, which were in sharp contrast to those of the middle-aged men, augur sociohistorical changes in sex roles and stereotypes, or whether they merely reflect the transient intimacies of newlyweds. We have also seen that interpersonal and expressive values were held by the oldest men, but without a cross-sequential design we cannot conclude whether this is a developmental or a "survival" factor.

In addition, we believe that we have demonstrated the richness of insights to be gained from a combination of prestructured and qualitative data (the latter, in turn, quantitatively analyzed). Quantitative assessment of open-ended material is a time-consuming and grueling task, but several important findings would have escaped us if we had not undertaken it. Among these findings are the nature of constructions, renunciations, and changes in goal and value systems; the relevance for adaptation of preoccupation with stress as well as exposure to stress; the practicality and value of a dual model of adaptation, which takes into account resources as well as deficits; and the functional dimensions of friendship. Despite its arduous nature, systematic analysis of in-depth material is, we are convinced, a very important method for detecting salient issues relating to the little-studied field of change across the adult life course. Only in this way can we locate key issues to be eventually subjected to the comparatively simpler procedures of hypothesis testing in the laboratory or in real-life situations. Furthermore, the quantification of detailed qualitative data has provided a sound empirical base for developing prestructured research instruments (such as those for the measurement of presumptive stress, of life style, and of the meaning of friendship) to be utilized in the longitudinal phase of the study.

Finally, such substantive areas as the following, we believe, hold promise for future research.

1. Further research, among lower and higher socioeconomic groups than those included here, on the relationship between adaptation and complexity (of life style, cognition, self-concept, affective and adaptive balance, and goal-value structure). Such studies would enable us further to test the validity and the extent of the univer-

sality of our finding that such complexity, in our present culture, tends to be maladaptive in the later stages of life, as indicated by lower levels of physical and mental health, morale, and life satisfaction.

2. Quantitative studies of presumptive stress, perceived stress, and preoccupation with stress, with large enough samples to explore differences across a wider range of socioeconomic groups and ethnic groups. (We have preliminary evidence that, for the young at least, ethnic and national identifications and conflicts play a critical role in relation to anticipatory adaptation to future transitions.)

3. Studies, with larger samples, of the relationship between early deprivation and adaptation at successive stages of the adult life course. Such studies would draw careful subsamples of women (including the work-committed and the noncommitted, the married with and without children, and single women). With such subsamples, investigators can more adequately test the hypothesis that family-centered women (in comparison with their male counterparts or with women who have more involvement with the outside world) are likely to continue to suffer from the psychic consequences of such early deprivation in the later stages of adult life.

4. Further operationalization of the concepts of mutuality and intimacy, which, as in our earlier studies of older subjects, have again proven decisive as buffers between life stress and adaptation. There is also a need for further testing of the significance of these concepts for adaptation in other social classes and ethnic groups than those reported on here.

5. Study of length of life-span projections as a diagnostic and predictive tool. Such a study should also include analysis of the extent to which changes in life-span projections are associated with changes in self-concept.

6. Study of the effect of the sense of continuity or discontinuity in values and goals on adaptive level of the middle-aged and elderly, with special attention to sex differences.

Implications for Public Policy

While this study represents a somewhat pioneering effort to explore the nexus between personal and social systems, it has not gone far enough. One of the most critical areas for research—if not for human survival—is how men and women of various life stages and ethnic origins *perceive* the institutions, norms, and values in the social world in which they grow up and grow old, because it is their individual perceptions that influence their behavior. In any case, it seems eminently clear from the findings of this report that a social theory bearing on the widening gap between the needs of the individual and the broader social context in which he lives can be refined by empirical data. We shall here focus primarily on the persons who will be, to use Neugarten's (1974) distinctions, "young-old" and "old-old" in fifteen years or so, and whose dilemmas are also relevant to the young, since they will presumably go through these stages not long after the turn of the century. Whether cohorts in these life stages increase or decrease in the proportion of the total population they represent, medical and actuarial knowledge suggests that half or more of the cohort to which our middle-aged and preretirement groups belong will survive into the 1990s, and a few of the women, perhaps, beyond the year 2000. As these people summarize their own anticipations of the future, they reveal some of the lacunae between individual needs, on the one hand, and social institutions and prevailing value systems on the other. In many sectors, the widening gaps threaten to produce not only an unconscionable waste of social resources but a large population at risk from both mental and physical health perspectives. For the growing cohorts of people now in relatively good health and facing an unprecedented fifteen to thirty years of the postparental and retirement periods, the times are seriously out of joint.

That these people and the many like them in the population are not likely to have much political impact on issues vital to them now or in the future is a conclusion based on their lagging interest in any social and political problems beyond those relating directly to their economic welfare and their safety in the streets. They professed doubts about the efficacy of any conceivable role for people like themselves, even at the community level. It should be borne in mind that they reported their suspicions about politics and political figures on the local, state, national, and international levels before Watergate and the "energy crisis" intensified political apathy among voters of all ages and classes across the country. Although we cannot confirm our thesis until the longitudinal data are in, we predict that the impact of these events, on our two older groups especially, will prove to be profound and traumatic. In concluding that these cohorts of middle-aged and late-middle-aged people are not likely to do much about improving their possibilities for a satisfying and productive postparental stage themselves, we are of course agreeing with Maddox (1974) and others who consider a gerontocracy in Western civilization to be an unlikely possibility.

This study was at the outset designed in part to test the rather optimistic self-actualization concepts of such theorists as Allport, Maslow, Erikson, Bühler, and Fromm—concepts largely evolved from studies of talented and privileged individuals. People in our sample, however, are in that increasingly mixed (blue- and white-collar) segment which may in part be beginning to assimilate values of professional and artistic elites but remain primarily job- and family-oriented. The dominance of these concerns became apparent when we inspected the nature of what they considered stressful when they adopted a life-course perspective, both retrospective and prospective. In general, the sheer volume of events and circumstances so perceived declined across the four stages, with a sharp demarcation between newlyweds and the middle-aged and only slight differences between the middle-aged confronting the postparental stage and those about ten years older, who were facing imminent retirement. Women at all stages reported more stress than men.

On nearly all counts, middle-aged women confronting the postparental period were more clearly in a critical period than were their male counterparts. The older women were, on most measures of adaptation, considerably better off. At the same time, they reported a curious mixture of positive and negative self-concepts, as though they were having role conflicts, and were almost as diffuse about what they might actually do outside of the home as were the younger. Their motivations seemed stronger, but realistic planning was blocked—perhaps as much by their husbands' needs and demands as by social strictures and a deficiency of perceived options outside the world of the family.

We noted among men an increase across the four stages in the importance of interpersonal characteristics as mitigating factors against stress and, conversely, as resources associated with a relatively positive orientation toward their most important future transition and the future in general. The resources of women were less clear. For about half of them, familial roles, emotional involvement with family, and feminine self-concept were important at all four stages. For others intrapersonal characteristics, such as competence and a more positive self-image, were significant mediators between stress and adaptation.

The differences between the middle-aged and the preretirement women, together with the signs of identity diffusion among the former, suggest the possibility of a developmental crisis in the cohort of women facing the postparental stage. There is some support for Freud's thesis ([1933] 1965) that they may be working through a resurgence of oedipal problems. Those who more or less succeed in doing so become free to shift roles and—were educational and occupational channels open—to make an active contribution to society. Their frustrations resembled those of the challenged men, and presumably their potential life-course trajectories might be similar were they not confronted with sociostructural roadblocks. The realistic problems of these women reinforce our conclusion that the psychologically simplistic, who have sought and developed self-protective, stress-avoidant life styles, are likely to age most comfortably in our present culture. Trajectories of many such women in their late fifties were in opposite directions from those of the less gifted and more stress-avoidant men, who seemed content with what they had already accomplished, who primarily wanted to relax into a life style best described as an admixture of ease and contentment. Among these older (perhaps newly ambitious) women, those who are married to men of this stress-avoidant type will probably find their role conflicts resolved—or, more likely, suppressed—as the need for nurturance on the part of their husbands supplants that of the departed children. These are the women whose husbands will begin to complain (as some already are complaining) about their wives' becoming too bossy, and whose children may complain about interference.

This state of affairs among the challenged men and the more enterprising women is not only a waste of human resources from a social point of view but threatens misery on the familial level as well. The mellowed wisdom to be transmitted to the younger generation,

which represents the ideal later life stage as postulated by the
theorists of self-actualization, is not likely to emanate from such
cohorts. Among older men, the less gifted may well be the most
likely to survive, and a notable segment of women are essentially
frustrated in what appear to be developmental needs by social and
economic constraints and the traditional sex-role stereotypes espoused
by society (as well as by many, if not all, of their husbands). While
the great majority of these people were in very good or moderately
good health at the time of our interviews with them, many were
almost obsessively preoccupied with health-related issues, perhaps
for sheer lack of other outlets.

The policy and planning implications of this waste of potential of mature women, as well as of that of "self-actualizing" and
often gifted men ready for second careers or other types of commitments, are self-evident. But the mere offering of educational opportunities and preventive mental health programs to these cohorts who
have already entered the later stages of life is not likely to alleviate
the situation very much. Indeed, many would not know how to go
about researching the options even if many were available and they
themselves were powerfully motivated. What is needed is a life-
course orientation in all of our social, educational, and economic
institutions, one which will have its impact on adolescents and
young adults, so that, when they approach the twenty- or thirty-
year postparental stage, they will not be forced to project as empty
a future as do most people who now make up the postparental and
retirement cohorts.

In spite of reports from women's liberation groups and prevailing observations about secular changes in sex roles and in attitudes toward aging, we saw few signs of such phenomena among our
adolescents and young adults, who indeed most likely represent the
majority of their age peers. The present and projected life styles of
these young people of both sexes were family-centered and male
dominant. As though reflecting on their parents' prospects, their
hopes for themselves at postparental and retirement stages amounted
to little more than financial security, a modicum of comfort, and
freedom from occupational and parental responsibilities.

On the other hand, one does detect a difference among a
substantial proportion of college and university students (regardless

of their socioeconomic background). It is especially notable among those at the graduate level in academic and professional settings (whom we have an opportunity to observe, although they do not comprise a significant segment of our sample). It is they who seem to be making innovative changes in traditional sex roles and who also are giving thought to later stages of adulthood. Some are beginning to demand that a life-course perspective be introduced not only in the social science curricula but in professional schools as well. There is some encouraging evidence that their interests are beginning to be attended by the educational establishment itself. One or two medical schools, for example, now require life-span-oriented courses for their students. And Albert Bandura, current president of the American Psychological Association, has recently noted: "As the composition of our population undergoes further changes, lifelong learning is likely to take precedence over degree-seeking in a pre-scribed period of study" (1974, p. 2).

Such trends bode well for the possibilities of a society in which those beyond the so-called prime of life are integrated within its vital institutions rather than withdrawn to the tranquilizing or escapist consolations of television, or segregated in housing develop-ments and institutions limited to their own age groups. Until this developmental change takes place in our social institutions, we must hasten to provide some temporary stopgaps. These might include well-advertised educational programs for the middle-aged and the elderly, not excluding ethnic minorities and the poor, and serious exploration of the possibilities of a voluntary (instead of mandatory) retirement age. Further, in service organizations, business, industry, and the civil service, training facilities might be developed, so that middle-aged men and women on all occupational levels can prepare for a second career if they so wish. And, perhaps most important, industry and the mass media might conduct a campaign to combat the predilection for youth. Otherwise, we may well soon find our-selves with an increasing proportion of frustrated, self-deprecating, or even self-hating late-middle-aged and older people whose personal way out of their dilemmas may be to adopt the sick role, thus wreaking a legitimate if not deliberate revenge on a society that has denied them any challenging alternatives.

Interview Schedule
and Description of
Structured Instruments

The interview schedule consisted of a focused interview (Merton, Fiske [Lowenthal], and Kendall, [1948] 1956), intended to elicit the respondent's own frame of reference and subjective perspectives, and several structured instruments. Interviews took an average of eight and a half hours, usually divided into three sessions. Most interviews were conducted in the homes of the respondents. Interviewer and respondent usually found privacy alone, but occasionally some parts of the interview were conducted with another family member present.

Sections of the interview guide were as follows:

I. *Demographic and Sociostructural Data.* Structured and semistructured questions dealing with such standard variables as ethnic identity, religious affiliation, education, economic and occupational status, work history, geographic mobility, and basic socio-demographic data on families of origin and procreation.

II. *Health History.* (1) Structured questions designed to elicit basic information on subject's past and present physical and emotional status and the history of physical and emotional illness of immediate family members; (2) a forty-two-item Symptoms Checklist.

III. *Behavioral Domain.* (1) Open-ended questions designed to elicit the patterning of daily, weekly, and yearly activities and the problems, satisfactions, and meanings attached to these activities; (2) a thirty-three-item Checklist of Activities.

IV. *Values and Goals Domain.* (1) Open-ended questions dealing with past, present, and future values and goals, determinants of goal choice, perceived supports and hindrances to goal attainment, and implementation of goals and outcome; (2) a seven-item value card sort.

V. *Family, Social Networks, and Social Perceptions.* Open-ended questions focused on relationships with members of family of origin and procreation; dating experiences and events preceding marriage; attitudes toward sex and sexual experience; friendship patterns; organizational membership and participation; and perceptions of neighborhood, social groups, and local and national problems and issues.

VI. *Evaluation of Life.* (1) Open-ended questions dealing with the timing, nature, and evaluation of past life events and transitions, including experience with death and modes of coping with loss, anticipated future events and changes, and perceptions of the best and worst periods of the life course; (2) a Life Evaluation Chart (see text, Figure 2), on which subjects rated each year of past and future life on a nine-point scale of satisfaction/dissatisfaction. (This chart is an adaptation of one developed by Jean MacFarlane of the Institute of Human Development, University of California, Berkeley.)

VII. *Psychological Domain.* Structured instruments and tests including (1) Bradburn Morale Scales (Bradburn and Caplovitz, 1965); (2) projective tests consisting of Murray (1943) Thematic Apperception cards (1, 2, 3GF, 7BM, 8BM, 10, 11, 17BM, 19, and 20) and Kansas City card (Neugarten and Gutmann, 1964);

(3) WAIS Vocabulary and Block Design subtests (Wechsler, 1955);
and (4) Adjective Rating List of personality traits derived from
Block's Modified Q Sort for Nonprofessional Sorters (Block, 1961).

VIII. *Interview Experience.* (1) Subjects were asked about
their feelings about the interview experience; (2) interviewers rated
subjects on two scales designed to assess overall interview behavior
and reaction to various sections of the interview, and also on the
Adjective Rating List; in addition, interviewers wrote a narrative
account of the interview and their impressions of and personal attitude toward subjects.

✂︎✂︎ Appendix B ✂︎✂︎

Scales, Typologies, Ratings, Derived Variables

✂︎ ✂︎ ✂︎ ✂︎ ✂︎ ✂︎ ✂︎ ✂︎

Accommodation, Judged (adaptive rating). A judgment of the degree to which the respondent accommodates others. Anchor points include "primarily accommodates others" and "primarily behaves in a way that disregards the needs of others." A four-point rating, with higher scores indicating greater accommodation. (Compare with Accommodation, Perceived.)

Accommodation, Perceived (adaptive rating). A rating, based on the entire protocol, of accommodation as perceived by the respondent. The scale points include "primarily accommodates others," "tends to accommodate others," "tends to disregard the needs, interests, and demands of others," and "primarily behaves in a way that disregards the needs of others." A four-point scale, with higher scores indicating greater accommodation. (Compare with Accommodation, Judged.)

Activity Scope. Each activity listed in the thirty-three-item Checklist of Activities was coded from 0 (representing no participation) to 3 (representing "frequent" participation). Ratings were summed and divided by the number of activities possible (33).

Activity Types. Respondents were asked to list their regular or scheduled activities; they were also asked to list what they did "yesterday." The number of mentions of activities falling in the seven categories used for value types (see Value Types) was recorded. A residual category, nongoal-directed activity, which indicated routine maintenance activities such as getting up, eating, bathing, and so on, was used.

Adaptive-Balance Typology. Psychological resources (see below) and psychological deficits (see below) were trichotomized and respondents cast into the resulting ninefold table. Individuals in the top third for both resources and deficits were called "complex"; those in the bottom third on both were called "simple."

Adaptive Ratings. Two sociologists, an anthropologist, a psychoanalyst, a psychologist, and a human developmentalist rated each of the respondents on fifteen characteristics which had been selected and defined for this purpose in a series of seminars. The resource characteristics are familial mutuality, extrafamilial mutuality, contextual perspective, life-cycle perspective, growth, intrapersonal competence, insight, perceived accommodations, judged accommodation, hope, resolution of losses, satisfaction with intrapersonal competence, satisfaction with interpersonal competence, and satisfaction with self. The deficit characteristics are degree of psychological impairment and direction of impairment. (For descriptions of each of these items, see the separate alphabetical listings in this Appendix.)

Adjective Rating List (Block, 1961). Seventy adjectives were coded 0 if the respondent indicated that the description was like him, 2 if the description was unlike him, and 1 if the description was not characteristic one way or the other. Respondents were also asked to indicate the descriptions that were unlike them but that they wished *were* like them and the descriptions that were like them but that they wished were *not*.

Affect-Balance Score. Following the example of Bradburn (1969), we computed an affect-balance score by subtracting a negative-affect score (see below) from a positive-affect score (see below). The scores in Table 8 have had a constant of 13 added in order to make all scores positive.)

Affect Toward Spouse. A three-point rating of general affect toward spouse. See Familial-Affect Summary Scores.

Affect Typology. The frequency distributions for the Bradburn positive and negative emotions (see Affect-Balance Score, above) were dichotomized at the median and respondents cast into the resulting fourfold table. Respondents falling above the median on both positive and negative emotions were called the "volatile," those below the median on both emotions the "bland," those high on positive emotions and low on negative the "exultant," and those low on positive and high on negative the "beset."

Affiliation. The proportion of changes in the Life Evaluation Chart (see text, Figure 2) which were attributed to events in the lives of people other than the respondent.

Bradburn Overall Happiness. The subject's response to the question "Taking all things together, how would you say things are these days—would you say you are very happy, pretty happy, or not too happy?"

Competence. See Intrapersonal Competence.

Complexity of Death Thoughts. A rating of responses to the question "Do you ever find yourself thinking of death and dying?" Anchor points are "superficial," "average," and "complex."

Contextual Perspective (adaptive rating). A rating, based on the entire protocol, of the respondent's ability to see himself and his life in perspective. Anchor points range from "broad perspective" to "very restricted perspective."

Cumulative Stress. See Presumed Stress.

Degree of Psychological Impairment (adaptive rating). A global assessment of current psychological status based on the entire protocol except for the Symptoms Checklist. The scale, from 1 through 13, includes anchor points of "minimal," "mild," "moderate," and "severe."

Density of the Future. The number of anticipated changes indicated on the Life Evaluation Chart (see text, Figure 2).

Density of the Past. The number of changes in the Life Evaluation Chart up to the present.

Direction of Psychological Impairment (adaptive rating). A global assessment of trends in the degree of psychological impairment. The rating is based on the entire protocol except for the Symptoms Checklist. The scale, which ranges from 1 through 9, includes "decreasing impairment," "stabilized," and "increasing impairment."

Ego Diffusion. From the Adjective Rating List, the number of traits the respondent indicated that he "cannot decide" are like himself or not.

Extrafamilial Mutuality (adaptive rating). A mutuality rating (see Familial Mutuality) based on respondent's description of relationships with people who were not considered part of his extended family.

Extrafamilial Roles. The number of the following roles the respondent had at the time of the interview: friend, neighbor, church member, organization member.

Familial-Affect Summary Scores. Respondents were asked a series of questions aimed at eliciting feelings toward their families. Answers were rated as mostly positive, mostly negative, or neutral or ambivalent with regard to father, mother, siblings, spouse, and children, if any.

Familial Mutuality (adaptive rating). Mutuality was defined as the capacity for relationships characterized by respect, trust, support, empathy, responsibility, and interdependence. The anchor points of the thirteen-point scale include "has genuine understanding of others and of self; lack of self-centeredness; capacity for close and shared relationships" and "absence of mutuality, trusting, respecting relationships; relationships may have exploitative, parasitic, or paranoid overtones." The rating of familial mutuality is based on respondent's description of relationships with individuals whom the respondent considers part of his extended family.

Familial Roles. The number of the following roles the respondent had at the time of the interview: spouse, parent, grandparent, sibling, child, grandchild.

Feminine Self-Concept. See Femininity Index.

Femininity Index. There were a number of adjectives in the Adjective Rating List which significantly distinguished women from men. The Femininity Index is the number of such adjectives characteristic of women which the respondent felt described himself or herself.

Frequency of Death Thoughts. A rating (from "never or seldom" to "often") of the frequency with which the respondent thought of death. (Compare with Complexity of Death Thoughts.)

Friendship Complexity. The number of different attributes used in describing what was important to the respondent about his friends.

Goal Sort. See Value Sort.

Gottschalk Anxiety Score. From the TAT.

Gottschalk Hostility Score. From the TAT.

Growth (adaptive rating). A rating, based on the entire protocol, of the capacity for growth and renewal. An individual who has this capacity shows a propensity to seek out new areas of self-expression, productivity, and relatedness; he finds meaning and pleasure in the application and improvement of skills and abilities; he shows readiness to acquire new roles as well as the ability to modify old ones. Individuals with the capacity for growth and renewal may be further characterized by curiosity, openness to experimentation, and some tolerance for ambiguity. They are alert to and keep pace with changes in the sociocultural environment. The anchor points include "seeks out new experiences," "open to new experiences," "resists new experiences," and "refuses new experiences." The scale ranges from 1 through 13.

Hope (adaptive rating). Hope, defined as the feeling that what is desired is also possible, was rated on a thirteen-point scale in terms of expectations for the ten years following the interview.

Horizons Complexity. See Social-Horizons Complexity.

Immediate Goal. A judgment of the respondent's most immediate and salient goal in life, based on a series of questions about present plans, goals, and concerns. Coded in the same categories as used in the value types (see below).

Insight (adaptive rating). Anchor points for this rating include "keen awareness of own strengths, weaknesses, conflicts, effect on others; insightful about all salient aspects of self," "moderate self-awareness; while insight may not be profound, there are no discernible distortions," "little self-awareness," and "no self-aware-

ness; realistic assessments limited to superficial aspects of self."
The scale ranges from 1 through 13.

Intrapersonal Competence (adaptive rating). A rating, based on
the entire protocol, of the respondent's degree of competence (defined as the capacity, fitness, or ability to carry on those transactions with the environment which result in the respondent's
maintaining himself, growing, and flourishing). The anchor
points include "high degree of competence in organization and
performance in work and nonwork spheres," "moderate," "somewhat inept," and "very inept." The scale ranges from 1 through
13.

Involvement with Family of Procreation. See Procreation-Family
Involvement.

Life Career Styles. See Life-Style Typology.

Life-Cycle Perspective (adaptive rating). An individual with a developed life-cycle perspective has a sense of personal biography, of
continuity with his past self, and draws on past experience when
scanning or planning for the future. In general terms, such an
individual has an overview of his entire life span. The rating is
based on the entire protocol, and the anchor points on the
thirteen-point scale are "broad perspective," "fair perspective,"
"limited," and "very restricted."

Life Satisfaction Index. A weighted combination of the codes for
"dissatisfied" and "unhappy" on the Adjective Rating List, self-
report on overall happiness, and self-report for the present year on
the Life Evaluation Chart (see text, Figure 2). Scores range from
10 to 36, with higher numbers indicating higher satisfaction and
greater happiness.

Life-Style Typology. From the Checklist of Activities, the distribution
of the number of activities plus political activity (dichotomized)
was dichotomized at the median; role scope (see below) was also
dichotomized at the median. Respondents were cast into the resulting fourfold table. Respondents above the median on both
roles and activities were called "complex"; those low on both
were called "simplistic." Respondents above the median on activities and below the median on roles were called "intense," and
those below the median on activities and above on roles were
called "diffuse."

Masculine Self-Concept. See Masculinity Index.

Masculinity Index. The number of adjectives characteristic of men which the respondent felt characterized himself or herself. (See also Femininity Index.)

Mutuality. The sum of the codes for the adjectives *considerate, co-operative, friendly, likeable, sincere, sympathetic,* and *warm* from the Adjective Rating List.

Negative-Affect Score. The sum of the ratings for the items "very lonely," "depressed," "bored," and "restless," where each was coded 1 for "not felt during past week," 2 for "felt once during past week," 3 for "felt several times during past week," and 4 for "felt often during past week." (Compare with Positive-Affect Score.)

Negative Self-Concept. From the Adjective Rating List, the number of the following traits attributed by the respondent to himself: absentminded, affected, cruel, defensive, dissatisfied, dull, easily embarrassed, easily hurt, hostile, impulsive, jealous, lazy, rebellious, resentful, restless, unhappy, uninterested, unworthy, withdrawn, worried. These traits were identified in a principal components analysis and had loadings of .30 or higher. (Compare with Positive Self-Concept.)

Occupational Roles. The number of the following roles the respondent had at the time of the interview: employee/employer, student.

Overall Happiness. See Bradburn Overall Happiness.

Overall Value Discrepancy. See Value Discrepancy.

Perceived Stress. A rating of the respondent's perception of the presence of loss in his life as it appears in the "Evaluation of Life" section of the protocol. The concept of loss is broadly defined. It includes prolonged separation from a love object; loss of a source of self-esteem; disillusionment about the worth of an idea, a person, or an institution; disruption of a life style or the enforced abandonment of a goal; or a state of deprivation resulting from the perceived lack of adequate and appropriate interpersonal and/or environmental experiences. The anchor points on the nine-point rating scale include "The mention of loss is a theme in the respondent's evaluation of his past life," "Some significant loss is mentioned by the respondent in his past life, but it is not thematic in his presentation," and "Loss is not present or is only incidentally mentioned in his evaluation of past life."

Physical Problems. A summary measure based on the health section of the interview schedule. Categories are "has health problem which affects behavior," "has health problem which does not affect behavior," and "no health problem."

Positive-Affect Score. The sum of the ratings for the items "feeling on top of the world," "excited or interested," "pleased about an accomplishment," and "proud," where each was coded 1 for "not felt during past week," 2 for "felt once during past week," 3 for "felt several times during past week," and 4 for "felt often during past week." (Compare with Negative-Affect Score.)

Positive Self-Concept. From the Adjective Rating List, the number of the following traits attributed by the respondent to himself: calm, confident, cooperative, energetic, fair-minded, friendly, intelligent, likeable, reasonable, poised, self-controlled, wise. These traits were identified in a principal components analysis and had loadings of .30 or higher. (Compare with Negative Self-Concept.)

Preoccupation with Stress. See Perceived Stress.

Presumed Stress. The number of stressful events occurring in the respondent's lifetime as judged on the basis of the entire protocol. A ninety-four-item modification of the Holmes and Rahe (1967) Social Readjustment Rating Scale was used as a checklist.

Procreation-Family Involvement. Familial-affect summary scores (see above) averaged over spouse and children.

Prospective Value Discrepancy. See Value Discrepancy.

Psychiatric Rating. A seventeen-point rating by a psychiatric resident on the seriousness of the constellation of psychological symptoms presented in the Symptoms Checklist.

Psychological Deficits. A composite index based on self-assessment of psychological problems, psychiatrist's rating of symptoms, Gottschalk anxiety score and Gottschalk hostility score (from the TAT), self-criticism (from the Adjective Rating List), staff rating of degree of impairment, and staff rating of predicted outcome of impairment.

Psychological Resources. A composite index based on staff ratings of contextual perspective, life-cycle perspective, intrapersonal competence, insight, satisfaction with intrapersonal competence, satisfaction with interpersonal competence, self-satisfaction, perceived and judged accommodation, growth, hope, familial and extrafamilial mutuality, and on the WAIS Vocabulary and Block Design scores.

Psychological Symptoms. The number of psychological symptoms which were rated "mild," "moderate," or "severe" on the Symptoms Checklist.

Respondent-Interviewer Agreement Score. The correlation between the respondent's description of himself on the Adjective Rating List and the interviewer's description of the respondent on the Adjective Rating List.

Retrospective Value Discrepancy. See Value Discrepancy.

Role Scope. The number of the following roles the respondent had at the time of the interview: spouse, parent, grandparent, sibling, child, grandchild, friend, neighbor, churchgoer, organization member, employee/employer, student.

Satisfaction with Interpersonal Competence (adaptive rating). A rating, based on the entire protocol, of the degree to which the respondent is satisfied with his or her interpersonal competence. The scale includes "very satisfied," "somewhat satisfied," "somewhat dissatisfied," and "dissatisfied," and ranges from 1 through 13.

Satisfaction with Intrapersonal Competence (adaptive rating). A rating, based on the entire protocol, of the degree to which the respondent is satisfied with his own competence. The scale includes "very satisfied," "somewhat satisfied," "somewhat dissatisfied," and "dissatisfied," and ranges from 1 through 13.

Satisfaction with Self (adaptive rating). A rating, based on the entire protocol, of the degree to which the respondent is satisfied with himself. The scale includes "very satisfied" (which does not necessarily indicate smugness), "somewhat satisfied," "somewhat dissatisfied," and "dissatisfied," and ranges from 1 through 13.

Self-Criticism. The number of characteristics the respondent indicated were true of himself but wished he did not have (see Adjective Rating List).

Self-Diffusion. See Ego Diffusion.

Social-Horizons Complexity. Respondents were asked what they thought were the major social problems and issues. They were asked which of the problems and issues they were personally most concerned with and what they were doing or planned to do about the issue or problem. They were asked whether their concern for social issues had changed recently and, if so, why. Social-horizons complexity is the sum of the ways each individual felt his life was affected by the issues and the problems mentioned, the number of solutions envisioned, the number of actions he had taken or planned to take, and the number of reasons he presented for his own change in concern about social conditions.

Social-Role Involvement. The following roles weighted by frequency of participation or contact: spouse, child, parent, friend, grandparent, sibling, organization member.

Socioeconomic Status. A composite of occupation, coded according to Bogue (1963); education; and income. High school students were assigned the status of their fathers; nonworking women were assigned the status of their husbands.

Stress Typology. Perceived stress (see above) and presumed stress (see above) were dichotomized, and individuals were classified on the resulting fourfold table. Individuals with frequent or severe presumptive stress and thematic (perceived) stress were called "overwhelmed," those with severe presumptive stress and no thematic stress were called "challenged," those with little presumptive stress and themes of loss were called "self-defeated," and those with little presumptive stress and little preoccupation with stress were called "lucky."

TAT Affect. A four-point rating of the intensity of feelings expressed in the TAT stories. The rating ranges from "absent" (no explicit or implicit indication of feelings) to "high" (much attention to feelings; seeks to bring out nuances of feelings).

Temporal Perspective. See Life-Cycle Perspective.

Thematic Stress. See Perceived Stress.

Time Extension. From the Life Evaluation Chart (see text, Figure 2), the number of years the respondent projected his predictions into the future.

Time Orientation. Based on the question "Do you tend to think

more about the past or the future?" Responses were coded "past,"
"past-present," "present," "present-future," "future," and "all."

Total Role Scope. See Role Scope.

Value Discrepancy. Measures designed to assess changes in values
were derived from the value sorts (see below) for past, present,
and future. Retrospective value consistency (between past and
present) was defined as the rank correlation coefficient between
the value sorts for past and present; prospective value consistency
(between present and future) was the correlation between value
sorts for present and future. Value discrepancy was defined as
(1–rho) in each case. Overall value discrepancy was defined as
the mean of retrospective discrepancy and prospective discrepancy.

Value Sort. Respondents were asked to rank seven different types of
goals (see Value Types) for their importance at the time of the
interview, at the time when respondents were eighteen years old,
and ten years in the future. (See also Value Summary Score.)

Value Summary Score. Respondents were asked questions directed
toward eliciting their values and goals. A tally was added for each
of the value types (see above) for each time it was given as the
first or second goal in the value sort (see above); as the first or
second want out of life; as an objective for the next five years;
as an immediate objective; or as the main task in life. Each respondent thus had a score ranging from 0 to 5 for each of the
seven values.

Value Types. Include: (a) instrumental (economic or occupation
productivity or achievement, social status, household chores); (b)
interpersonal-expressive (intimacy, friendship, and sociability);
(c) philosophical-religious (religious or spiritual activity, concern
with the meaning of existence, adherence to an ethical or behavioral code); (d) social service (helping others, community
service); (e) ease-contentment (simple comforts, security, relaxa-
tion); (f) hedonistic; (g) personal growth.

Appendix C

Variables Examined in Relation to Stance Toward Transitions

Circumstantial Variables
  WAIS: Vocabulary
  WAIS: Block Design
  WAIS: total
  Religion
  Education
  Socioeconomic status*
Interpersonal Variables
  Familial role scope
  Role scope
  Frequency of religious
    participation*
  Involvement with family of
    procreation*
  Friendship complexity

Familial mutuality
Extrafamilial mutuality*
Activity scope
Affect toward spouse*
Intrapersonal Variables
  Social-horizons Complexity
  Subjective sense of religion
    (religiosity)*
  Positive self-concept
  Negative self-concept
  Feminine self-concept
  Masculine self-concept
  Ego diffusion
  Self-criticism
  Long time extension*

261

Frequency of death thoughts
Complexity of death thoughts[a]
Density of past time
Density of future time
Time orientation (past-present-future)
Immediate goal[a]
Retrospective value discrepancy
Prospective value discrepancy
Overall value discrepancy
Intrapersonal-competence rating

Affective Variables
Life satisfaction
Affect balance
Overall happiness[a]
TAT affect
Adaptive Variables
General adaptive rating
Psychiatric rating
Psychological symptoms
Physical symptoms
Stress type

[a] Not significantly related to stance toward the transition.

Bibliography

ADAMS, B. N. *Kinship in an Urban Setting*. Chicago: Markham, 1968.

AISENBERG, R. "What Happens to Old Psychologists? A Preliminary Report." In R. Kastenbaum (Ed.), *New Thoughts on Old Age*. New York: Springer, 1964. Pp. 116–135.

ALLPORT, G. W. *Pattern and Growth in Personality*. New York: Holt, [1937] 1961.

ANGYAL, A. *Neurosis and Treatment: A Holistic Theory* (edited by E. Hanfmann and R. M. Jones). New York: Wiley, 1965.

BABCHUK, N. "Primary Friends and Kin: A Study of the Associations of Middle Class Couples." *Social Forces*, May 1965, *43*, 483–493.

BACK, K. W. "Transition to Aging and the Self-Image." *Aging and Human Development*, Nov. 1971, 2, 296–304

BALTES, P. B. "Longitudinal and Cross-Sectional Sequences in the Study of Age and Generation Effects." *Human Development*, 1968, *11*(3), 145–171.

BANDURA, A. Editorial. *APA Monitor*, Feb. 1974, *5*, 2.

BARRON, F. *Creativity and Psychological Health*. Princeton, N. J.: Van Nostrand, 1963.

BECKER, H., AND STRAUSS, A. "Careers, Personality, and Adult Social-

263

ization." In B. L. Neugarten (Ed.), *Middle Age and Aging.* Chicago: University of Chicago Press, 1968. Pp. 311–320.

BEISER, M. "A Study of Personality Assets in a Rural Community." *Archives of General Psychiatry,* March 1971, *24,* 244–254.

BENGTSON, V. L. "Differences Between Sub-Samples in Level of Present Role Activity." In R. J. Havighurst and others (Eds.), *Adjustment to Retirement: A Cross-National Study.* Assen, Netherlands: Van Gorkum, 1969.

BENGTSON, V. L. "Inter-Age Perceptions and the Generation Gap." *The Gerontologist,* 1971, *11*(4), Part 2, 85–89.

BENGTSON, V. L., CHIRIBOGA, D. A., AND KELLER, A. C. "Occupational Differences in Retirement: Patterns of Role Activity and Life-Outlook Among Chicago Retired Teachers and Steelworkers." In R. J. Havighurst and others (Eds.), *Adjustment to Retirement: A Cross-National Study.* Assen, Netherlands: Van Gorkum, 1969.

BENGTSON, V. L., AND KUYPERS, J. A. "Generational Difference and the Development Stake." *Aging and Human Development,* Nov. 1971, *2,* 249–260.

BERGER, P. L., AND BERGER, B. "The Blueing of America." *Intellectual Digest,* Sept. 1971, *2,* 25–27.

BIRREN, J., AND OTHERS. (Eds.) *Human Aging: A Biological and Behavioral Study.* Public Health Service Bulletin 986. Washington, D. C.: U. S. Government Printing Office, 1963.

BLAU, Z. S. "Structural Constraints on Friendships in Old Age." *American Sociological Review,* June 1961, *26,* 429–439.

BLAU, Z. S. *Old Age in a Changing Society.* New York: Franklin Watts, 1973.

BLOCK, J. *The Q-Sort Method in Personality Assessment and Psychiatric Research.* Springfield, Ill.: Thomas, 1961.

BLOCK, J. *Lives Through Time.* Berkeley: Bancroft, 1971.

BLOCK, J. H., HAAN, N., AND SMITH, M. B. "Socialization Correlates of Student Activism." *Journal of Social Issues,* Autumn 1969, *25,* 143–177.

BLOOD, R. O., JR., AND WOLFE, D. M. *Husbands and Wives: The Dynamics of Married Living.* New York: Free Press, 1960.

BOGUE, D. J. *Skid Row in American Cities.* Chicago: Community and Family Study Center, University of Chicago, 1963.

BOHANNAN, P. "Dyad Dominance and Household Maintenance." In F. L. K. Hsu (Ed.), *Kinship and Culture.* Chicago: Aldine, 1971. Pp. 43–65.

BOHANNAN, P. "Before Divorce: Some Comments About Alienation in Marriage." In L. Nader and T. W. Maretzki (Eds.), *Cultural Illness and Health: Essays in Human Adaptation*. Anthropological Studies 9. Washington, D.C.: American Anthropological Association, 1973. Pp. 43–55.

BOOTH, A. "Sex and Social Participation." *American Sociological Review*, April 1972, *37*, 183–192.

BORTNER, R. W., AND HULTSCH, D. F. "Personal Time Perspective in Adulthood." *Developmental Psychology*, Sept. 1972, *7*, 98–103.

BRADBURN, N. M. *The Structure of Psychological Well-Being*. Chicago: Aldine, 1969.

BRADBURN, N. M., AND CAPLOVITZ, D. *Reports on Happiness: A Pilot Study of Behavior Related to Mental Health*. Chicago: Aldine, 1965.

BRIM, O. G., JR. "Socialization Through the Life Cycle." In O. G. Brim, Jr., and S. Wheeler, *Socialization After Childhood: Two Essays*. New York: Wiley, 1966. Pp. 3–49.

BRIM, O. G., JR. "Adult Socialization." In J. A. Clausen (Ed.), *Socialization and Society*. Boston: Little, Brown, 1968. Pp. 182–226.

BROOKS, J. B., AND ELLIOTT, D. M. "Prediction of Psychological Adjustment at Age Thirty from Leisure Time Activities and Satisfactions in Childhood." *Human Development*, 1971, *14*(1), 51–61.

BÜHLER, C. *Der Menschliche Lebenslauf als Psychologisches Problem*. Göttingen, Germany: Verlag für Psychologie, 1959.

BÜHLER, C. *Values in Psychotherapy*. New York: Free Press, 1962.

BÜHLER, C. "The General Structure of the Human Life Cycle." In C. Bühler and F. Massarik (Eds.), *The Course of Human Life: A Study of Goals in the Humanistic Perspective*. New York: Springer, 1968. Pp. 12–26.

BÜHLER, C., BRIND, A., AND HORNER, A. "Old Age as a Phase of Human Life." *Human Development*, 1968, *11*(1), 53–63.

BUNZEL, J. H. "Note on the History of a Concept—Gerontophobia." *The Gerontologist*, 1972, *12*(2), Part 1, 116, 203.

BURR, W. R. "Satisfaction with Various Aspects of Marriage over the Life Cycle: A Random Middle Class Sample." *Journal of Marriage and the Family*, Feb. 1970, *32*, 29–37.

BURR, W. R. "Role Transitions: A Reformulation of Theory." *Journal of Marriage and the Family*, Aug. 1972, *34*, 407–416.

BUTLER, R. N. "The Life Review: An Interpretation of Reminiscence in the Aged." *Psychiatry*, Feb. 1963, *26*, 65–76.

BUTLER, R. N. "Looking Forward to What? The Life Review, Legacy, and Excessive Identity Versus Change." *American Behavioral Scientist,* Sept.–Oct. 1970, *14,* 121–128.

BYRNE, D. E. *The Attraction Paradigm.* New York: Academic Press, 1971.

CAMERON, P. "The Generation Gap: Time Orientation." *The Gerontologist,* 1972, *12*(2), Part 1, 117–119.

CANTRIL, H. *The Pattern of Human Concerns.* New Brunswick, N.J.: Rutgers University Press, 1965.

CAPPON, D. "Attitudes on Death." *Omega,* May 1970, *1,* 103–108.

CARLSON, R. "Understanding Women: Implications for Personality Theory and Research." *Journal of Social Issues,* 1972, *28*(2), 17–32.

CHINOY, E. *Automobile Workers and the American Dream.* New York: Random House, 1955.

CHIRIBOGA, D. A., AND LOWENTHAL, M. F. "The Correlates of Social Stress." Paper presented at the 52nd Annual Meeting of the Western Psychological Association, Portland, Ore., April 1972.

CLARK, M., AND ANDERSON, B. G. *Culture and Aging: An Anthropological Study of Older Americans.* Springfield, Ill.: Thomas, 1967.

CLAUSEN, J. A. "Methodological Issues in the Measurement of Mental Health of the Aged." In M. F. Lowenthal and A. Zilli (Eds.), *Interdisciplinary Topics in Gerontology: Colloquium on Health and Aging of the Population.* Vol. 3. Basel (Switzerland)/New York: S. Karger, 1969. Pp. 111–127.

CLAUSEN, J. A. "The Life Course of Individuals." In M. W. Riley, M. Johnson and A. Foner (Eds.), *Aging and Society.* Vol. 3: *A Sociology of Age Stratification.* New York: Russell Sage Foundation, 1972. Pp. 457–514.

COLEMAN, J. V. "Adaptive Integration of Psychiatric Symptoms in Ego Regulation." *Archives of General Psychiatry,* Jan. 1971, *24,* 17–21.

CONSTANTINOPLE, A. "An Eriksonian Measure of Personality Development in College Students." *Developmental Psychology,* 1969, *1*(4), 357–372.

CUMMING, E., AND HENRY, W. E. *Growing Old: The Process of Disengagement.* New York: Basic Books, 1961.

CUTLER, S. J. "Voluntary Association Participation and Life Satisfaction: A Cautionary Research Note." *Journal of Gerontology,* 1973, *28*(1), 96–100.

CYRUS-LUTZ, C., AND GAITZ, C. M. "Lifetime Goals: Age and Ethnic

Considerations." Paper presented at the 24th Annual Meeting of the Gerontological Society, Houston, Texas, Oct. 1971.

DIXON, W. J. (Ed.) *BMD: Biomedical Computer Programs.* (2nd ed.) Berkeley: University of California Press, 1970.

DOHRENWEND, B. S. "Life Events as Stressors: A Methodological Inquiry." *Journal of Health and Social Behavior,* June 1973, *14,* 167–175.

DOUVAN, E., AND ADELSON, J. *The Adolescent Experience.* New York: Wiley, 1966.

DUNN, H. L. "Dynamic Maturity for Purposeful Living." *Geriatrics,* July 1966, *21,* 205–208.

EDWARDS, J. N., AND KLEMMACK, D. L. "Correlates of Life Satisfaction: A Re-examination." *Journal of Gerontology,* 1973, *28*(4), 497–502.

ELDER, G. H., JR. *Children of the Great Depression.* Chicago: University of Chicago Press, 1974.

EPSTEIN, C. F. "Women vs. Success." *Intellectual Digest,* Sept. 1973, *4,* 26–27.

ERIKSON, E. H. *Identity and the Life-Cycle. Psychological Issues, 1*(1). Monograph 1. New York: International Universities Press, 1959.

ERIKSON, E. H. *Childhood and Society.* (2nd ed.) New York: Norton, 1963.

ERIKSON, E. H. *Identity: Youth and Crisis.* New York: Norton, 1968.

ERIKSON, E. H. "Reflections on the Dissent of Contemporary Youth." *International Journal of Psychoanalysis,* 1970, *51* (Part 1), 11–22.

FAUNCE, D., AND BEEGLE, J. A. "Cleavages in a Relatively Homogeneous Group of Rural Youth: An Experiment in the Use of Sociometry in Attaining and Measuring Integration." *Sociometry,* Aug. 1948, *11,* 207–216.

FEIFEL, H. "Attitudes Toward Death in Some Normal and Mentally Ill Populations." In H. Feifel (Ed.), *The Meaning of Death.* New York: McGraw-Hill, 1959. Pp. 114–130.

FEIFEL, H. Comments on "Attitudes Toward Death in Older Persons: A Symposium." *Journal of Gerontology,* 1961, *16*(1), 61–63.

FENGLER, A. P. "The Effects of Age and Education on Marital Ideology." *Journal of Marriage and the Family,* May 1973, *35,* 264–271.

FOGARTY, M. P., RAPOPORT, R., AND RAPOPORT, R. N. *Sex, Career and*

Family: Including an International Review of Women's Roles.
Beverly Hills, Calif.: Sage, 1971.

FOOTE, N. N. "The Movement from Jobs to Careers in American Industry." *Transactions of the Third World Congress of Sociology,* 1956, *2,* 30–40.

FRAISSE, P. *The Psychology of Time.* (Trans. by J. Leith.) New York:
Harper, 1963.

FRENCH, T. M. *The Integration of Behavior.* Vol. 1: *Basic Postulates.*
Chicago: University of Chicago Press, 1952.

FREUD, S. "Femininity." In *New Introductory Lectures on Psycho-
analysis.* (Trans. and ed. by J. Strachey.) New York: Norton,
[1933] 1965. Pp. 112–135.

FREUD, S. "Thoughts for the Times on War and Death." (Originally
published 1915.) In *The Complete Psychological Works of
Sigmund Freud.* Vol. 14. London: Hogarth Press, 1957. Pp.
273–302.

FRIED, M., AND LINDEMANN, E. "Sociocultural Factors in Mental Health
and Illness." *American Journal of Orthopsychiatry,* Jan. 1961,
31, 87–101.

FRIEDMAN, M., AND ROSENMAN, R. H. *Type A Behavior and Your Heart.*
New York: Knopf, 1974.

FROMM, E. "The Problem of the Oedipus Complex." Paper presented
at Langley Porter Neuropsychiatric Institute Staff Meeting, San
Francisco, April 20, 1966.

GANS, H. J. *The Urban Villagers: Group and Class in the Life of
Italian Americans.* New York: Free Press, 1962.

GANS, H. J. *The Levittowners.* New York: Pantheon Books, 1967.

GARAI, J. E. "Sex Differences in Mental Health." *Genetic Psychology
Monographs,* May 1970, *81,* 123–143.

GIEDT, F. H., AND LEHNER, G. F. J. "Assignment of Ages on the Draw-
a-Person Test by Male Neuropsychiatric Patients." *Journal of
Personality,* June 1951, *19,* 440–448.

GOLDFARB, A. I. "A Psychosocial and Sociophysiological Approach to
Aging." In N. E. Zinberg and I. Kaufman (Eds.), *Normal
Psychology of the Aging Process.* New York: International Uni-
versities Press, 1963. Pp. 72–92.

GOLDSTEIN, K. *Human Nature in the Light of Psychopathology.* Cambridge: Harvard University Press, 1940. (Republished: New
York: Schocken Books, 1963.)

GOODE, W. J. *World Revolution and Family Patterns.* New York: Free
Press, [1963] 1970.

GOTTSCHALK, L. A., WINGET, C. N., AND GLESER, G. C. *Manual of Instructions for Using the Gottschalk-Gleser Content Analysis Scales: Anxiety, Hostility, and Social Alienation–Personal Disorganization.* Berkeley: University of California Press, 1969.

GOULD, R. L. "The Phases of Adult Life: A Study in Developmental Psychology." *American Journal of Psychiatry,* Nov. 1972, *129,* 521–531.

GRANICK, R., AND NAHEMOW, L. D. "Preadmission Isolation as a Factor in Adjustment to an Old Age Home." In P. H. Hoch and J. Zubin (Eds.), *Psychopathology of Aging.* New York: Grune and Stratton, 1961. Pp. 285–302.

GRANT, C. H. "Age Differences in Self-Concept from Early Adulthood Through Old Age." *Proceedings of the 77th Annual Convention of the American Psychological Association,* 1969, *4*(2), 717–718.

GRINKER, R. R., SR. (with the collaboration of R. R. Grinker, Jr., and J. Timberlake) " 'Mentally Healthy' Young Males (Homoclites)." *Archives of General Psychiatry,* June 1962, *6,* 405–453.

GURIN, G., VEROFF, J., AND FELD, S. *Americans View Their Mental Health.* Joint Commission on Mental Illness and Health, Monograph Series No. 4. New York: Basic Books, 1960.

GUTMANN, D. L. "An Exploration of Ego Configurations in Middle and Later Life." In B. L. Neugarten and Associates, *Personality in Middle and Late Life.* New York: Atherton, 1964. Pp. 114–148.

GUTMANN, D. L. "Mayan Aging—A Comparative TAT Study." *Psychiatry,* Aug. 1966, *29,* 246–259.

GUTMANN, D. L. *The Country of Old Men: Cultural Studies in the Psychology of Later Life.* Occasional Papers in Gerontology, No. 5. Ann Arbor: Institute of Gerontology, University of Michigan–Wayne State University, 1969.

HAAN, N. "A Tripartite Model of Ego Functioning Values and Clinical and Research Applications." *Journal of Nervous and Mental Disease,* Jan. 1969, *148,* 14–30.

HABERLAND, H. W., AND LIEBERMAN, M. A. "Psychological Dimensions of Hope: Relationship to Survival." Paper presented at the 8th International Congress of Gerontology, Washington, D.C., Aug. 28, 1969.

HARMON, D. K., MASUDA, M., AND HOLMES, T. H. "The Social Readjustment Rating Scale: A Cross-Cultural Study of Western Europeans and Americans." *Journal of Psychosomatic Research,* Dec. 1970, *14,* 391–400,

HAUSER, S. T., AND SHAPIRO, R. L. "Differentiation of Adolescent Self-Images." *Archives of General Psychiatry,* July 1973, *29,* 63–68.

HAVIGHURST, R. J. "Successful Aging." In R. H. Williams, C. Tibbitts, and W. Donahue (Eds.), *Processes of Aging.* Vol. 1. New York: Atherton, 1963. Pp. 299–320.

HAVIGHURST, R. J., NEUGARTEN, B. L., AND TOBIN, S. S. "Disengagement and Patterns of Aging." In B. L. Neugarten (Ed.), *Middle Age and Aging.* Chicago: University of Chicago Press, 1968. Pp. 161–177.

HENRY, W. E. *The Analysis of Fantasy.* New York: Wiley, Science Editions, [1956] 1967.

HENRY, W. E. "The Role of Work in Structuring the Life Cycle." *Human Development,* 1971, *14*(2) 125–131.

HERBERG, W. *Protestant-Catholic-Jew.* New York: Doubleday, 1955.

HINTON, J. *Dying.* Middlesex, England: Penguin, 1967.

HOCHSCHILD, A. R. "A Review of Sex Role Research." In J. Huber (Ed.), *Changing Women in a Changing Society.* Chicago: University of Chicago Press, 1973. Pp. 249–267.

HODGES, R. "Ego Mastery Styles and the Adult Life Course." Presented at the 80th Annual Convention of the American Psychological Association, Honolulu, Hawaii, Sept. 1972.

HOLMES, T. H., AND RAHE, R. H. "The Social Readjustment Rating Scale." *Journal of Psychosomatic Research,* Aug. 1967, *11,* 213–218.

HOMANS, G. C. *Social Behavior: Its Elementary Forms.* New York: Harcourt, Brace, 1961.

HOOPER, T., AND SPILKA, B. "Some Meanings and Correlates of Future Time and Death Among College Students." *Omega,* Feb. 1970, *1,* 49–56.

HORNEY, K. *Feminine Psychology.* New York: Norton, 1967.

HOROWITZ, M. J., AND BECKER, S. S. "Cognitive Response to Stress: Experimental Studies of a 'Cumpulsion to Repeat Trauma.' " *Psychoanalysis and Contemporary Science,* 1972, *1,* 258–305.

HUTSCHNECKER, A. A. "Personality Factors in Dying Patients." In H. Feifel (Ed.), *The Meaning of Death.* New York: McGraw-Hill, 1959. Pp. 237–250.

HUTT, C. "Sex Differences in Human Development." *Human Development,* 1972, *15,* 153–170.

IRISH, D. P. "Sibling Interaction: A Neglected Aspect in Family Life Research." *Social Forces,* March 1964, *42,* 279–288.

JAHODA, M. *Current Concepts of Positive Mental Health.* Joint Commission on Mental Illness and Health, Monograph Series No. 1. New York: Basic Books, 1958.

JAMES, W. "The Emotions." In C. G. Lange and W. James (Eds.), *The Emotions*. Vol. 1. Baltimore: Williams and Wilkins, 1922. Pp. 93–105.

JOURARD, S. M. "Healthy Personality and Self-Disclosure." *Mental Hygiene*, Oct. 1959, *43*, 499–507.

JOURARD, S. M. *Self-Disclosure: An Experimental Analysis of the Transparent Self*. New York: Wiley-Interscience, 1971.

JUNG, C. G. "The Stages of Life." In *Modern Man in Search of a Soul*. (Trans. by W. S. Dell and C. F. Baynes.) New York: Harcourt, Brace, 1933. Pp. 95–114.

JUNG, C. G. "The Relations Between the Ego and the Unconscious." (Originally published 1916.) In *Collected Works*. Vol. 7: *Two Essays on Analytical Psychology*. Princeton, N.J.: Princeton University Press, 1953. Pp. 123–304.

KAPLAN, H. B. "Age-Related Correlates of Self-Derogation: Contemporary Life Space Characteristics." *Aging and Human Development*, 1971, *2*(4), 305–313.

KAPLAN, M. "Toward a Theory of Leisure for Social Gerontology." In R. W. Kleemeier (Ed.), *Aging and Leisure*. New York: Oxford University Press, 1961. Pp. 389–412.

KASTENBAUM, R. "The Structure and Function of Time Perspective." *Journal of Psychological Researches*, 1964, *8*(3), 1–11.

KELLY, H. H. "Attribution Theory in Social Psychology." *Nebraska Symposium on Motivation*, 1967, *15*, 192–238.

KENISTON, K. *The Uncommitted: Alienated Youth in American Society*. New York: Harcourt, Brace, 1965.

KENISTON, K. *Young Radicals: Notes on Committed Youth*. New York: Harcourt, Brace, 1968.

KEPHART, W. M. "The 'Dysfunctional' Theory of Romantic Love: A Research Report." *Journal of Comparative Family Studies*, Autumn 1970, *1*, 26–36

KERCKHOFF, A. C., AND BEAN, F. D. "Social Status and Interpersonal Patterns Among Married Couples." *Social Forces*, Dec. 1970, *49*, 264–271.

KING, C. E., AND HOWELL, W. H. "Role Characteristics of Flexible and Inflexible Retired Persons." *Sociology and Social Research*, Jan. 1965, *49*, 153–165.

KLEIN, M. "On Mental Health." *British Journal of Medical Psychology*, 1960, *33*(4), 237–241.

KLUCKHOHN, C., AND OTHERS. "Values and Value-Orientations in the Theory of Action: An Exploration in Definition and Classification." In T. Parsons and E. A. Shils (Eds.), *Toward a General Theory of Action.* New York: Harper Torchbooks, 1962. Pp. 388–433.

KLUCKHOHN, F. R. "Dominant and Variant Value Orientations." In C. Kluckhohn, H. A. Murray, with the collaboration of D. M. Schneider (Eds.), *Personality in Nature, Society, and Culture.* New York: Knopf, 1953. Pp. 342–357.

KLUCKHOHN, F. R., AND STRODTBECK, F. L. *Variations in Value Orientations.* Evanston: Row, Peterson, 1961.

KOCH, H. L. "The Relation in Young Children Between Characteristics of Their Playmates and Certain Attributes of Their Siblings." *Child Development,* 1957, *28,* 175–202.

KOMAROVSKY, M. *Blue Collar Marriage.* New York: Random House, 1962.

KOMAROVSKY, M. "Cultural Contradictions and Sex Roles: The Masculine Case." In J. Huber (Ed.), *Changing Women in a Changing Society.* Chicago: University of Chicago Press, 1973. Pp. 111–122.

KORCHIN, S. J. "Some Psychological Determinants of Stress Behavior." In S. Z. Klausner (Ed.), *The Quest for Self-Control.* New York: Free Press, 1965, Pp. 247–266.

KÜBLER-ROSS, E. *On Death and Dying.* New York: Macmillan, 1969.

KUHLEN, R. G. "Developmental Changes in Motivation During the Adult Years." In B. L. Neugarten (Ed.), *Middle Age and Aging.* Chicago: University of Chicago Press, 1968. Pp. 115–136.

KUHLEN, R. G., AND JOHNSON, G. H. "Change in Goals with Adult Increasing Age." *Journal of Consulting Psychology,* 1952, *16,* 1–4.

LANGNER, T. S., AND MICHAEL, S. T. *Life Stress and Mental Health: The Midtown Manhattan Study.* New York: Free Press, 1963.

LAXER, R. M. "Relation of Real Self-Rating to Mood and Blame, and Their Interaction in Depression." *Journal of Consulting Psychology,* Dec. 1964, *28,* 538–546.

LAZARSFELD, P., AND MERTON, R. "Friendship as a Social Process: A Substantive and Methodological Analysis." In M. Berger, T. Abel, and C. Page (Eds.), *Freedom and Control in Modern Society.* New York: Octagon Books, [1954] 1964. Pp. 18–66.

LAZARUS, R. S. "Cognitive and Personality Factors Underlying Threat and Coping." In S. Levine and N. A. Scotch (Eds.), *Social Stress*. Chicago: Aldine, 1970. Pp. 143–164.

LAZARUS, R. S., AND ALFERT, E. "Short-Circuiting of Threat by Experimentally Altering Cognitive Appraisal." *Journal of Abnormal and Social Psychology*, Aug. 1964, *69*, 195–205.

LAZARUS, R. S., OPTON, E. M., JR., AND AVERILL, J. R. "The Management of Stressful Experiences." Paper presented at the Foundations' Fund for Research in Psychiatry Conference on Adaptation to Change, Dorado, Puerto Rico, June 1968.

LECKY, P. *Self-Consistency: A Theory of Personality*. Garden City, N.Y.: Doubleday Anchor, 1969.

LEIGHTON, A. H. *My Name Is Legion*. New York: Basic Books, 1959.

LEMON, B. W., BENGTSON, V. L., AND PETERSON, J. A. "An Exploration of the Activity Theory of Aging: Activity Types and Life Satisfaction Among In-Movers to a Retirement Community." *Journal of Gerontology*, 1972, *27*(4), 511–523.

LEWIN, K. "Field Theory and Experiment in Social Psychology: Concepts and Methods." *American Journal of Sociology*, May 1939, *44*(6), 868–896.

LEWIN, K. *Field Theory in Social Science* (selected theoretical paper. Edited by D. Cartwright). New York: Harper, 1951.

LEWIS, A. "Between Guesswork and Certainty in Psychiatry." *Lancet*, Jan. 25, 1958, *1*, 170–175.

LIDZ, T. *The Person: His Development Throughout the Life Cycle*. New York: Basic Books, 1968.

LIEBERMAN, L. R. "Life Satisfaction in the Young and the Old." *Psychological Reports*, Aug. 1970, *27*, 75–79.

LIFTON, R. J. "Protean Man." *Archives of General Psychiatry*, April 1971, *24*, 298–304.

LINDEN, M. E., AND COURTNEY, D. "The Human Life Cycle and Its Interruptions. A Psychologic Hypothesis. Studies in Gerontologic Human Relations I." *American Journal of Psychiatry*, June 1953, *109*, 906–915.

LINDZEY, G. "Psychoanalytic Theory: Paths of Change." *International Journal of Psycho-Analysis*, 1968, *49*, 656–661.

LINTON, R. *The Study of Man*. New York: Appleton-Century, 1936.

LIPSET, S. M., AND BENDIX, R. *Social Mobility in Industrial Society*. Berkeley: University of California Press, 1959.

LOTT, A. J., AND LOTT, B. E. "Group Cohesiveness as Interpersonal Attraction: A Review of Relationships with Antecedent and

Consequent Variables." *Psychological Bulletin,* Oct. 1965, *64*
(4), 259–309.

LOWENTHAL, M. F. "Social Isolation and Mental Illness in Old Age."
American Sociological Review, Feb. 1964, *29,* 54–70.

LOWENTHAL, M. F. "Intentionality: Toward a Framework for the Study
of Adaptation in Adulthood." *Aging and Human Development,*
May 1971, *2,* 79–95.

LOWENTHAL, M. F. "Some Potentialities of a Life-Cycle Approach to
the Study of Retirement." In F. M. Carp (Ed.), *Retirement.*
New York: Behavioral Publications, 1972. Pp. 307–336.

LOWENTHAL, M. F., BERKMAN, P. L., AND ASSOCIATES. *Aging and Mental Disorder in San Francisco: A Social Psychiatric Study.* San
Francisco: Jossey-Bass, 1967.

LOWENTHAL, M. F., AND CHIRIBOGA, D. "Stress and Affective Reactions:
A Lifecycle Perspective." Paper presented at 51st Annual Meet-
ing of the Western Psychological Association, San Francisco,
April 1971.

LOWENTHAL, M. F., AND CHIRIBOGA, D. "Transition to the Empty Nest:
Crisis, Challenge, or Relief?" *Archives of General Psychiatry,*
Jan. 1972a, *26,* 8–14.

LOWENTHAL, M. F., AND CHIRIBOGA, D. "Correlates of Susceptibility to
Stress." Presented in Symposium, Personality and Developmental Factors in Adaptation to Stress, 80th Annual Convention
of the American Psychological Association, Honolulu, Hawaii,
Sept. 1972b.

LOWENTHAL, M. F., AND CHIRIBOGA, D. "Social Stress and Adaptation:
Toward a Life-Course Perspective." In C. Eisdorfer and M. P.
Lawton (Eds.), *The Psychology of Adult Development and
Aging.* Washington, D.C.: American Psychological Association,
1973. Pp. 281–310.

LOWENTHAL, M. F., AND HAVEN, C. "Interaction and Adaptation: Intimacy as a Critical Variable." *American Sociological Review,*
Feb. 1968, *33,* 20–30.

LURIE, E. E. "An Exploration of Orientation to Roles, Satisfaction with
Roles, and Effects of Support and Conflict Among Roles in a
Sample of Aged Persons." Unpublished doctoral dissertation,
Columbia University, 1970.

LURIE, E. E. "Role Scope and Social Participation." San Francisco:
University of California, Human Development Program. Unpublished paper #10 A. 11, 1972.

MACCOBY, E. E. "Women's Intellect." In S. M. Farber and R. H. L.

Wilson (Eds.), *The Potential of Women*. New York: McGraw-Hill, 1963. Pp. 24–39.

MADDOX, G. L. "Activity and Morale: A Longitudinal Study of Selected Elderly Subjects." *Social Forces*, 1963, *42*(2), 195–204.

MADDOX, G. L. "Is Senior Power the Wave of the Future?" Presented at the 140th Annual Meeting of the American Association for the Advancement of Science, San Francisco, Feb. 1974.

MASLOW, A. H. *Toward a Psychology of Being*. New York: Van Nostrand, 1962. (Rev. ed., 1968.)

MASLOW, A. H. *Motivation and Personality*. New York: Harper, [1954] 1970.

MASON, E. P. "Some Correlates of Self-Judgments of the Aged." *Journal of Gerontology*, 1954, *9*(3), 324–337.

MASUDA, M., AND HOLMES, T. H. "The Social Readjustment Rating Scale: A Cross-Cultural Study of Japanese and Americans." *Journal of Psychosomatic Research*, Aug. 1967, *11*, 227–237.

MC CALL, G. J., AND OTHERS. *Social Relationships*. Chicago: Aldine, 1970.

MC CALL, G. J., AND SIMMONS, F. L. *Identities and Interactions*. New York: Free Press, 1966.

MEAD, G. H. *Mind, Self, and Society*. Chicago: University of Chicago Press, 1934.

MENDELSOHN, G. A., AND GALL, M. D. "Personality Variables and the Effectiveness of Techniques to Facilitate Creative Problem Solving." *Journal of Personality and Social Psychology*, Oct. 1970, *16*, 346–351.

MERTON, R. K., FISKE (LOWENTHAL), M., AND KENDALL, P. L. *The Focused Interview*. New York: Free Press, [1948] 1956.

METTEE, D. R. "Happiness Is a Mystery, Still." Review of N. Bradburn, *The Structure of Psychological Well-Being*. *Contemporary Psychology*, April 1971, *16*, 245–246.

MICHAELS, J. J. "Character Structure and Character Disorders." In S. Arieti (Ed.), *American Handbook of Psychiatry*. Vol. 1. New York: Basic Books, 1959. Pp. 353–377.

MILLER, J. B. "Conclusion: New Issues and New Approaches." In J. B. Miller (Ed.), *Psychoanalyses and Women, Contribution to New Theory and Therapy*. New York: Brunner/Mazel, 1973. Pp. 379–406.

MITSCHERLICH, A., AND OTHERS. "On Psychoanalysis and Sociology." *International Journal of Psycho-Analysis*, 1970, *51* (Part 1), 33–48.

MORRIS, C. *Varieties of Human Value*. Chicago: University of Chicago Press, 1956.

MORSE, S., AND GERGEN, K. J. "Social Comparison, Self-Consistency, and the Concept of Self." *Journal of Personality and Social Psychology*, 1970, *16*(1), 148–156.

MOULTON, R. "The Myth of Femininity: A Panel Discussion." *American Journal of Psychoanalysis*, 1973, *33*(1), 45–49.

MURRAY, H. A. *Thematic Apperception Test*. Pictures and Manual. Cambridge: Harvard University Press, 1943.

NEUGARTEN, B. L. "A Developmental View of Adult Personality." In J. E. Birren (Ed.), *Relations of Development and Aging*. Springfield, Ill.: Thomas, 1964. Pp. 176–208.

NEUGARTEN, B. L. "The Awareness of Middle Age." In B. L. Neugarten (Ed.), *Middle Age and Aging*. Chicago: University of Chicago Press, 1968a. Pp. 93–98.

NEUGARTEN, B. L. "Adult Personality: Toward a Psychology of the Life Cycle." In B. L. Neugarten (Ed.), *Middle Age and Aging*. Chicago: University of Chicago Press, 1968b. Pp. 137–147.

NEUGARTEN, B. L. "Age Groups in American Society and the Rise of the Young-Old." Presented at the 140th Annual Meeting of the American Association for the Advancement of Science, San Francisco, Feb. 1974.

NEUGARTEN, B. L., AND ASSOCIATES. *Personality in Middle and Late Life*. New York: Atherton, 1964.

NEUGARTEN, B. L., AND GUTMANN, D. L. "Age-Sex Roles and Personality in Middle Age: A Thematic Apperception Study." In B. L. Neugarten and Associates, *Personality in Middle and Late Life*. New York: Atherton, 1964. Pp. 44–89.

NEUGARTEN, B. L., AND GUTMANN, D. L. "Age-Sex Roles and Personality in Middle Age: A Thematic Apperception Study." In B. L. Neugarten (Ed.), *Middle Age and Aging*. Chicago: Chicago University Press, 1968. Pp. 58–71.

NEUGARTEN, B. L., AND MILLER, D. L. "Ego Functions in the Middle and Later Years: A Further Exploration." In B. L. Neugarten and Associates, *Personality in Middle and Late Life*. New York: Atherton, 1964. Pp. 105–113.

NEUGARTEN, B. L., MOORE, J. W., AND LOWE, J. C. "Age Norms, Age Constraints, and Adult Socialization." *American Journal of Sociology*, May 1965, *70*, 710–717.

NIE, N. H., POWELL, G. B., JR., AND PREWITT, K. "Social Structure and

Political Participation: Developmental Relationships, Part I."
American Political Science Review, June 1969a, *63,* 361–378.

NIE, N. H., POWELL, G. B., JR., AND PREWITT, K. "Social Structure and
Political Participation: Developmental Relationships, Part II."
American Political Science Review, Sept. 1969b, *63,* 808–832.

NOWLIS, V. "Research with the Mood Adjective Check List." In S. S.
Tomkins and C. E. Izard (Eds.), *Affect, Cognition, and Personality: Empirical Studies.* New York: Springer, 1965. Pp.
352–389.

OFFER, D. *The Psychological World of the Teen-Ager.* New York:
Basic Books, 1969.

ORGAN, D. W. "Locus of Control and Clarity of Self-Concept." *Perceptual and Motor Skills,* Aug. 1973, *37,* 100–102.

PARKES, C. M. "Psycho-Social Transitions: A Field for Study." *Social
Science and Medicine,* April 1971, *5,* 101–115.

PARSONS, T., AND FOX, R. "Illness, Therapy and the Modern Urban
American Family." *Journal of Social Issues,* 1952, *8*(4), 31–44.

PARSONS, T., AND SHILS, E. A., with the assistance of J. Olds. "Systems
of Value-Orientations." In T. Parsons and E. A. Shils (Eds.),
Toward a General Theory of Action. New York: Harper Torchbooks, 1962. Pp. 159–189.

PFEIFFER, E., VERWOERDT, A., AND DAVIS, G. C. "Sexual Behavior in
Middle Life." *American Journal of Psychiatry,* April 1972, *128,*
1262–1267.

PHILLIPS, D. L. "Social Participation and Happiness." *American Journal
of Sociology,* March 1967, *72,* 479–488.

PIAGET, J. "Time Perception in Children." In J. T. Fraser (Ed.), *The
Voices of Time.* New York: Braziller, 1966. Pp. 202–216.

PRESSEY, S. L., AND KUHLEN, R. G. *Psychological Development Through
the Life Span.* New York: Harper, 1957.

RILEY, M. W., AND FONER, A. *Aging and Society.* Vol. 1: *An Inventory
of Research Findings.* New York: Russell Sage Foundation,
1968. Pp. 13–184.

RILEY, M. W., AND OTHERS. "Socialization for the Middle and Later
Years." In D. A. Goslin (Ed.), *Handbook of Socialization
Theory and Research.* Chicago: Rand McNally, 1969. Pp.
951–982.

ROGERS, C. R. *Becoming a Person.* Oberlin College Nellie Heldt Lecture
Series. Oberlin, Ohio: Oberlin College Printing Co., 1954.

ROLLINS, B. C., AND FELDMAN, H. "Marital Satisfaction over the Family

Life Cycle." *Journal of Marriage and the Family.* Feb. 1970, *32,* 20–28.

ROSE, A. M. "The Subculture of the Aging: A Framework for Research in Social Gerontology." In A. M. Rose and W. A. Peterson (Eds.), *Older People and Their Social World.* Philadelphia: Davis, 1965. Pp. 3–15.

ROSENBERG, G. S. *The Worker Grows Old.* San Francisco: Jossey-Bass, 1970.

ROSENBERG, G. S., AND ANSPACH, D. F. "Sibling Solidarity in the Working Class." *Journal of Marriage and the Family,* Feb. 1973, *35,* 108–113.

ROSENFELT, R. H. "The Elderly Mystique." *Journal of Social Issues,* Oct. 1965, *21,* 37–43.

ROSENKRANTZ, P., AND OTHERS. "Sex-Role Stereotypes and Self-Concepts in College Students." *Journal of Consulting and Clinical Psychology,* June 1968, *32,* 287–295.

ROSOW, I. "Adjustment of Normal Aged." In R. H. Williams, C. Tibbitts, and W. Donahue (Eds.), *Processes of Aging.* Vol. 2. New York: Atherton, 1963. Pp. 195–223.

ROSOW, I. "Forms and Functions of Adult Socialization." *Social Forces,* Sept. 1965, *44,* 35–45.

ROSOW, I. *Social Integration of the Aged.* New York: Free Press, 1967.

ROSOW, I. "Housing and Local Ties of the Aged." In B. L. Neugarten (Ed.), *Middle Age and Aging.* Chicago: University of Chicago Press, 1968. Pp. 382–389.

ROTHENBERG, A. "The Process of Janusian Thinking in Creativity." *Archives of General Psychiatry,* March 1971, *24,* 195–205.

SARASON, I. G., AND SMITH, R. E. "Personality." In P. Mussen and M. Rozenzweig (Eds.), *Annual Review of Psychology.* Vol. 22. Palo Alto, Ca.: Annual Reviews Inc., 1971. Pp. 393–446.

SARBIN, T. R. "Role Theory." In G. Lindzey (Ed.), *Handbook of Social Psychology.* Reading, Mass.: Addison-Wesley, 1954. Pp. 223–258.

SCHAIE, K. W. "A General Model for the Study of Developmental Problems." *Psychological Bulletin,* 1965, *64*(2), 92–107.

SCHAIE, K. W., AND STROTHER, C. R. "A Cross-Sequential Study of Age Changes in Cognitive Behavior." *Psychological Bulletin,* Dec. 1968, *70,* 671–680.

SCHNEIDER, D. M. *American Kinship: A Cultural Account.* Englewood Cliffs, N.J.: Prentice-Hall, 1968.

SEELEY, J. R., SIM, R. A., AND LOOSLEY, E. W. *Crestwood Heights: A*

Study of the Culture of Suburban Life. New York: Basic Books, 1956.

SELYE, H. *The Stress of Life.* New York: McGraw-Hill, 1956.

SELYE, H. *Stress Without Distress.* Philadelphia: Lippincott, 1974.

SHAKOW, D. "The Education of the Mental Health Researcher." *Archives of General Psychiatry,* July 1972, *27,* 15–25.

SHANAS, E., AND OTHERS. "The Psychology of Health." In B. L. Neugarten (Ed.), *Middle Age and Aging.* Chicago: University of Chicago Press, 1968. Pp. 212–219.

SHAPIRO, D. "Psychological Factors in Friendship Choice and Rejection." Unpublished doctoral dissertation, University of Michigan. In *Dissertation Abstracts,* 1953, *13*(3), 437.

SHERIF, M., AND CANTRIL, H. *The Psychology of Ego-Involvements.* New York: Wiley, 1947.

SIMMEL, G. "The Web of Group Affiliation." *Conflict and the Web of Group Affiliation.* New York: Free Press, 1955.

SINGER, M. T. "Personality Measurements in the Aged." In J. E. Birren and others (Eds.), *Human Aging.* Washington, D.C.: U. S. Government Printing Office, 1963. Pp. 217–249.

SKOLNICK, A. S., AND SKOLNICK, J. H. "Rethinking the Family." In A. S. Skolnick and J. H. Skolnick (Eds.), *Family in Transition.* Boston: Little, Brown, 1971. Pp. 1–32.

SMITH, M. B. *Social Psychology and Human Values.* Chicago: Aldine, 1969.

Social Science Research Council. "Description of Proposed Activities, Committee on Work and Personality in the Middle Years," New York, 1973.

SPANIER, G. B. "Romanticism and Marital Adjustment." *Journal of Marriage and the Family.* Aug. 1972, *34,* 481–487.

SPENCE, D., AND LONNER, T. "The 'Empty Nest': A Transition Within Motherhood." *The Family Coordinator,* Oct. 1971, *20,* 369–375.

STOTLAND, E. *The Psychology of Hope.* San Francisco: Jossey-Bass, 1969.

TAYLOR, M. C. "Postponing the First Child: A Proposal for Research in the Field of Fertility and Family Planning." Unpublished master's thesis, University of California, San Francisco, May 1972.

TEAHAN, J., AND KASTENBAUM, R. "Subjective Life Expectancy and Future Time Perspective as Predictors of Job Success in the 'Hard-Core Unemployed.' " *Omega,* 1970, *1*(3), 189–200.

TEC, N., AND GRANICK, R. "Social Isolation and Difficulties in Social

Interaction of Residents of a Home for the Aged." *Social Problems,* Winter 1959–1960, *7,* 226–232.

TEMPLER, D. I. "Death Anxiety as Related to Depression and Health of Retired Persons." *Journal of Gerontology,* 1971, *26*(4), 521–523.

THOMAE, H. "Theory of Aging and Cognitive Theory of Personality." *Human Development,* 1970, *13,* 1–16.

THOMAS, D. L., FRANKS, D. D., AND CALONICO, J. M. "Role-Taking and Power in Social Psychology." *American Sociological Review,* Oct. 1972, *37,* 605–614.

THURNHER, M. "Goals, Values, and Life Evaluations at the Preretirement Stage." *Journal of Gerontology,* 1974, *29*(1), 85–96.

THURNHER, M., SPENCE, D., AND LOWENTHAL, M. F. "Value Confluence and Behavioral Conflict in Intergenerational Relations." *Journal of Marriage and the Family,* May 1974, *36,* 308–319.

TOBIN, S. S., AND NEUGARTEN, B. L. "Life Satisfaction and Social Interaction in the Aging." *Journal of Gerontology,* 1961, *16*(4), 344–346.

TREANTON, J.-R. "The Concept of Adjustment in Old Age." In R. H. Williams, C. Tibbitts, and W. Donahue (Eds.), *Processes of Aging.* Vol. 1. New York: Atherton, 1963. Pp. 292–298.

TROLL, L. E. "The Family of Later Life: A Decade Review." *Journal of Marriage and the Family.* May 1971, *33,* 263–290.

VAILLANT, G. E. "Theoretical Hierarchy of Adaptive Ego Mechanisms: A Thirty Year Follow-Up of Thirty Men Selected for Psychological Health." *Archives of General Psychiatry,* Feb. 1971, *24,* 107–118.

VEROFF, J., AND FELD, S. *Marriage and Work in America: A Study of Motives and Roles.* New York: Van Nostrand, 1970.

WALLACH, M., AND KOGAN, N. "Aspects of Judgment and Decision Making: Interrelationships and Changes with Age." *Behavioral Science,* Jan. 1961, *6,* 23–36.

WEBER, M. *The Theory of Social and Economic Organization.* (Trans. by A. M. Henderson and T. Parsons.) New York: Free Press, 1947.

WECHSLER, D. *Manual for the Wechsler Adult Intelligence Scale.* New York: Psychological Corporation, 1955.

WEINSTEIN, J., AND OTHERS. "Defensive Style and Discrepancy Between Self-Report and Physiological Indexes of Stress." *Journal of Personality and Social Psychology,* Dec. 1968, *10,* 406–413.

WEISBERG, P. S., AND SPRINGER, K. J. "Environmental Factors in Creative Function." *Archives of General Psychiatry*, Dec. 1961, *5*, 554–564.

WERNER, H. *Comparative Psychology of Mental Development*. New York: International Universities Press, [1940] 1948.

WESSMAN, A. E., AND RICKS, D. F. *Mood and Personality*. New York: Holt, 1966.

WESTLEY, W. A., AND EPSTEIN, N. B. *The Silent Majority: Families of Emotionally Healthy College Students*. San Francisco: Jossey-Bass, 1969.

WILSON, W. R. "An Attempt to Determine Some Correlates and Dimensions of Hedonic Tone." Unpublished doctoral dissertation, Northwestern University, 1960. (In *Dissertation Abstracts, 21* (3), 1961, 2814.)

WILSON, W. R. "Correlates of Avowed Happiness." *Psychological Bulletin*, April 1967, *67*, 294–306.

YOUNG, M., AND WILLMOTT, P. *Family and Kinship in East London*. New York: Free Press, 1957.

ZBOROWSKI, M., AND EYDE, L. "Aging and Social Participation." *Journal of Gerontology*, 1962, *17*(4), 424–430.

ZILLER, R. "Self-Other Orientation: Theory and Communication." Presented at American Research Association Meetings, New York, Feb. 1967.

ZINBERG, N. E., AND KAUFMAN, I. "Cultural and Personality Factors Associated with Aging: An Introduction." In N. E. Zinberg and I. Kaufman (Eds.), *Normal Psychology of the Aging Process*. New York: International Universities Press, 1963. Pp. 17–71.

Indexes

Name Index

Indexes

287

W

WALLACH, M., 62, 280
WEBER, M., 49, 280
WECHSLER, D., 112, 113, 280
WEINSTEIN, J., 161, 280
WEISBERG, P. S., 120, 280
WERNER, H., 80, 281
WESSMAN, A. E., 85, 86, 88, 281
WESTLEY, W. A., 3, 40, 281
WILLMOTT, P., 6, 281

WILSON, W. R., 85, 91, 281
WINGET, C. N., 101, 269
WOLFE, D. M., 32, 264

Y

YOUNG, M., 6, 281

Z

ZBOROWSKI, M., 11, 281
ZILLER, R., 62, 281
ZINBERG, N. E., 105, 281

Subject Index

A

Absentmindedness, 73, 78
Acceptance, 55, 57
Accommodation, 108-109, 250
Activity, 251; morale and, 98; and satisfaction, 92; social, 85
Adaptation: complexity of, 99-121, 239; and deprivation, 240; dual model of, 100, 116-117, 119-121, 228; indicators of, 159-160; and stress, 163; and time perspective, 135-138
Adaptive-balance typology, 251; correlates of, 117-119
Adaptive level, 84
Adaptive rating, 100, 108, 194
Adjective Rating List, 63, 67, 74, 75, 76, 80, 81, 86, 101, 154, 160n, 251
Adolescence, 90, 133; recollection of, 33
Affect: characteristics associated with, 91-96, 228; and social interaction, 97-98; typology of, 96-98, 252
Affect-balance score, 90, 137
Affiliation, 36, 37, 38
American Psychological Association, 245
Anxiety, 106; score of, 101
Assertiveness, 66, 67, 73
Authority, 70, 74

B

Beset, the, 96-98

Bland, the, 96-98
Bradburn Overall Happiness Measure, 117, 159n, 252

C

Career: family, 15-18; leisure, 15-16, 20-21; occupational, 15-16, 18-20
Career configuration, 15-16, 18, 21-23
Challenged, the, 147, 199; and physical health, 161-162; and psychiatric impairment, 161; and stress, 156-157; and well-being, 159
Checklist of Activities, 6, 13
Children, 172
Close other, 158
Communication: difficulties in, 41; and friendship, 53, 57
Competitiveness, 66, 67
Complexity, 225; and adaptation, 99-121, 239; of death thoughts, 142-143, 252; of friendship, 59-61; psychic, 228, 236; of social horizons, 8-10, 148, 259
Conflict-evoking behavior, 63
Consolation, 36, 37, 38
Contextual perspective, 252
Coping with external circumstances, 177, 178, 179, 180, 181
Counterculture, 8, 196

D

Death: attitude toward, 228, 229; concern with, 138-144; mea-